Language Acquisition and Learnability is an accessible introduction to learnability theory and its interactions with linguistic theories. Working within the Principles and Parameters framework, the book surveys general concepts from formal learning theory and complexity theory, together with important findings from developmental psycholinguistics, historical linguistics and language processing. Written by a team of leading researchers, it examines important techniques that can be used to obtain interesting and empirically testable predictions from parametric theories of language variation and includes chapters on syntax, diachronic syntax and the relationship between linguistic complexity and the form of parameters. Fully integrated, and complete with a large number of exercises to test readers on their understanding of the material, this book will become essential reading for students and researchers in linguistic theory.

STEFANO BERTOLO has taught at Rutgers University and the Massachusetts Institute of Technology and has presented the results of his research on learnability and parametric linguistics at several international conferences. His published work includes the article "Maturation and Learnability" (1995) in the journal *Language Acquisition* and the entry "Formal Models of Language Acquisition" in *The MIT Encyclopedia of the Cognitive Sciences* (1999).

Language Acquisition and Learnability

Edited by
STEFANO BERTOLO

CAMBRIDGE
UNIVERSITY PRESS

P
118
.L2527
2001

PUBLISHED BY THE PRESS SYNDICATE OF THE UNIVERSITY OF CAMBRIDGE
The Pitt Building, Trumpington Street, Cambridge, United Kingdom

CAMBRIDGE UNIVERSITY PRESS
The Edinburgh Building, Cambridge CB2 2RU, UK   www.cup.cam.ac.uk
40 West 20th Street, New York, NY 10011-4211, USA   www.cup.org
10 Stamford Road, Oakleigh, Melbourne 3166, Australia
Ruiz de Alarcón 13, 28014 Madrid, Spain

First published 2001

Printed in the United Kingdom at the University Press, Cambridge

Typeface *Times*   System *3B2*

A catalogue record for this book is available from the British Library

ISBN 0 521 64149 7 hardback
ISBN 0 521 64620 0 paperback

44794914

Contents

Contributors

Martin Atkinson, Department of Language and Linguistics, University of Essex

Stefano Bertolo, 8849 Mountain Ridge Circle, Austin, Texas TX 78759

Robin Clark, Department of Linguistics, University of Pennsylvania

Janet Dean Fodor, Ph.D. Program in Linguistics, Graduate Center, City University of New York

Ian Roberts, Department of Linguistics, University of Stuttgart

William Gregory Sakas, Department of Computer Science, Hunter College and Ph.D. Program in Computer Science, Graduate Center, City University of New York

Preface

Language learning is considered by many to be one of the central problems of linguistics and, more generally, cognitive science. Yet, the very same interdisciplinary nature that makes this field of study so interesting, makes it somehow difficult for researchers to reach a thorough understanding of the issues at play. This follows from the fact that research in the field by necessity has to draw on techniques and results that come from traditionally disparate fields such as linguistics, psychology and computer science.

This book has been conceived as a companion to learnability for the benefit of those linguists that base their work on Chomsky's *Principles and Parameters Hypothesis*. General concepts from formal learning theory and complexity theory and important facts from developmental psycholinguistics, historical linguistics and language processing have been introduced in a tutorial and completely self-contained fashion, so as to introduce linguists of the parametric persuasion to important techniques that can be used (and indeed have been used in the recent research literature) to obtain interesting and empirically testable predictions from parametric theories of language variation.

The tutorial nature of the book is demonstrated by the large number of exercises that can be used by readers to test their understanding of the material. In the editing of the book a conscious effort has been made in order to integrate the five chapters as tightly as possible by means of extensive cross-referencing.

S. Bertolo

Acknowledgments

This book started as a tutorial prepared by the authors for the Fall 1996 meeting of the Linguistic Association of Great Britain, in Cardiff. The support of the Linguistic Association of Great Britain allowed us to start this project and we are very pleased to be able to express our gratitude here.

In addition, the editor of the volume wishes to thank Dr Andrew Winnard, his editor at Cambridge University Press, for waiting patiently while the editing of the manuscript was being delayed by the ever growing time demands of a fast paced non-academic work environment on one side and a young family on the other.

1 A brief overview of learnability

Stefano Bertolo

Applications of formal learning theory to the problem of human language learning can be described as an exercise in which three parties – linguists, psychologists and learnability researchers – cooperatively construct a theory of human language learning and, in so doing, constrain their space of hypotheses by ruling out all the theories that violate one or more of the constraints that each party brings to bear on the problem.

The interaction among these three parties is similar to the interaction that would take place if a rich patron were to ask an architect and a structural engineer to work together to design a museum: the architect would start by designing very bold and innovative plans for the museum; the engineer would remind him or her, calculator in hand, that some of those designs would be physically impossible to build and the patron would visit every so often to make sure that the plans the engineer and the architect have agreed upon would result in a museum that could be built within budget and according to a specified construction schedule. In our case, linguists would correspond to the architect: based on their study of human languages or on more speculative reasons, they specify what they take the possible range of variation among human languages to be. Psychologists would correspond to the patron: they collect experimental data to show that it is not just that humans learn the language(s) of the linguistic community in which they are brought up, but that they do so according to a typical time schedule and relying on linguistic data of a certain, restricted, kind. Finally, learnability researchers correspond to the engineer: some theories of language variation they would be able to rule out directly, by showing that no conceivable mechanism could single out a correct hypothesis from such a large and dense range of choice; some other theories they would pronounce tenable, but only under certain assumptions on the resources available for learning, assumptions that need to be empirically validated by work in developmental psycholinguistics.

The goal of this introductory chapter is to provide linguists subscribing to Chomsky's *Principles and Parameters Hypothesis* (PPH) with a general understanding of the learnability concepts that need to be digested in order to study with profit research work at the intersection of linguistics, psychology and learnability and so, in particular, to provide the background that is required to understand the remaining essays in this collection.

1.1   The five components of a learning problem

Just like a structural engineer could not even *begin* to perform an analysis until a plan of the building has been provided together with the properties of the materials to be used in building it, a learnability researcher cannot even *begin* to work alongside linguists and psychologists until certain general properties of the learning problem to be solved are known:[1]

(i)   What is being learned, exactly?
(ii) What kind of hypotheses is the learner capable of entertaining?
(iii) How are the data from the target language presented to the learner?
(iv) What are the restrictions that govern how the learner updates her conjectures in response to the data?
(v)   Under what conditions, exactly, do we say that a learner has been successful in the language learning task?

We will briefly look at each of them in turn.

1.1.1   The end state of language learning

Since we are dealing with human language learning, the end state of this process is, by definition, a human language. In this section we will see, however, two things: that this fact itself has a number of interesting consequences and that there is disagreement of a rather interesting kind on what counts as knowledge of a human language.

First of all, since humans understand and produce utterances *productively* – i.e. they are able to understand and produce sentences they were never exposed to – having learned a human language cannot be equated with having memorized the list of all the sentences that one has ever encountered, but it must amount instead to having internalized a system of rules (a grammar). Under this view, the final state of the learning process encodes grammatical knowledge that can be used to classify every possible sentence as grammatical or ungrammatical in the target language. This observation might give the impression that learnability may only address the problem of learning the surface syntax of a language. This is in fact not the case. One could easily annotate an utterance with all the relevant syntactic and semantic information. As long as this annotation results in a finite object that can be the input/output of a computation (see Wexler and Culicover (1980) for an example of how such an annotation can be carried out), the learning problem of finding a grammar for the given data remains essentially the same. It is for this reason that often in formal work learning problems are cast as problems of learning sets of natural numbers, the assumption being that appropriate coding could turn any learning problem into such a problem.

It is important to note that there is a fecund research tradition dating back to Horning (1969) that takes a different view of what the end state of the learning process is. Researchers in the field of stochastic grammars would claim that a grammar that explains the data and can be used productively is only part of what humans learn when they learn a natural language. In addition human learners also learn a probability distribution describing the applicability of the rules in the grammar. To exemplify, a learner would not only learn that two rules A and B are part of her grammar but also that, say, A is twice as likely to be used than B is. It is easy to see that the probability of every surface sentence in a language can thus be obtained by first determining how many possible structural interpretations the sentence can have and then adding all the values obtained by multiplying together the probabilities of each of the rules recruited in each interpretation. In this view, therefore, learners do not simply try to identify the grammar of their linguistic community but, rather, they try to approximate the ambient probability distribution on possible linguistic events.

All the contributions in this book proceed under the assumptions corresponding to the first view, but the reader must be aware of the fact that alternative views exist that are possibly better placed to explain certain facts about human language learning.

1.1.2   Available hypotheses

One of the idealizations on which much work on learnability relies is that learners must entertain hypotheses about the language they are trying to learn at every step of the way, so that, in effect, their learning history can be viewed as a data driven trajectory in a space of hypotheses, with the last state hopefully being (one of) the correct hypothesis(es).

For a learner to be successful, this space must contain at least a correct conjecture for each of the possible targets (if, while trying to learn Hungarian, you were not allowed to hypothesize a grammar equivalent to the grammar for Hungarian, you would naturally fail), but can otherwise be limited in many other ways. For example, it has been conjectured that, because humans converge on *productive* hypotheses about their target languages, it is perhaps a feature of their learning psychology that they cannot hypothesize any grammar that allows only finitely many sentences. The PPH has a very strong impact on this component of the learning problem. Its central idea is that human languages differ from each other only in finitely many respects (the *parameters*) and, in these respects, only in finitely many ways (the *values* of the parameters). But if this is so, all the hypothesis space needs to include are all the possible combinations of parameter values.

1.1.3   Learning environments

Generally speaking, given a possible sentence *s*, there are three kinds of clues the learner can receive about it from the environment: he or she can either be told, correctly or incorrectly, that *s* is part of her target language; or he or she can be told, correctly or incorrectly, that *s* is not part of her target language; or, finally he or she may not be told anything at all about *s*. In other words the environment, even when accurate, may provide less than complete information about the language to be learned. Martin Atkinson will show in his chapter that children learn language using evidence that comes from a rather constrained subset of the target language.

Finally, a common assumption in learnability is that learners are not aware of the rule – if any – according to which the environment is presenting the data. Why knowing such a rule would help for learning in the form of indirect negative evidence will be explained by the example on page 24 in the next chapter.

1.1.4   Learners

A finite sequence of sentences from the target language can be seen as an *evidential state* a learner could be in. Accordingly, learners can be broadly characterized by how they behave as a function of their present conjecture and evidential state.

For example, some learners base their next move in hypothesis space on the whole content of their evidential state (they have *perfect memory* of past data) while others only remember parts of it. Some learners change their conjecture only when it is incompatible with their evidential state, others are not so constrained. Some try to modify their conjectures as little as possible in order to fit their evidential state, others take "wild guesses"... For at least one of the criteria of success we are going to examine, *identification in the limit*, there exists an impressive body of work detailing how the class of learnable languages changes when one or more of these restrictions are imposed on learners. The interested reader can consult Jain et al. (1999). Here we just mention the fact that, as we will see below when discussing *identification by enumeration*, while it is often easy to point out which parts of a learning procedure are at odds with one's best guess about the resources available to human language learners, it is often quite difficult to give a general characterization of the learning procedures one is comfortable with as far as developmental psycholinguistics is concerned.

1.1.5 Criteria of success

When can we say that a language learning strategy is successful? We will consider here three alternative criteria of success that are all compatible with the implicit premise of all the essays in this collection, the premise, that is, that what is learned is a grammar with no attached information about the probability distribution of the sentences that can be generated by it. As we introduce them we will show that it is very easy to prove that any class of languages that can be generated by a class of grammars consistent with the PPH is learnable under each of the three criteria.

The point of this exercise, which will be carried out using each time the same learning function, *identification by enumeration*, is to show that *all* PPH-consistent classes of languages are trivially learnable under *all* of the best understood criteria of success unless some rather substantial restrictions are imposed on what kind of learners humans are. The whole history of the last fifteen years of interaction between parametric linguistics and learnability (the essays in this volume included) can then be understood as an attempt to flesh out, using whatever evidence is available from empirical work in linguistics or psychology, what would follow from the assumption that human learners do not learn by enumeration but by some other, possibly independently motivated, mechanism. As mentioned above, no general consensus of what those mechanisms ought to be has emerged in the last fifteen years. As a result, rather than establishing general results, most recent studies have confined themselves to the analysis of individual learning algorithms, that as a consequence appear to the (ever shrinking) interested public as distant and isolated points in a vast and otherwise uncharted design space.

With all this in mind, let us start with our first criterion of success, *identification in the limit* (Gold, 1967).

1.1.5.1 Identification in the limit

Gold defines a *text* for a language *L* as an *infinite* sequence of sentences such that every sentence of *L* appears at least once in it and no sentence not in *L* ever appears in it. Let's consider now a procedure that takes as input *finite* initial segments of a *text* for a language and returns a conjecture (a grammar) about the language it is observing. Such a procedure is said to *identify* a *text* for *L* if and only if, after presentation of finitely many initial segments of the text it stabilizes on a single conjecture and that conjecture generates exactly *L*. The procedure is said to *identify* an entire language *L* if it is able to identify every possible text for it and, finally, it is said to identify a class of languages $\mathcal{L}$ if it identifies every *L* in it.

Given these definitions, in order to find out whether a class of languages $\mathcal{L}$ is learnable under the criterion of *identification in the limit* we either need to show the existence of a learning procedure that would *identify* every text for every language in $\mathcal{L}$, or show that no such learning procedure can exist.

We will immediately show that if a class of languages $\mathcal{L}$ has been generated by a set of grammars consistent with the PPH, then such a learning procedure does indeed exist. The procedure in question is called *identification by enumeration* (IBE) and was first described in Gold's (1967) seminal paper. We will describe it in detail because the very same learning procedure will be later employed to prove that PPH-consistent classes of languages are also learnable under the other two criteria of success we are going to discuss.

This is how IBE works for a finite class of languages such as those that result from any theory consistent with the PPH: the learner starts by writing down an enumeration $G_1, G_2 \ldots G_n$ of all her possible conjectures. The enumeration must have the property that, if $k > j$, then either $L(G_k) = L(G_j)$ (the language generated by grammar/hypothesis G_k is the same language as that generated by grammar/hypothesis G_j) or there is at least a sentence in $L(G_k)$ that is not in $L(G_j)$. She then initializes her hypothesis *H* to G_1 and the set of data observed *D* to the empty set. After presentation of each sentence s_i the learner first determines whether s_i is part of $L(H)$, the language resulting from her current hypothesis *H*. If so, she adds s_i to *D* and waits for a new sentence. Otherwise she adds s_i to *D* and changes her current conjecture *H* to the first G_i in the enumeration such that *D* is a subset of $L(G_i)$.

Now, let's see why IBE works for every finite class of languages. Suppose the target is $L(G_t)$, with $1 \leq t \leq n$ and σ is a text for the target. All we need to show is that: (a) IBE will never abandon the conjecture G_t – or any conjecture equivalent to it – if it ever happens to entertain it, and (b) there is a finite initial segment of σ in response to which IBE will hypothesize G_t or something equivalent. (a) follows immediately from the definition of IBE. As for (b) we can prove it by establishing that: (c) IBE will never hypothesize a G_k with $k > t$; (d) it will abandon every incorrect conjecture G_j after finitely many strings from σ, and (e) it will only entertain finitely many incorrect conjectures prior to hypothesizing G_t or one of its equivalents. Now, (e) directly follows from the fact that the enumeration $G_1 \ldots G_n$ is finite and (c) from the definition of IBE. As for (d), we can reason by contradiction: suppose that, in response to the first m sentences $s_1 \ldots s_m$ of σ, the learner conjectured a G_j such that $j < t$ and $L(G_j) \neq L(G_t)$ and never changed her conjecture thereafter. By definition of IBE, all of $s_1 \ldots s_m$ must be members of $L(G_j)$. Also, from the definition of the enumeration $G_1 \ldots G_n$ and the assumption that $j < t$ it follows that there is a sentence s_t in $L(G_t)$ that is not in $L(G_j)$. Now, since by assumption σ is a text for $L(G_t)$, s_t must appear somewhere in σ. And since s_t cannot be one of the $s_1 \ldots s_m$ sentences that caused the learner to hypothesize G_j, it must appear after the learner has hypothesized G_j. So, when the learner encounters s_t she is forced to abandon her conjecture, by the definition of IBE and the assumption that s_t is not a member of $L(G_j)$. But this contradicts the initial hypothesis that the learner could stick to the hypothesis G_j forever and so the proof by contradiction is completed.

So we now know that IBE is all that is needed to learn (identify in the limit) any parametric class of languages. With this established, we must hasten to add that identification in the limit is far too idealized a criterion of success to be used to model human language learning.

First of all it assumes complete and perfectly reliable information about the target language. In the following chapter, Martin Atkinson will show in detail what one would have readily suspected: the environment in which children learn their target language is *noisy* and fairly restrictive in the kind of information it makes available.

Second, it places no bounds of any kind on the amount of data learners are allowed to use to converge on their target: all that matters is that they do so *in the limit*. What we really would like is a criterion that would require the target to be reached after exposure to a number of sentences of the same order of magnitude as the number of sentences children are normally exposed to.

Finally, identification in the limit requires identification to be *exact*. But, as the whole chapter by Ian Roberts will explain, it is natural to argue that languages change over time precisely because there are situations in which learners get very close to the language of the previous generation, without, however, quite identifying it.

1.1.5.2 Wexler and Culicover's criterion

We'll take the cue from this last observation to introduce a second criterion of success on which a fair amount of research in linguistics and learnability depends. We will call it the Wexler and Culicover criterion, as it was most extensively used in Wexler and Culicover's (1980) seminal study on the learnability of transformational grammars. In more recent times it has been used as the criterion of choice in Gibson and Wexler's (1994) study and in all the research papers that extended their original idea, including the chapter by Sakas and Fodor in the present book.

While in identification in the limit it was possible for a sentence to appear exactly *once* in a text for a language, here we will require that at every time step in the learning process, every sentence in the target language have a nonzero probability of being presented to the learner. At the same time, instead of requiring *exact* identification of the target language we will just require that, for every $0 < \epsilon < 1$, for every language L in the class to be learned and every presentation sequence satisfying the condition above, there must be a finite number n such that, after presentation of n strings, the learner is guaranteed to output a conjecture that has probability less than ϵ to be incorrect.

Now, it is very easy to show that IBE can also learn every finite class of languages (and so every class of languages generated by a PPH theory) under the Wexler and Culicover criterion. The proof goes like this: since every text satisfying the Wexler and Culicover criterion is also a text in Gold's sense, it follows that after finitely many strings IBE can identify exactly, that is with error $\epsilon = 0$, every text in the sense of Wexler and Culicover. But if it can do so for $\epsilon = 0$, it can do so for every $0 < \epsilon < 1$.

1.1.5.3 PAC learning

Still, even in the Wexler and Culicover criterion, there is no requirement that the number of sentences that are used to attain convergence with less-than-ϵ error be a *small* number for every language in the class to be learned. This concern is, on the contrary, at the heart of the last criterion we will consider here, *Probably Approximately Correct* (PAC) learning, a criterion first proposed by Valiant (1984).

According to the PAC criterion, a learner is successful if and only if she has a *very high probability* of producing a conjecture that is *very close* to the target language when using only *reasonably few* sentences from the target language.

The general idea underlying PAC learning is that data are presented to the learner according to a probability distribution unknown to her and different for each target language. In other words, every language has, associated with it, a function that, for each sentence in it, determines how likely the given sentence is to be presented to the learner at any one time.[2]

PAC captures the idea that learners are successful if and only if they rapidly produce conjectures that would misclassify only a set of sentences from the target language that has a negligible chance of appearing in the learner's environment. How rapidly they are required to produce such a conjecture is a function of how negligible the chance of error is required to be: the smaller the chance of error required, the larger the size of the sample that can be used. Larger samples, naturally, take longer to be collected.

Moreover, unlike the Wexler and Culicover criterion, PAC does not require that a less-than-ϵ-error conjecture be *always* arrived at, but only that the probability of it not being arrived at be smaller than a certain confidence parameter δ ($0 \leq \delta < 1/2$).

However, as mentioned before, PAC is rather strict on the size of the sample that can be consumed to produce a conjecture that has less than δ probability of being in error by more than ϵ: it requires that, for every choice of δ and ϵ, the size of the sample consumed be a polynomial function of $1/\delta$ and $1/\epsilon$. In other words, the size of the sample should not grow *very fast* as $1/\delta$ and $1/\epsilon$ grow.

Once again, IBE can be used to show that every finite class of languages is PAC learnable. This follows directly from a theorem proved by Blumer et al. (1987) which states that a class of languages is PAC learnable if an *Occam learning algorithm* can be found for it.

Blumer defines an Occam learning algorithm for a class of languages $\mathcal{L}$ as an algorithm that, in response to data from any L in $\mathcal{L}$ always outputs a conjecture that has two properties, it is consistent with the sample received and has a complexity not exceeding a certain value that is a function of the least complex hypothesis available for the language to be learned and the size of the sample itself. The interested reader can find the precise statement of this second requirement in Blumer's original article. For the purpose of the present discussion, it is sufficient to note that the requirement in question is designed to disqualify hypotheses that, even if consistent with the data, consist simply of an enumeration of the sample itself. It will soon be clear, however, that the details of this requirement are not important for our proof. So, we want to show that IBE is an Occam learning algorithm for every finite class of languages (when the space of hypotheses is equally finite). That its conjectures are always consistent with the sample presented follows immediately from the definition of IBE. As for the second requirement, it is sufficient to observe that since the learner can entertain only finitely many hypotheses, there exists an upper bound on the complexity of the possible conjectures. The reader may consult Robin Clark's chapter in this book for a tutorial on how the complexity of hypotheses may be defined. Here we just note that this upper bound is a constant and that this is sufficient to meet the second part of Blumer's requirement for Occam learning algorithms. The reader can refer to Blumer's original paper to be convinced that this is indeed the case. This completes the proof that every finite class of languages, and so any class that is consistent with the PPH, is PAC learnable.

1.2   Moving away from identification by enumeration

Our insistence on using IBE in the proof that PPH-informed classes of languages are learnable under each of the success criteria we examined is due to the importance of driving home the following point: proving the learnability of PPH-informed classes of languages is generally speaking a trivial enterprise, whichever criterion of success one decides to adopt. The task becomes challenging only once one decides to reject as part of a model of human language learning the two very features that make IBE as successful as it is: complete memory of all past data and access to an initial enumeration that allows for hypotheses to be searched in the *correct order*.

Even in the absence of much substantive work in developmental psycholinguistics showing how much memory for past data children can be expected to have in the process of language learning, it is quite reasonable to reject the hypothesis that they have recall of their entire learning sample. It is interesting to note that most recent models of parametric language acquisition such as Dresher and Kaye's cue based learner, Gibson and Wexler's TLA, Clark's Genetic Algorithm and Fodor's STL (see Martin Atkinson's and Fodor and Sakas' chapters for detailed discussion of each of them) make the exact opposite assumption and attempt to show how learnability may be proved even using learners that have no explicit memory whatsoever of their learning sample although some of them cleverly encode some of it in the conjectures they entertain at any given time.

But it is when we start exploring what it would mean to abandon the *other* important feature of IBE, the prescient enumeration of all possible hypotheses, that we finally get to the heart of what makes the interaction between parametric linguistics, psychology and learnability interesting. IBE was repeatedly proved to work under the assumption that only finitely many hypotheses are available to the learner. But the PPH is a much stronger hypothesis than that: it not only implies that the class of possible (hypotheses about) human languages is finite but, most importantly, that variation among human languages can be expected to be systematic and take place along several, largely orthogonal dimensions. What this suggests, in effect, is that, although it is unrealistic to expect that human learners rely on a space of hypotheses that is nicely linearized as seen in IBE, it is perhaps not unreasonable to suppose that it is organized according to other principles that may make it possible to search it reliably and efficiently. The last fifteen years of work on the subject could be fairly reconstructed as a sustained investigation of what those principles might be. The entire line of research on the so called *Subset Principle* initiated by Wexler and Manzini (1987) and summarized by Martin Atkinson in the next chapter can be seen as an investigation of the structure of the space of hypotheses that would result if all parameter values except one were kept constant.

More recent work has concentrated on the possible patterns of overlapping among target languages that result from alternative settings of the parameters and allow algorithms as diverse as Gibson and Wexler's TLA and Fodor's STL to search the resulting space of hypotheses reliably and efficiently.

Because such patterns, which will form the subject of the discussion in much of the rest of this book, are often quite intricate, this introductory chapter will end by introducing a formal definition of parameter spaces that will, in effect, serve as a specialized vocabulary designed to make it possible to describe those patterns precisely and concisely. All the contributors to this book will then be able to use this vocabulary as a *lingua franca* that will facilitate the understanding of several, interrelated arguments by translating them from their original formulation into a common standard.

1.3   A formal model of parameter spaces

In this final section we will proceed as follows: we will first give a definition of parameter spaces that is general enough to cover any conceivable theory of language variation consistent with the PPH. We will then introduce the notation that is necessary to isolate regions of interest in any parameter space of interest.

Definition 1.1 *A parameter space* $\mathcal{P}$ *is a triple* $\langle par, L, \Sigma \rangle$, *where* Σ *is a finite alphabet of symbols and par is a finite set of parameters* $\{p_1 \ldots p_n\}$. *The parameters themselves can be seen as sets. In particular, given a parameter* p_i, *its members, which we enumerate as* $v_i^1 \ldots v_i^{|p_i|}$, *are just the "possible values" of* p_i. *Given the cartesian product* $\mathbf{P} = p_1 \times p_2 \times \cdots \times p_n$, *a parameter vector* $\overline{P}$ *is a member of* $\mathbf{P}$, *namely a possible way of choosing one value for every parameter. Let* Σ^* *be the set of all finite strings over the alphabet* Σ *and* 2^{Σ^*} *its power set (the set of all subsets of* Σ^*). *The function* $L : \mathbf{P} \mapsto 2^{\Sigma^*}$ *assigns a possibly empty subset of* Σ^* *to each vector* $\overline{P} \in \mathbf{P}$, *that is it associates every possible parameter setting (vector) with a language (set of strings).*

As it turns out, in order to analyze a parametric learning algorithm it is important to have a way of referring to portions of a parameter space that share a certain value assignment to certain selected parameters. This can be achieved in two steps by first defining the notion of a *partial* parameter assignment and then showing how a parameter space can be *sliced* according to a particular parameter assignment.

Definition 1.2 *Let* $\mathcal{P}$ *be a parameter space. A partial assignment in* $\mathcal{P}$ *is any subset B of*

$$\bigcup_{p_i \in par} \{p_i\} \times p_i$$

such that for every p_i *in par there is at most one* $\langle p_i, v_i^m \rangle$ *in B. Given two partial assignments A and B in* $\mathcal{P}$, *B is said to be A-consistent iff* $A \cup B$ *is also a partial assignment in* $\mathcal{P}$.

For example, suppose we have a parameter space with two binary valued parameters p_1 and p_2. If $p_1 = \{0, 1\}$, then the cartesian product $\{p_1\} \times p_1$ is the set of all ordered pairs such that the first element is the parameter p_1 and the second element is one of its values, 0 or 1. The cartesian product $\{p_1\} \times p_1$ therefore turns out to be $\{\langle p_1, 0 \rangle, \langle p_1, 1 \rangle\}$. Each of the elements of the cartesian product can be seen as a particular assignment of value to p_1. If p_2 is also equal to the set $\{0, 1\}$, then we have that

$$\bigcup_{p_i \in par} \{p_i\} \times p_i = \{\langle p_1, 0 \rangle, \langle p_1, 1 \rangle, \langle p_2, 0 \rangle, \langle p_2, 1 \rangle\}.$$

By definition 1.2 the subsets $\{\langle p_1, 0\rangle, \langle p_2, 0\rangle\}$, $\{\langle p_1, 0\rangle\}$ and $\{\langle p_2, 0\rangle\}$ are all partial assignments in $\mathcal{P}$. In particular, $\{\langle p_2, 0\rangle\}$ is $\{\langle p_1, 0\rangle\}$-consistent.

Finally, the following definition formalizes the notion of concentrating only on a part of a parameter space, a part that is picked up by choosing a partial assignment. The function π_i is a "projection" function: it takes a vector (parameter assignment) and returns the i-th element of the vector.

Definition 1.3 *Let $\mathcal{P}$ be a parameter space and A a partial assignment in it. If $A = \varnothing$, then $\mathcal{P}[A] = \mathcal{P}$. If $\mathcal{P}[A]$ is a parameter space $\langle par^A, L, \Sigma\rangle$ (with $par^A = \{p_1^A \ldots p_n^A\}$) and B is an A-consistent partial assignment in $\mathcal{P}$, then the subspace $\mathcal{P}[A \cup B]$ is the parameter space $\langle par^{A \cup B}, L, \Sigma\rangle$ such that, given*

$$H = \bigcup_{x \in B} \pi_1(x),$$

if $p_j \notin H$ then $p_j^{A \cup B} = p_j^A$ and if $p_j \in H$ then $p_j^{A \cup B} = \{v_j^m\}$ where v_j^m is the only $v \in p_j$ such that $\langle p_j, v_j^m\rangle \in B$. Finally, $\mathcal{P}[A \cup \overline{B}]$ is the parameter space $\langle par^{A \cup B}, L, \Sigma\rangle$ where, for every p_i in H, $p_i^{A \cup B} = p_i^A - p_i^{A \cup B}$ and, for every p_i not in H, $p_i^{A \cup B} = p_i^A$.

This definition looks more formidable than it really is. All it says is that, given a parameter space $\mathcal{P}$, and a partial assignment A, it is possible to define the "$\mathcal{P}[A]$ corner" of $\mathcal{P}$ to consist of all and only those languages in $\mathcal{P}$ that have their parameters set exactly as dictated by A. So, if $A = \{\langle p_i, 0\rangle, \langle p_j, 1\rangle\}$, the "$\mathcal{P}[A]$ corner" of $\mathcal{P}$ contains all and only those languages that have p_i set to value 0 and p_j set to value 1. Similarly, $\mathcal{P}[\overline{A}]$ can be seen as the "mirror image" of the "$\mathcal{P}[A]$ corner" since it is the set of all languages that have all the parameters listed in A set differently than is dictated by A.

It is worth noting that the larger the partial assignment A, the smaller the "$\mathcal{P}[A]$ corner" of $\mathcal{P}$ one is looking at. This means that, when we take a partial assignment A and we expand it to a larger partial assignment $A \cup B$, the "$\mathcal{P}[A \cup B]$ corner" of $\mathcal{P}$ is smaller than the original "$\mathcal{P}[A]$ corner".[3]

This is all the descriptive apparatus that we will need for the discussion that follows. So, for example, using the notation

$$s \in \bigcup_{\overline{P} \in \mathbf{P}^A} L(\overline{P}) - \bigcap_{\overline{P} \in \mathbf{P}^{A \cup B}} L(\overline{P})$$

we can avoid the cumbersome expression "s belongs to at least one of the languages whose parameters have been set as dictated by A but it is not the case that it belongs to every language that has its parameters set as dictated by *A* and at variance with all the parameter assignments listed in *B*". Hopefully, the reader will soon appreciate the advantages of the notation.

NOTES

1 Sadly, much work on language learning is published in which entire theories are established and conclusions are drawn with disregard for these very basic requirements.
2 PAC is really able to represent a more general scenario, where what is assigned a probability is the event that a given sentence is presented to the learner as a positive *or* negative example of the target language.
3 This obviously assumes that *B* is not empty and that *B* is not properly included in *A*.

2 Learnability and the acquisition of syntax

Martin Atkinson

2.1 Introduction

...there is no a priori reason to expect that the languages permitted by UG be learnable – that is, attainable under normal circumstances. All that we can expect is that some of them may be; the others will not be found in human societies. If proposals within the P[rinciples] & P[arameters] approach are close to the mark, then it will follow that languages are in fact learnable, but that is an empirical discovery, and a rather surprising one. (Chomsky and Lasnik, 1995: 18)

The above passage appears in a discussion in which Chomsky and Lasnik argue against the proposition that an adequate grammar of a language must provide an efficient basis for parsing the language's sentences. Well-known examples of well-formed sentences which are not efficiently parsable provide the crucial cases for the argument, which, of course, is ultimately based on the importance of the competence–performance distinction. Consistency then requires that skepticism be extended to another aspect of linguistic performance, that of acquiring a natural language. Just as there is no reason to believe that a grammar is well-designed to parse over an infinite range, so it is not necessary for universal grammar (UG) to be designed so as to make available only learnable languages. The optimism which appears in Chomsky and Lasnik's final sentence is closely linked to the theme of this book, since it is based on an accumulation of evidence indicating that linguistic variation, at least that obtaining within core grammar, can be accommodated by a finite number of finitely valued parameters.

The previous chapter has introduced a wide range of formal considerations and has illustrated some of the consequences which flow from the finiteness guaranteed by the human language faculty. In these circumstances, learnability is assured by some learning function or other, e.g. enumeration of hypotheses. However, as was noted, it does not follow that human learners embody such a learning function, so we should not infer from this perspective that considerations of learnability have no work to do.

In this chapter, we shall be focusing on learnability issues which arise in the context of the acquisition of syntax, seeking to establish the relevance of some of the ideas from the previous chapter to the study of natural languages and of children acquiring these languages. There currently exists a large gap in vocabulary between formal learning theory and linguistics. Chapter 1 has begun to bridge this gap, starting from formal learning theory; here, our bridge-building operation will start from the opposite side of the chasm, with the topics we consider all arising within the framework of Principles and Parameters Theory (PPT). A consequence of this starting point is that I shall lean towards the informal and intuitive whenever the opportunity presents itself, although a certain amount of formalism will at times be necessary. As will become apparent, while a small part of our discussion will be directly based on empirical work with children acquiring languages, most of it will be at a more abstract level, where we consider learnability problems and their solution in the context of specific *grammatical* proposals. Some of the methodological and interpretive difficulties which arise when we try to move from this level of abstraction to studies of real-time acquisition will be raised as we proceed.

The chapter has three major sections, which can incidentally be seen as providing a historical tour through the recent development of learnability theory. One component of a learning paradigm, as introduced in section 1.1.3, is an *environment*, and in section 2.2, I shall briefly review what is known about children's linguistic environments. The notion of a *text* has played a fundamental role in much formal learnability work, and in the previous chapter it was acknowledged that text presentation does not approximate to the situation confronted by a child learner. Because it will provide a backdrop for some of the subsequent discussion, it is appropriate to sketch the empirical findings here.

Historically, concern with this question predates any developments in formal learnability theory. It seems that some psychologists, suspicious of the innateness claims which have provided the intellectual backdrop to so much of the progress in modern linguistics, have found it difficult to give up on the belief that linguistic environments really do have properties (if only we could identify them) which would enable us to see them as providing a sufficient basis for grammar induction. We can be fairly confident in our conclusions under this heading, but we owe it to the skeptics to provide some justification for this confidence.

Turning to parameterization and the specific learnability problems it poses, the most accessible of these conceptually is the *Subset Problem*. It is therefore almost certainly no accident that the first, and probably still best-known, work on learnability within PPT is Wexler and Manzini's detailed discussion of Binding Theory parameters and their claim that these parameters do raise Subset Problems for the learner. Here we meet a very straightforward illustration that, even with only a finitely bounded space of possibilities, it is necessary to equip the human learning function with special properties if it is to succeed. Section 2.3 will introduce the most important aspects of Wexler and Manzini's work and will attempt to assess its current relevance in the light of ongoing work in linguistics and child language acquisition.

Where Subset Problems do not arise, an immediate response might be that the learning task for a PPT learner should be straightforward. In such cases, there ought to be diagnostic sentences in each language which will immediately direct the learner to the target parameter setting. However, this optimism is not well-founded. It turns out that an intriguing set of problems emerges as soon as we begin to look carefully at the ways in which parameters can interact, while at the same time remaining alert to the fact that a human learner is computationally limited and working within a rather short time frame. The work which has established itself as a benchmark in this area is Gibson and Wexler (1994), and section 2.4 is largely devoted to examining some of the linguistic consequences of their Triggering Learning Algorithm (TLA), including some of the work which has been directly stimulated by this development. A rather different approach to the problems raised by interacting parameters has been developed by Clark (1992), and this section will also include an introduction to the major aspects of his "selective" model of parameter setting, embodied in his Genetic Algorithm (GA). Since this model has been employed as the basis for an account of a specific set of historical changes in French (Clark and Roberts, 1993), section 2.4 will conclude by briefly examining the relationship between language acquisition and language change, comparing Clark and Roberts' approach to change with that advocated by Lightfoot (1997).

2.2   The child's linguistic environment

There are at least three aspects of the child's linguistic environment which have been subjected to some scrutiny and which are of importance in discussions of learnability. These are: the availability of negative evidence, the "complexity" of the language directed at small children and the question of whether the structural characteristics of this language change in any systematically ordered way as development proceeds.

2.2.1 *Negative evidence*

It must be noted that the availability of negative evidence can radically alter the nature of a learnability problem. Therefore we really need to have a clear view on the empirical availability of negative information to take into our discussion of how syntactic parameters might be fixed.

Before turning to empirical studies, it is important to be clear that learnability proofs relying on the existence of negative evidence typically require such evidence to be *systematically* available, just like positive evidence is. Indeed, along with the notion of a *text*, introduced in 1.1.5.1, it is also possible to consider an *informant sequence* (Gold, 1967), where the latter is a sequence such that *all* sentences from the target language and *all* non-sentences on the appropriate vocabulary are guaranteed to be eventually presented, along with the information (which could be supplied by an informant, hence the name) as to whether they are sentences or not. If children were systematically supplied with negative information in this way, the nature of the acquisition task would be radically changed. Indeed, Gold was able to prove that the class of languages identifiable in the limit from informant presentation properly included the class of context sensitive languages.[1] For text, on the other hand, not even the class of regular languages is identifiable in the limit, so the shift in learnability capacity which is contingent on this changed environment is very significant.

Obviously, the occasional correction of grammatical errors which occurs as children acquire their native language does not turn a child's linguistic environment into an informant sequence; indeed, we can rely on the finiteness of children's linguistic environments to categorically assert that these environments do not constitute informant sequences (as we have seen, for the same reason, they do not constitute texts). Given such certainty, why spend time considering the availability of negative data? There are at least two reasons for this.

First, a substantial literature has appeared in which the view that negative data of one sort or another do exist has been supported. The findings reported in this literature must be critically examined and their consequences for learnability questions assessed. Second, while the formal implications of systematic exposure to negative data are clear, this is not the case for what we might term "occasional" exposure to such data. If we were to be entirely open-minded, we might suppose that the learning problem, rather than being cast in the context of a whole language or a complete set of parameters, could be "modularized" into subproblems, with any negative data which do occur having a valuable function within one of the "modules." While an entirely speculative suggestion, this is perhaps sufficient to motivate an interest in the extent (if there is one) to which negative data are available to the child.

Having advocated open-mindedness in the previous paragraph, let me now immediately close off one area of enquiry by proposing that explicit correction is a phenomenon which occurs too infrequently and unsystematically and does not have any causal role in guiding acquisition. I don't know whether this is true, but there is well-known anecdotal evidence which raises severe doubts about causal role. These are the interchanges cited by McNeill (1966) and Braine (1971), where they sought to explicitly correct grammatical errors in the speech of their own children with no success at all.

What other source of negative data might we consider? Imagine that there are two signals S_1 and S_2 such that whenever children produce a grammatical utterance, S_1 occurs, and whenever they produce an ungrammatical utterance, they are presented with S_2 – where S_2 might be no more than lack of S_1. Such a contingency could provide children with *feedback*, enabling them to mark their own utterances as grammatical or not, and might be an important component of the learning task. Do such signals exist? The classic study in this area (Brown and Hanlon, 1970) examined the notions of "contingent approval" and "contingent appropriateness" in mothers' responses to their children's well- and ill-formed utterances. For the former, the authors were interested in whether approval (S_1) followed grammatical child utterances and disapproval (S_2) ungrammatical utterances; for the latter, they asked whether it was the case that comprehension and appropriate behavior (S_1) followed grammatical utterances, whereas bewilderment and *nonsequiturs* (S_2) followed ungrammatical forms. In neither case did they find any significant correlation. In short, mothers were no more likely to respond to an ill-formed utterance than to a well-formed utterance with some variant of "no, that's not right" or to produce behavior, linguistic or otherwise, inconsistent with the perceived purpose of the ongoing dialogue. Conversely, the frequency of occurrence of approval and appropriate behavior was not skewed in the direction of well-formed utterances. What did appear to govern these contingencies was truth-value, with mothers being anxious to applaud their children's insights and to offer negative evaluations and semantic corrections for their false utterances.

Since 1970, the search for contingencies which might be linked to grammaticality has gone on. For example, the suggestion that *repetition* of ill-formed strings (with corrections) is more likely than repetition of well-formed strings was investigated by Hirsh-Pasek, Treiman and Schneiderman (1984), with what were presented as positive results. Particularly, it was found that for two-year-olds, 20 percent of ill-formed utterances were repeated by mothers, whereas only 12 percent of well-formed utterances evoked this behavior. A number of other discourse-based types of signal have been investigated from a similar perspective (Demetras, Post and Snow 1986; Penner, 1987; Bohannon and Stanowicz 1988). Overall, while some of the investigated cor-relations have reached statistical significance, there have been severe difficulties in comparing categories of discourse signals across studies as well as differing reporting techniques, whereby some investigators present their results as averages over mother–child pairs and others report individual dyad data. A trenchant critique of the methodology of these studies is Marcus (1993), where most of the issues mentioned below are also discussed in some detail.

Setting aside methodological reservations, what are we to make of figures such as those presented by Hirsh-Pasek et al.? At least two observations should be made. First, the asymmetric use of repetition by the parents in this study was restricted to mothers of two-year-olds; mothers of older children did not produce significantly different numbers of repetitions following their children's grammatical and ungrammatical utterances. As a consequence, even if we suppose that parental repetition is a source of negative data for two-year-old children, it appears that this source is not available for older children. Of course, children entering their third year are still producing ungrammatical utterances and it would be absurd to suggest that acquisition is complete at this point. Second, it is important to note that contingent repetition of this type does *not* amount to the adult *reliably* signalling the grammatical status of children's utterances, as was envisaged in the introduction of S_1 and S_2 above. To use Marcus' (1993) term, it is conceivable that repetition provided the children with *noisy feedback*, an appropriate characterization for all the various discourse variables which have been put forward as potential suppliers of negative information, but it certainly did not provide them with *complete feedback*, i.e. a signal which would enable them to immediately conclude that their preceding utterance was or was not grammatical.[2] As noisy feedback is not completely reliable, it becomes important to ask *how much* noisy feedback children would need in order to be confident in their assessment of the grammatical status of their repeated utterances. Making reasonable assumptions about confidence levels, Marcus concludes that for a child to categorize a string as ungrammatical on the basis of the Hirsh-Pasek et al. figures, tokens of the string would need to be uttered by the child 446 times! To be fair, this is not the least absurd figure Marcus derives from the discourse studies he considers; this honor goes to a figure of 85 based on Bohannon and Stanowicz (1988), but this is unlikely to provide much consolation to those who would believe that discourse contingencies can, even in principle, provide effective sources of negative evidence.

It seems, then, that we can conclude that it has not been established that negative evidence exists in any plausible form – overt correction is infrequent and unsystematic, discourse signals appear to lack the reliability necessary for children to be able to confidently *categorize* their utterances as grammatical or ungrammatical. But suppose we still want to leave options open – perhaps the overt corrections really are systematic in ways we haven't realized; perhaps there are reliable discourse signals that we simply haven't spotted yet. As is argued by Pinker (1989) and Grimshaw and Pinker (1989), the *existence* of negative evidence of the types contemplated here is only the first of three properties which must be considered. With existence established, it would still be necessary to show that overt correction or the discourse signal is *effective* in acquisition, and this has never been done. In this connection, we can again cite McNeill (1966) and Braine (1971) on the ineffectiveness of correction, while Morgan and Travis (1989) is a revealing study of the failings of the discourse-based work to even address this question.

Finally, even if negative evidence existed and its effectiveness had been demonstrated, it would remain to show that it is *necessary* in acquisition. Note that this would not be achieved if the demonstration of effectiveness involved no more than facilitation of acquisition, say by speeding up some aspect of structural development relative to a group which did not benefit from the negative evidence. For necessity to be established, it would have to be shown that the group denied the negative evidence did not develop the relevant structures at all, or perhaps developed them in some fashion which could be diagnosed as "abnormal." Not surprisingly, there are no experimental results which would justify this conclusion. Furthermore, the existence of cultures in which not even noisy feedback exists to any significant extent suggests that any plausible argument for the necessity of negative information is an extremely remote possibility (Marcus, 1993: 71). In conclusion, then, it seems that we are entirely justified in proceeding with the *No Negative Data Assumption*, which has been a feature of most work in learnability.[3]

2.2.2   Complexity

In the 1970s, a great deal of work was done on the characteristics of Motherese, the register which mothers and others use in addressing small children (see Snow and Ferguson, 1977, for a representative collection of articles). One suggestion emerging from this (Brown, 1977) was that the "simplicity" exhibited by this register made first language acquisition easier and obviated the need for an innate UG. In some sense, which was never made precise, Motherese was to provide a database which would enable the child to formulate a grammar inductively. Challenges to this concept of "simplicity" were not long in coming (Newport, Gleitman and Gleitman, 1977), along with the observation that a reduction of the information provided by the child's linguistic environment, rather than shedding instant light on the process of language development, ought to make the problem of acquiring grammar more mysterious – to the extent that information about the grammar of a language was exhibited only in "complex" constructions, denying children access to these constructions would only make their task more difficult. This observation has proved to be of considerable importance, since one aspect of "simplicity" did survive critical scrutiny.

In a statistical study of mothers' speech to children, Morgan (1989) reports that more than 90 percent of the utterances in the available corpora were degree-0 utterances, with fewer than 1 percent being degree-2 or more (in this report, the degree of an utterance was computed in terms of sentential embeddings). Now, of course, we have no idea whether the small number of degree-2 utterances played any significant role in the acquisition process, but it is at least *a priori* plausible that had they not been present, there would have been no consequences for the children's acquisition. If this is so, it follows that acquisition must be possible on the basis of data which exhibit at most a single degree of embedding, and the implications of this sort of thinking have been pursued in two different ways.

First, it can be maintained that observations on the complexity of the data available to the child will have an impact on PPT itself. If, in fact, children acquire grammars (that is, establish the values of a set of parameters) on the basis of data which are subject to an identifiable complexity restriction, then the parameters *must be settable on this basis*. In short, if we have a parameter p_i with values v_i^1 and v_i^2, then it must be the case that the "effects" of setting p_i at v_i^1 or v_i^2 are "visible" on data which respect the complexity restriction. Responding to this challenge, Lightfoot (1989, 1991) has proposed that parameters should be constrained so as to be settable on the basis of degree-0 data.

To illustrate, the claim that UG should include a Bounding Nodes Parameter in the theory of movement was originally based on consideration of differences in the behavior of WH-questions in English, French and Italian (Sportiche, 1981; Rizzi, 1982). A French example cited in Sportiche's discussion is (1):

(1)   Voilà quelqu'un à qui je crois que je sais lequel j'offrirais
        "Here's someone to whom I think that I know which I would give"

The English translation of (1) is not well-formed and this is put down to the fact that it violates the Subjacency Principle, which requires that no token of movement should cross more than one bounding node. With the set of bounding nodes specified as {NP, IP}, the violation induced by the movement of *to whom* follows. However, the movement of *à qui* in the French sentence has exactly the same trajectory.

In the face of this type of observation, rather than abandon the Subjacency Principle, Sportiche and Rizzi proposed that the set of bounding nodes should be parameterized, with grammars having (possibly constrained) choices from the set {NP, IP, CP}. Then, French and Italian can be seen as making the selection {NP, CP}, from which it follows that only one bounding node is crossed by the movement of *à qui* in (1).[4]

Crucially, for Lightfoot's thesis, examples such as those in (1) are degree-2, and in the light of his hypothesis, the logic is stark: he can reject the Bounding Nodes Parameter as a legitimate parameter in PPT, or he can show how the effects of the Bounding Nodes Parameter are exhibited on degree-0 data. Taking the latter option, he cites the degree-0 sentence in (2):

(2)   Combien$_i$ as-tu vu [$_{NP}$ t$_i$ de personnes]?
        "How many people did you see?"

If, as seems reasonable, *combien* originates in the NP-specifier position in (2), in order to move to the CP-specifier position, it will have to cross NP and IP. But, assuming Subjacency, this will be sufficient to show a child that {NP, IP} is not the appropriate setting for the Bounding Nodes Parameter in French. Supposing, for the sake of argument, that {NP, CP} is the only option, the child will be able to set this parameter on the basis of exposure to degree-0 data.[5]

The second consequence of taking seriously the "simplicity" of the child's linguistic environment has focused on how this might shape an appropriate conception of a text for learnability purposes. We have already met the unconstrained notion of text which informs much of the classic learnability work and noted its empirical weakness. It is of interest, therefore, that Robin Clark has been able to develop a concept of a *fair text* on the basis of certain assumptions about the process of parameter setting and the way in which parameter values must be *expressed* in sentences which are appropriately "simple" (see section 2.4 for some background discussion and chapter 4 for extensive development). We thus see that an emphasis emerges from these considerations which is quite contrary to that initially adopted by Brown. The "simplicity" of Motherese utterances, at least in so far as this is assessed by computations of degree, provides a valuable constraint on the nature of parameters, rather than an inductive basis for traditional learning. That parameters, once set, will exhibit their effects over arbitrarily complex data, simply serves to underwrite the misguidedness of Brown's initial position.

2.2.3   Ordered data

Linked to complexity is the view that the data presented to children come in a particular *order* and that children are capable of exploiting this order in their acquisition of the target language – Levelt (1975) contemplates the possibility of Motherese providing "graded language lessons" for small children. The intuitive idea seems to be that children may be led to focus on different aspects of language in an ordered and systematic way, but again no firm proposals to back up this intuition have ever been presented.

We should note immediately that if a learner is equipped with whatever principles determine the order in which data are presented, this can be a powerful aid to acquisition, converting an insoluble learnability problem into a tractable one. We can see this by considering again the following, infinite, class of languages $\mathcal{L}$:

$$L_0 = \{a, aa, aaa, aaaa, \ldots\}$$
$$L_1 = \{a\}$$
$$L_2 = \{a, aa\}$$
$$L_3 = \{a, aa, aaa\}$$
$$\ldots$$

As it happens, $\mathcal{L}$ is not identifiable in the limit on text. To see why, consider that any learner able to identify L_0 would do so after inspecting finitely many sentences from it with a_i being the longest ($a_i = a$ repeated i times). But any learner that identified L_0 would then fail to identify the finite language L_i, one of whose texts does indeed begin exactly as the text in response to which the learner conjectured L_0.

But now suppose that we constrain the mode of data presentation so that sentences are presented according to the following rule, and suppose further that the learner knows this rule:

(3)   Data are presented in order of increasing length; for the finite languages L_i ($i \neq 0$), once the longest sentence has been presented, the sequence begins again with the shortest sentence.

It is easy to see that a learner equipped with (3) can now identify $\mathcal{L}$ in the limit. We offer an informal description of a procedure which such a learner can follow. A learner starting with the hypothesis L_0 will retain it so long as data go on increasing in length. This will ensure that L_0 is identified if it is the target. If one of the finite languages is the target, there will be a point in the data sequence (corresponding to the $(i + 1)$-th datum for L_i) at which the length of data reverts to 1 and at this point, the learner switches hypotheses to L_i and stays there. Of course, what the reduction in length indicates is that certain strings are *not* in the target language, so this kind of order information is an indirect source of negative evidence.

What might the issues be empirically? Obviously, the above illustration does not link to empirical considerations in any direct way. We shall meet some issues concerning order of parameter setting in section 2.4, but it is not clear that the sorts of ordering questions which have been considered in the acquisition literature can be linked to any explicit learnability framework. For instance, Newport, Gleitman and Gleitman (1977) investigated the proposal that the speech addressed to young children is grammatically homogeneous, when compared to adult–adult talk, the idea being that such homogeneity might enable a child to focus on one or a small number of grammatical aspects of the target language at a time, thereby making acquisition more readily explicable. We need not agonize over whether enhanced learning would be the outcome of such homogeneity, as Newport et al.'s results were uniformly negative across a number of measures. It appears, then, that with the exception of the degree-n variable, where speech addressed to children might exhibit a developmental pattern, there is no intelligible sense of order which a learnability model might exploit.[6]

With our views on the child's linguistic environment in place, we can now turn to studies of parameter setting in PPT.

2.3   Subset parameters

As we shall see in the next section, serious difficulties emerge for learners constrained in ways which are not psychologically implausible as soon as we begin to take account of the possibility of parameters interacting in unhelpful ways. In this section, however, we shall focus on parameters which succeed in being badly behaved and creating learning problems without any assistance from other parameters.

Wexler and Manzini (1987) and Manzini and Wexler (1987) are the classic studies of subset parameters in a learnability context. To come to terms with the issues they raise, we begin by considering the set-theoretic relations which can obtain between languages which result from setting parameters in various ways.

So, suppose that we have a parameter p_i with values v_i^1 and v_i^2 and two parameter settings $\overline{Pv_i^1}$ and $\overline{Pv_i^2}$ that differ only in the value assigned to p_i (v_i^1 and v_i^2, respectively). We will assume for the moment that p_i can be studied while all the other parameters are kept fixed as dictated by $\overline{P}$. This assumption will be discussed below, in section 2.3.2. Consider the languages $L(\overline{Pv_i^1})$ and $L(\overline{Pv_i^2})$ which are generated by these alternative parameter settings. There are four possible set-theoretic relations between $L(\overline{Pv_i^1})$ and $L(\overline{Pv_i^2})$. These are set out in (4):

(4)   a. $L(\overline{Pv_i^1}) \cap L(\overline{Pv_i^2}) = \varnothing$

    b. $L(\overline{Pv_i^1}) \cap L(\overline{Pv_i^2}) \neq \varnothing$ and
        neither $L(\overline{Pv_i^1}) \supset L(\overline{Pv_i^2})$ nor $L(\overline{Pv_i^2}) \supset L(\overline{Pv_i^1})$

    c. $L(\overline{Pv_i^1}) \supset L(\overline{Pv_i^2})$

    d. $L(\overline{Pv_i^2}) \supset L(\overline{Pv_i^1})$

In the cases of (4a) and (4b), where $L(\overline{Pv_i^1})$ and $L(\overline{Pv_i^2})$ are disjoint or have a nonempty intersection without either being properly contained in the other, we shall assume for now that there is no immediate learnability problem. *Prima facie* evidence for this is easy to come by. Suppose that learners set parameters at random and that in the situation depicted by (4a), the target value for p_i is v_i^1. If the learner's choice is v_i^1 and we suppose that shifts in hypotheses occur only when a sentence is presented which cannot be analyzed by the grammar, and if we further suppose that all evidence is positive, the learner will stay with this correct hypothesis. If, on the other hand, we suppose that the initial choice is (incorrectly) v_i^2, then, assuming that the only parameter that can be reset is p_i, the very first datum to be presented from $L(\overline{Pv_i^1})$ will force a change to what we are assuming is the correct alternative.

For (4b), the situation is identical if the learner's initial choice is v_i^1. If, however, the learner incorrectly chooses v_i^2, it will not necessarily be the case that the first presented datum will exhibit this incorrectness – this datum could be from $L(\overline{Pv_i^1}) \cap L(\overline{Pv_i^2})$. Nevertheless, supposing some analogue of text presentation, eventually a datum from $L(\overline{Pv_i^2}) - L(\overline{Pv_i^1})$ will be presented and this will be sufficient to cause a hypothesis switch for the learner. Again, the learner having switched, all subsequent data will be consistent with the revised hypothesis and the language will be successfully identified.

But now consider (4c) and (4d). They are symmetrical in the relevant respects, so we will take just (4c). Suppose that the target value for p_i is v_i^2. Again, if the learner's initial guess is correct, this value will never be changed and $L(\overline{Pv_i^2})$ will be identified. If an incorrect guess of v_i^1 is made, the situation is analogous to that in (4b) and is resolved in an identical fashion. Suppose, on the contrary, that the target is v_i^1, which gives rise to the subset language $L(\overline{Pv_i^1})$. Once more, a correct initial guess will be maintained, but the crucial case allows the learner to guess v_i^2. This puts the learner in the superset language $L(\overline{Pv_i^2})$ and now the absence of negative data becomes crucial. All data presented to the learner are, of course, from $L(\overline{Pv_i^1})$. However, because of the subset–superset relation in (4c), they are also from $L(\overline{Pv_i^2})$. Accordingly, if we suppose that learners only switch their hypotheses on the presentation of unanalyzable data, our learner will never abandon the choice of v_i^2 and will be stuck with the wrong hypothesis for ever. $L(\overline{Pv_i^1})$ is not identifiable on this scenario and the small class of languages characterized by the parameter P is also *not* identifiable, as one of its members fails to have this property.

This informal description raises a number of questions. Most obviously, we should ask what we can do to overcome the difficulty created by the Subset Problem. Also, however, there is the simplifying assumption we have made about all other parameters being set in the same way, which deserves careful scrutiny. Third, and most urgently for the linguist, one needs to determine whether the predicament raised by the Subset Problem ever arises. We consider these issues in the next three subsections.

2.3.1   The Subset Principle

Responding to the difficulty created by the Subset Problem is straightforward. This difficulty only arises if we allow the learner the option of setting parameters randomly. If we remove this option, then the problem will be resolved. To this end, Wexler and Manzini (1987: 61) formulate the *Subset Principle* as follows.[7]

(5)   The learning function maps the input data to that value of a parameter which generates a language:
   a. compatible with the input data; and
   b. *smallest* among the languages compatible with the input data.

To see how this works in the simple case we started with, consider again the situation depicted by (4c). If the target value of p_i is v_i^2, it will again always be possible to converge on this value from a text, although (5b) will now require the learner to assume the incorrect value v_i^1 so long as the text contains only data from $L(\overline{Pv_i^1})$. This, of course, is the key to the situation when the target is v_i^1. Then, only data from $L(\overline{Pv_i^1})$ are ever presented, and (5b) requires that in these circumstances v_i^1 is the learner's choice. We thus see that if we constrain the learning function in this simple way, the learner will never end up in a superset language from which retreat is impossible.

Before going further, it is important to observe that Wexler and Manzini see the Subset Principle as providing an explanatory basis for a theory of linguistic markedness. Obviously, what (5) does is order the values of subset parameters based on the inclusion relations of the sets they generate. Wexler and Manzini suggest that this ordering should in turn be linked to statements of relative markedness, governed by (6):

(6)   If p_i is a parameter with values $v_i^1, v_i^2 \ldots v_i^n$ such that, for some parameter assignment $\overline{P}$, $L(\overline{Pv_i^1}) \subset L(\overline{Pv_i^2}) \subset \ldots \subset L(\overline{Pv_i^n})$, then v_i^m is unmarked relative to v_i^{m+1} for every $1 \leq m \leq n-1$.

As we shall see, this and related notions of markedness have provoked considerable discussion.

2.3.2   The Independence Principle

Moving next to our simplifying assumption, we can arrive at an understanding of the problem by restricting attention to the two-parameter case. Suppose we have two parameters p_i and p_j with values v_i^1, v_i^2 and v_j^1, v_j^2 respectively. Again supposing that all other parameters are fixed in value as dictated by $\overline{P}$, we can refer to the languages generated by the possible combinations of these parameter values as $L(\overline{Pv_i^m v_j^n})$ where

m and n take on the values 1, 2. Now, suppose that we compute subset relations between these languages and derive the results in (7):

(7)   a. $L(\overline{Pv_i^1 v_j^1}) \subset L(\overline{Pv_i^2 v_j^1})$

b. $L(\overline{Pv_i^2 v_j^2}) \subset L(\overline{Pv_i^1 v_j^2})$

Such a situation creates a dilemma for the Subset Principle; if we suppose that p_j is set at the value v_j^1, then, according to the Subset Principle, p_i should be set at v_i^1 unless the data require the setting v_i^2 – this is because of (7a). Alternatively, via (7b), if p_j is set at the value v_j^2, then p_i should be set at v_i^2 unless the data demand the setting v_i^1. Thus, it appears that the Subset Principle cannot apply in these circumstances. If this is the case, however, it is easy to see that there is nothing to prevent the learner from becoming trapped in a superset. For suppose that the target is $L(\overline{Pv_i^2 v_j^2})$ and that the learner initially relies on (7a) in conservatively approaching the value of p_i. Subsequently, p_j is set to its correct value of v_j^2, which leaves the learner in the superset language $L(\overline{Pv_i^1 v_j^2})$ with respect to the target. Alternatively, suppose that the target is $L(\overline{Pv_i^1 v_j^1})$ and the learner relies on (7b) to get started. Correct fixing of the value of p_j as v_j^1 moves the learner into the language $L(\overline{Pv_i^2 v_j^1})$, which is again a superset with respect to the target.[8] To rule out the possibility of this situation arising, Wexler and Manzini (1987:65) formulate the *Independence Principle*:

(8)   The subset relations between languages generated under different values of a parameter remain constant whatever the values of the other parameters are taken to be.

Thus, a slight modification of the simplifying assumption with which we started turns out to be necessary if the Subset Principle is to do its work as part of the learning function: while we do not need to assume that all other parameters are set at the same value, we must assume that any differences in their settings are immaterial as far as the relevant set inclusion relations are concerned. It is noteworthy that whereas the Subset Principle is properly construed as part of the learning function, the Independence Principle is actually a constraint on UG, providing an example of how considerations of learnability can have implications for linguistic theory.[9]

2.3.3   The empirical status of the Subset Problem: Binding Theory

It is all very well to appreciate the force of the Subset Problem in the abstract, but without illustration from reasonably plausible parameter spaces, it remains a tool without a purpose. Perhaps all parameters in PPT give rise to the situations depicted in (4a) and (4b), with the Subset Problem never arising in practice.

Wexler and Manzini locate an application for the Subset Principle in the Binding Theory. It would not be appropriate here to go into the full complexities which they explore, but it is easy enough to illustrate the general direction of their argument. Consider the English examples in (9):

(9)   a. John$_i$ says that [Maria$_j$ loves herself$_j$/*himself$_i$]
        b. John$_i$ ordered Harald$_j$ [PRO$_j$ to shave himself$_{*i/j}$]

Simplifying slightly, here we see illustrations of the fact that the English reflexive anaphors *himself/herself* must be bound from inside the clause within which they occur. This clause constitutes a local domain known as a governing category (GC) and Principle A of the Binding Theory (Chomsky, 1981a) is formulated as (10):

(10)   An anaphor must be bound within its GC.

To yield a fully explicit account of the data in (9), (10) must be supplemented with a definition of GC, and this appears in (11):

(11)   The GC for α is the smallest category containing α and a subject.

Running these definitions on the examples in (9) quickly establishes that the bracketed strings are the GCs for the anaphors in each case; then, the ill-formed examples result from abortive attempted bindings from outside the anaphors' GCs.

It turns out that the Icelandic anaphor *sig* ("self") behaves rather differently to *himself/herself*. To see this, consider the examples in (12):[10]

(12)   a. Jón$_i$ segir að [Maria$_j$ elskar sig$_{*i/j}$]
           "Jon says that Maria loves self"
        b. Jón$_i$ skipaði Harald$_i$ að [PRO raka sig$_i$]
           "Jon ordered Harald to shave self"

The first of these examples is identical to English in the relevant respects and indicates that in a finite clause (*elskar* is a finite verbal form) *sig* cannot be bound outside the domain defined by its closest subject. In (12b), however, where the subordinate clause is infinitival, such long-distance binding is possible. This, along with other data, leads to the suggestion that the definition of GC should be parameterized to include the value in (13) alongside that in (11):

(13)   The GC for α is the smallest category containing α and an indicative tense.

Applying this definition to (12a) yields the local binding requirement; in (12b), however, there is no indicative tense in the subordinate clause and binding of the anaphor from outside that clause is permitted. Now, it is not too difficult to see that if we identify our parameter p_i from section 2.3.1 with the GC Parameter we have begun to construct in (11) and (13), regarding the English value in (11) as v_i^1 and the Icelandic value in (13) as v_i^2, then, *ceteris paribus* (that is for every parameter assignment $\overline{P}$) $L(\overline{Pv_i^1}) \subset L(\overline{Pv_i^2})$, i.e. with respect to the set of structures in question) English is a subset of Icelandic.

In fact, the proposals that Wexler and Manzini develop are considerably more elaborate than the above in a variety of ways. Specifically, they claim to identify *five* distinct values of the GC Parameter as shown in (14) (cf. Wexler and Manzini, 1987: 53):[11]

(14)   The GC for α is the smallest category containing α and
        a. a subject, or
        b. an INFL, or
        c. a TNS, or
        d. an indicative TNS, or
        e. a root TNS.

Above, we have seen that English reflexive anaphors instantiate (14a), whereas Icelandic *sig* illustrates (14d).[12] To take just one further example, consider the binding possibilities for Japanese *zibun* "self," as illustrated in (15) (Manzini and Wexler, 1987: 419):

(15)   John-wa$_j$ [Bill-ga$_i$ zibun-o$_{i/j}$ nikunde iru] to omotte iru
        John Bill self hates that thinks
        "John thinks that Bill hates self"

Obviously, it is no surprise that *zibun* can be bound here by *Bill*; however, it is also possible for it to be bound by *John*, and a moment's reflection shows that this requires the GC for *zibun* to be defined as in (14e).

Generalizing the observations we made above about English reflexives and Icelandic *sig*, it is fairly easy to see that, when all other parameters are kept fixed (so, for any choice of $\overline{P}$) the five values of the GC Parameter yield successively larger languages for anaphors, as indicated in (16):

(16) $L(\overline{P_{GC^a}}) \subset L(\overline{P_{GC^b}}) \subset L(\overline{P_{GC^c}}) \subset L(\overline{P_{GC^d}}) \subset L(\overline{P_{GC^e}})$

Taking just $L(\overline{P_{GC^a}})$ and $L(\overline{P_{GC^b}})$, an anaphor which must be bound in the domain of a subject *cannot* be bound outside an NP which has a subject. Thus, in English, (17) is ill-formed:

(17)   *John$_i$ resented [$_{NP}$ Mary's criticism of himself$_i$]

If, however, an anaphor is required to be bound in the domain of an INFL and NPs lack INFL, then binding from outside NP over an NP-subject will be possible, i.e. the analogue of (17) will be well-formed. Since *Mary* can bind an anaphor in the position of *himself* in (17) (the anaphor would normally be *herself* for unrelated reasons) irrespective of whether GCs are defined in terms of occurrences of subject or INFL, it follows that $L(\overline{P_{GC^a}})$ properly contains $L(\overline{P_{GC^b}})$.

Exercise

2.1   Construct informal arguments similar to those preceding this exercise to show that the other proper inclusions in (16) do indeed follow from the parameter values on which they are based.

So far, we have said nothing about pronouns, which are the subject of Principle B of the Binding Theory:

(18)   A pronoun must be free (= not bound) in its governing category.

The natural proposal for Wexler and Manzini to make is that GCs for pronouns are subject to the same parametric variation as they are for anaphors. Initial evidence for the correctness of this view can be gleaned from the distribution of the Icelandic pronoun *hann*, which Wexler and Manzini (1987: 54) present as in (19):[13]

(19)   a.   Jón$_i$ segir að [Maria elskar hann$_i$]
              "Jon says that Maria loves (ind) him"
        b.   Jón$_i$ segir að [Maria elski hann$_i$]
              "John says that Maria loves (subj) him"
        c.   *Jón$_i$ skipaði mér að [raka hann$_i$]
              "Jon ordered me to shave him]"

Here, (19c) indicates that the GC for *hann* must be defined by TNS. By assumption the infinitive clause lacks TNS, so the matrix clause is the pronoun's GC in (19c) and attempting to bind *hann* within this category leads to ill-formedness. Thus, Wexler and Manzini suggest that the GC for *hann* is determined by (14c).[14]

Again, it is easy to see that the five values of GC Parameter from (14) yield nested languages when applied to pronouns. In this case, however, the order of the inclusions is reversed, yielding (20):

(20) $L(\overline{P_{GC^e}}) \subset L(\overline{P_{GC^d}}) \subset L(\overline{P_{GC^c}}) \subset L(\overline{P_{GC^b}}) \subset L(\overline{P_{GC^a}})$

To illustrate, consider the extreme ends of this ordering. A pronoun for which the GC is specified by (14e) must be free everywhere. By contrast, a pronoun such as English *him* must only be free in the domain of a subject, as indicated in (21):

(21)   Bill$_i$ said that [John$_j$ chased him$_{i/*j}$]

If the GC of English *him* were determined by (14e), (21) with *Bill* binding *him* would be ill-formed, and informally, we can see that it follows that $L(\overline{P_{GC^a}})$ properly contains $L(\overline{P_{GC^e}})$.

The difference between (16) and (20) has an important consequence from the perspective of markedness (cf. (6) above). If the relative markedness of GC values were part of UG, we would expect this to be reflected in the same way for both anaphors and pronouns. That the markedness orderings are different for the two cases is seen by Wexler and Manzini as a powerful argument for locating the source of these orderings in the learning function itself. Furthermore, construed in this way, they are *explained* by the nature of the learning function rather than constituting stipulations in UG.

Exercises

2.2   Repeat Exercise 2.1 for the adjacent pairs in (20).

2.3   For each of the following, informally described parameters, ascertain whether its values give rise to a Subset Problem:

   (a) The Null Subject Parameter, which allows the subjects of finite clauses to be empty in some languages, e.g. Italian *(lui) parla* "(He) speaks" vs. English *He speaks/*speaks*.

   (b) The Head–Complement Parameter, which specifies the order V–NP, P–NP, etc. (English) vs. NP–V, NP–P, etc. (Japanese).

   (c) The Bounding Node Parameter, which specifies {NP, IP} as bounding nodes for English, {NP, CP} as bounding nodes for Italian and {NP, IP, CP} as bounding nodes for Russian. Some resulting contrasts between the three languages are illustrated in the examples below with the presumed movements of WH-expressions indicated using trace (the role of NP as a bounding node is not relevant to these examples):

(i) English: *Your brother, [to whom]$_i$ [$_{IP}$ I wonder [$_{CP}$ [which stories]$_j$ [$_{IP}$ they have told t$_j$ t$_i$]]]

(ii) Italian: Tuo fratello, [a cui]$_i$ [$_{IP}$ mi domando [$_{CP}$ [che storie]$_j$ [$_{IP}$ abbiano raccontato t$_j$ t$_i$]]]

(iii) English: [Who]$_i$ does [$_{IP}$ Ivan say [$_{CP}$ t$_i$ that [$_{IP}$ Mary loves t$_i$]]]

(iv) Russian: *Kavo   govorit Ivan cto Marija ljubit
who-acc says   Ivan that Mary loves

(d) The Preposition Stranding Parameter which permits prepositional heads of WH-expressions to be stranded in English but not in French:

(i) a. [To whom]$_i$ did you give the book t$_i$?
    b. [Who]$_i$ did you give the book to t$_i$?

(ii) a. [À qui]$_i$ as-tu donné le livre t$_i$?
     b. *[Qui]$_i$ as-tu donné le livre à t$_i$?

2.4   Manzini and Wexler (1987: 416) offer the following paradigm for the distribution of the Italian anaphor *sè* ("self")

(i) Alice$_i$ sapeva che [Mario$_j$ aveva guardato sè$_{*i/j}$ nello specchio]
"Alice knew that Mario had looked at (her)self in the mirror"

(ii) Alice$_i$ disse a Mario$_j$ [PRO$_j$ di guardare sè$_{*i/j}$ nello specchio]
"Alice told Mario to look at (her)self in the mirror"

(iii) Alice$_i$ guardó [i ritratti di sè$_{i/j}$ di Mario]
"Alice looked at Mario's portraits of (her)self"

With respect to (i) and (ii), Italian *sè* patterns like English *herself*, but the equivalent of (iii) with *Alice* binding *sè* is considered by many to be ill-formed in English. Assuming the correctness of this judgment, what is the value of the GC Parameter for Italian *sè*?

2.5   The following examples, from Thráinsson (1991: 56-7) illustrate further aspects of the distribution of Icelandic *sig*:

(i) *Jón yrði glaður [ef þú hjálpaðir sér]
"Jon would be glad if you helped (subj) self"

(ii) *Jón lykur þessu ekki [nema þú hjálpir sér]
"Jon finishes this not unless you help (subj) self"

(iii) Jón$_i$ sagði [að hann$_i$ yrði glaður [ef þú hjálpaðir sér$_i$]]
"Jon said that he would be glad if you helped (subj) self"

(iv) Jón$_i$ segir [að hann$_i$ ljúki þessu ekki [nema þú hjálpir sér$_i$]]
"Jon says the he finishes this not unless you help self"
What difficulties do these examples raise for the claim that
the GC for *sig* is defined as in (14d)?

The final issue we need to note in this exposition of the major
features of Parameterized Binding Theory is the existence of a second
parameter. This is the Proper Antecedent (PA) Parameter and its
impact can be readily understood via examples.

We have already met the claim that Japanese *zibun* "self" is an
anaphor with GC as defined by (14e), i.e. it must be bound in a root
clause. However, it turns out that *zibun* cannot be bound by *any*
element in this domain; this anaphor displays subject-orientation,
whereby it can be bound only by a subject. This is illustrated in (22)
(Manzini and Wexler, 1987: 431):

(22)   John-wa$_i$ Mary-ni$_j$ zibun-noi$_{i/*j}$ syasin-o mise-ta
        John Mary self pictures showed
        "John showed Mary pictures of self"

In (22), the GC for *zibun* is the matrix clause, but the anaphor cannot
be bound by the object *Mary* which occurs in this domain. It is therefore proposed that only subjects constitute *proper antecedents* for *zibun*.
Now, it is easy to see that an anaphor which is not restricted in this
way has a wider distribution than one which is. Thus, if we postulate
the PA Parameter in (23), we can also assert (24), showing that the
Subset Principle will be applicable in this case too:

(23)   A proper antecedent for α is:
        a. a subject, or
        b. any item

(24)   For anaphors, the PA Parameter yields: $L(\overline{P_{PA^a}}) \subset L(\overline{P_{PA^b}})$

Conversely, there is some evidence that pronouns can vary in terms of
items from which they must be free. Wexler and Manzini (1987: 431)
cite the examples involving Icelandic *hann* in (25):

(25)   a. *Jón$_i$ skipaði mér að raka hann$_i$
           "Jon ordered me to shave him"
        b. Ég lofaði Jón$_i$ að raka hann$_i$
           "I promised Jon to shave him"

Recall that the GC for *hann* is defined by TNS, so in these examples it
is the matrix clause. While (25a) shows that *hann* must indeed be free
of a subject in this domain, (25b) indicates that this restriction does

not extend to objects. This phenomenon of *subject obviation* indicates that the PA Parameter in (23) should be extended to pronouns. Clearly, for pronouns, the appropriate set inclusion is (26):

(26) $L(\overline{P_{PA^b}}) \subset L(\overline{P_{PA^a}})$

Exercise

2.6   Show that the GC Parameter and the PA Parameter satisfy the Independence Principle in (8).

To this point, there has been something inexorable about our progress. With the nature of Subset Problems understood and the existence of subset parameters plausibly established, the need for the Subset Principle is almost self-evident for a learner who is error-driven and does not benefit from negative evidence. The remainder of this section will be more studied. Specifically, as Wexler and Manzini themselves acknowledge, cross-linguistic variation in the behavior of anaphors and pronouns presents certain difficulties for a Binding Theory containing the GC and PA Parameters. It is necessary to evaluate their response to these difficulties. Second, it appears that parameterized Binding Theory ought to make some fairly explicit predictions about children's acquisition orders. The nature of these predictions and the empirical findings should be examined. Finally, the nature and scope of the Subset Principle have attracted discussion. As for its nature, its emphasis on the computation of subset relations between sets of sentences is not immediately consistent with the emphasis in PPT on I-language (Chomsky, 1986); regarding its scope, it will be helpful to assess the extent to which subset parameters infect linguistic systems.

2.3.4   *Extending the account*

Some intriguing issues arise when we consider the generalization, formulated by Safir (1987) among others, that anaphors, like Japanese *zibun* or Chinese *ziji*, which can be bound over long distances, typically are subject-oriented (Huang and Tang, 1991; Katada, 1991); conversely, anaphors which must be bound within the domain of a subject, such as English reflexives, are indifferent as to the grammatical function of their antecedent. To the extent that this generalization is true, it indicates that we should consider a "super-parameter" which simultaneously specifies domain and antecedent properties. Setting aside intermediate domains, we could formulate such a parameter along the lines of (27):

(27)   If α is an anaphor, it is bound
        a. in the domain of a subject by an antecedent bearing any grammatical function;
        b. in a long distance domain but only by a subject.

Wexler and Manzini reject any parameter such as (27) for two reasons. First, they observe that it does not satisfy the Subset Condition.[15]

Second, they maintain that the generalization on which it is based is false. Here we focus on the falseness claim.

The falseness of (27) is illustrated again by the distribution of the Icelandic reflexive *sig*. Consider the data in (28) and (29) (Manzini and Wexler, 1987: 437):

(28)   a. Jón$_i$ elskar sig$_i$
           "Jon loves self"
        b. Ég sendi Jón$_i$ föt a sig$_i$
           "I sent Jon clothes for self"

(29)   a. Jón$_i$ segir að Maria elski sig$_i$
           "Jon says that Maria loves (subj) self"
        b. *Ég sagði Jón$_i$ að Maria hefði boðið sér$_i$
           "I told Jon that Maria had (subj) invited self"

Recall that it has been claimed that *sig* must be bound in the domain of an indicative TNS. In (27), this counts as a long-distance domain, so if the generalization expressed in (27) is sound, *sig* should be subject-oriented. Now, (29) shows that this is correct, with binding by the object *Jón* in (29b) being ruled out. However, (28b) shows that object binding of *sig* is possible, and it follows that the distribution of *sig* does not fall under either clause of (27).

In order to deal with data such as those in (28) and (29), while at the same time capturing what they believe to be a correct generalization about the relationship between the values of the two parameters, Wexler and Manzini formulate (30):[16]

(30)   A token of an anaphor must be bound either in its unmarked governing category or by its unmarked proper antecedent.

It is important to be clear that (30) refers explicitly to token occurrences of anaphors. With this in mind, we can readily see how the examples in (28) and (29) are accommodated. In (28), tokens of *sig* are bound in the unmarked governing category for anaphors. Thus, they do not need to be bound by the unmarked proper antecedent and binding from the object in (28b) is possible. By contrast, in (29) the anaphors occur with antecedents which are not in the unmarked governing category for anaphors (although they are in the governing category for *sig*). In these circumstances, (30) permits binding only from the unmarked proper antecedent, that is, the subject, and (29b) is ill-formed.

At least two concerns have been expressed about (30). First, in Atkinson (1992: 150), I raised the question of its status with respect to the principles of PPT. Clearly, referring as it does to token occurrences, it is quite distinct from familiar grammatical principles; equally, unlike for the Subset Principle itself, there seems to be no motivation for locating it in a learning module.

Second, MacLaughlin (1995: 167) appears to believe that (30) could be causally involved in parameter setting with potentially dire consequences. Specifically, she raises the specter of a learner receiving positive evidence for long distance binding in connection with a particular anaphor and using this along with (30) to reset the PA Parameter value for the anaphor from its superset (marked) to subset (unmarked) value. Obviously, if this sort of process were available, the initial motivation for the Subset Principle would be seriously undermined, as the learner is now being provided with a means of retreat from supersets. But MacLaughlin's point is based on a misunderstanding, as (30) is not concerned at all with mechanisms for setting parameters. In the situation she envisages, all that (30) tells a learner who knows it is that *in this long-distance context*, the anaphor must be bound by the subject. If the learner has the superset setting for the PA Parameter, there is nothing in this conclusion to challenge this setting.

A rather obvious difficulty arises for the Wexler and Manzini account of parameterized binding if we juxtapose traditional views on markedness with what appear to be rather robust generalizations about the domain properties of pronouns. Quite simply, the vast majority of pronouns do not take the root clause as their binding domain, a condition which would forbid intrasentential binding for such pronouns. Indeed, most pronouns which have been systematically studied are like English personal pronouns with their domains defined by the closest subject, and in terms of (14) this domain is the *most marked* pronominal domain.

Now, we should note first that the generalization we have just noted does not, in itself, render the Wexler and Manzini account of pronominal binding domains incoherent. Nowhere do they suggest that their learnability-induced sense of markedness is intended to reconstruct traditional frequency-based notions. What it does do is signal a *gap* in the account; ideally, Wexler and Manzini should have some way of accounting for pronouns' affinity for the most marked value of the GC Parameter. They are aware of the problem and they propose an ingenious solution to it. To approach this, consider the schemas in (31) (Atkinson, 1992: 150):

(31) a. ... β ... [$_{GC(A)=GC(P)}$ ... γ ... α ...] ...
      b. ... δ ... [$_{GC(A)}$ ... β ... [$_{GC(P)}$ ... γ ... α ...] ...] ...
      c. ... δ ... [$_{GC(P)}$ ... β ... [$_{GC(A)}$ ... γ ... α ...] ...] ...

In (31), α may be either an anaphor or a pronoun, and β, γ and δ are potential antecedents for α. The binding domains for α are indicated by GC(A) for the case where α is an anaphor and GC(P) where α is a pronoun. Thus, in (31a), if α is an anaphor, it can be bound by γ and if it is a pronoun, it can be bound by β (and by elements which are "more distant" than β); in short, the position occupied by α can enter into binding relationships with any c-commanding position. The same conclusion obtains for (31b), where the GC for α, a pronoun, is smaller than the GC for α, an anaphor; the anaphor can be bound from β or γ and the pronoun from β, δ or any domain beyond δ. However, (31c) is different; in this configuration, where GC(P) is bigger than GC(A), binding of α from β is not possible, irrespective of whether α is a pronoun or an anaphor. Wexler and Manzini describe this situation by saying that whereas in (31a–b), the relevant domains are spanned by the binding possibilities, this is not so in (31c), and they formulate their Spanning Hypothesis to rule out (31c) (Manzini and Wexler, 1987: 440):[17]

(32) If β c-commands α, β can bind α, where α is either an anaphor, or a pronominal, or both.

It is now easy to see how the Spanning Hypothesis can account for the tendency for pronouns to be associated with the most marked value of the GC Parameter. Suppose a language has an anaphor associated with the unmarked GC value for anaphors, a common situation. By the Spanning Hypothesis, a pronoun cannot have a binding domain bigger than this anaphor, as this would give rise to the situation schematized in (31c). Thus, the pronoun must be associated with the same binding domain as the anaphor, even though this is the most marked domain for the pronoun.[18]

What are we to make of this account of the unexpected properties of pronouns? Again, an important question concerns the status of the

Spanning Hypothesis, and, while aware of this, Manzini and Wexler have nothing reassuring to say (Atkinson, 1992: 151). Second, as MacLaughlin (1995: 169) notes, even with the Spanning Hypothesis, the account is incomplete. This is because in order for the Spanning Hypothesis to yield the correct generalizations, the binding domains of anaphors must be established before the corresponding domains for pronouns. If the converse obtained with pronouns being initially linked to their unmarked binding domains, the Spanning Hypothesis requires anaphors to have equally large (in this case, maximally marked) domains; but while long-distance anaphors are widely attested, they do not exhibit the overwhelming frequency noted for marked pronouns, so it appears that the required asymmetry will have to be an additional component of an account relying on the Spanning Hypothesis.[19]

In the light of observations such as the above, some might think that it would be more comfortable to get along without the Spanning Hypothesis. Interestingly, in Wexler's (1993) response to Kapur et al. (1993), a perspective is raised which, if it could be sustained, might render the Spanning Hypothesis superfluous. Kapur et al. offer a number of examples from various languages where the binding domain for pronouns is determined by the closest subject, i.e. they provide examples to support the generalization which led to the Spanning Hypothesis. Wexler does not seek to defend the Spanning Hypothesis in his reply – Kapur et al. raise a number of objections to this hypothesis which there is not space to go into here. Instead, he suggests that many of the cited examples do *not* illustrate pronominal binding but accidental co-reference. To illustrate, consider the simple examples in (33):

(33)   a. That is him
         b. Everyone likes him

As regards (33a), it is interpreted with *him* and *that* co-referential. However, we would not wish to suggest that (33a) provides evidence that the GC for English pronominals is not determined by the closest subject. In short, Binding Theory, as a theory of co-indexing, associates (33a) with (34):

(34)   That$_i$ is him$_j$

It immediately follows that contra-indexing cannot always entail disjoint reference, so there must be another aspect of the interpretive capacity (at this point, it is customary to mention pragmatics!) which governs the conditions under which contra-indexing can yield co-referential interpretations. Now note that (33b) does not allow an interpretation that everyone likes themselves. Why should this be so? Suppose that Principle B applies to the representation in (35) after *everyone* has been raised by Quantifier Raising to an operator position (May, 1985):

(35)   everyone$_i$ [t$_i$ likes him]

By Principle B, we obtain (36):

(36)   everyone$_i$ [t$_i$ likes him$_j$]

But now note that t$_i$ here is a bound variable with no independent referential content; contra-indexing of the pronoun indicates that it cannot function as a token of the same bound variable, and a pragmatic theory of co-reference will be silent in a domain where items are not themselves referential. In conclusion, then, *him* cannot have a bound variable interpretation in (33b), a direct consequence of the Binding Theory alone. The lesson from all of this, Wexler maintains, is that to be sure of accurately assessing the binding domain of a pronoun, it is necessary to consider its behavior when its potential antecedent is a bound variable, contexts where the pronoun itself, if co-indexed with this antecedent, will have a bound variable interpretation. The pronouns Kapur et al. cite as exhibiting the most marked pronominal GC include Japanese *kare*. However, Wexler argues that *kare* can never function as a bound variable, and for this reason, its GC is actually given by (14e).[20] Whether this sort of argumentation could be extended to include significant numbers of pronouns which have been regarded as having marked GCs remains to be seen. As things stand, the binding behavior of pronominals and attendant complications such as those which surround the Spanning Hypothesis remains a worrying problem for Wexler and Manzini's account.

2.3.5   Children's acquisition of anaphors and pronouns

As the Subset Principle is a component of a theory aimed at accounting for how it is possible for human learners to acquire the intricacies encoded in parameterized Binding Theory, it is natural to expect that we can formulate predictions for the child's real-time acquisition of anaphors and pronouns. It is salutary that investigation of these issues has proved to be extremely difficult and uncomfortably inconclusive.

The obvious candidate for a developmental prediction based on parameterized Binding Theory appears in (37):[21]

(37)   If developmental sequences can be observed for Binding
        Theory parameters, they will indicate children moving from
        unmarked to marked values.

Thus, we might expect children confronted with long distance anaphors
to pass through stages in which such items must be locally bound;
similarly, we might anticipate children's pronouns to be initially free
everywhere, and for the development of their binding domain to that
determined by a subject to be discernible.[22] Note, however, that (37) is
cautiously phrased as a conditional, as there is no reason to be
optimistic that evidence for such developmental sequences will be
readily available. Specifically, the Subset Principle requires a learner to
immediately adopt marked values of parameters as soon as the
appropriate evidence appears; thus, on theoretical grounds, there is no
reason why children's adoption of marked binding domains should not
occur before they provide any evidence that they are operating with
unmarked domains. A nonconditional prediction can, of course, be
formulated, as in (38):

(38)   Children will not adopt marked parametric values before
        unmarked values.

How have empirical studies engaged these predictions?[23] Consider first
work on English. A consistent finding across a variety of age ranges
and methodological designs has been that children appear to have
difficulties in displaying adult-like behavior with pronouns. A robust
finding is that up to the age of about six years, children will allow a
local antecedent in simple examples such as (39) (Jakubowicz, 1984;
Grimshaw and Rosen, 1990; Chien and Wexler, 1990):

(39)   The bear is touching her

This result could be interpreted as showing either that children in this
age-range have a GC for pronouns which is even smaller than that
defined by a subject, or that they simply do not know Principle B of
the Binding Theory. If the latter is correct, then the observation is
irrelevant to the question of the markedness of the value of their GC
parameter, so it is important to have a view on this question first.

   Wexler and Chien (1990), Grimshaw and Rosen (1990) and
Grodzinsky and Reinhart (1993) argue from different perspectives that
the children in question *do* know Principle B. As we have already seen
(page 40), Principle B provides an account of contra-indexing, not
disjoint reference; accordingly, tests of knowledge of Principle B should
be based on examples where pronouns can or cannot be interpreted as

bound variables. When this was done by Chien and Wexler, using examples such as (40), it was discovered that five-year-olds, the youngest children who were competent with quantified noun phrases, produced behavior which was unambiguously consistent with their knowing Principle B:

(40)   Every bear touched her

As far as children's behavior in examples like (39) goes, this is then accounted for in terms of their not having developed the pragmatics of disjoint reference, suffering from a response bias which prevents them from selecting external referents, or some combination of these.[24]

So, we suppose that a marked Governing Category does exist for the pronouns of English five-year-olds. How does this bear on the predictions in (37) and (38)? Obviously, there is nothing here to embarrass (38), as there is no suggestion that children subsequently move to an unmarked value of this parameter. However, as the children are already five years old, we can unfortunately say nothing about any developmental sequence leading up to this point, so work such as this does not provide the sort of positive evidence which (37) seeks.

Consider next Chinese and the acquisition of the long-distance anaphor *ziji*. Here there is the potential for a developmental sequence and Chien and Wexler (1987) report an experiment in which Chinese children (aged 2;6 to 7;0) exhibited a preference for local antecedents in an act-out task using sentences like (41):

(41)   xiao-shizi yao xiaohua gei ziji yi-ge xiangjiao
        little-lion want Xiaohua (child's name) give self one-CL
        banana
        "Little lion wants Xiaohua to give self a banana"

However, as is correctly noted by MacLaughlin (1995: 174), such a *pre-ference* for a local antecedent can hardly be cited as evidence that the children are (or have been) operating with an unmarked GC for *ziji*: long-distance interpretations do occur, and they require a marked GC, unless they are to be explained in some other way. Again, note that such a result is not counter to (38), but once more it does not provide any evidence for (37). The Chinese third person pronoun *ta* was examined in the same study, but bound variable interpretations were not investigated. It is therefore impossible to conclude anything about pronominal domains on this basis.

Unfortunately, the indeterminacy which has been briefly described above appears to be an endemic feature of the relevant experimental work with children. The most sensible attitude we can adopt to developmental work of this type at the moment is that it is disappointingly uninformative.

2.3.6   *The status and scope of the Subset Principle*

An aspect of the Subset Principle which has provoked some disquiet is that, as stated in (5), it is an *extensional* principle, explicitly referring to sets of sentences and requiring computations over these sets. Some, such as Safir (1987), have seen this computational requirement as implausible. Others, such as Kapur et al. (1993), relying to a large extent on the properties of pronouns discussed above, have sought to defend the classic view of binding domains from Chomsky (1981a), suggesting that this makes available an *intensional* definition of markedness. Whether what Kapur et al. have to say about markedness can be defended is itself debatable (Wexler, 1993), but in introducing the contrast between *intensional* and *extensional*, they raise what may be an important issue for a linguistic theory which regards sets of sentences as E-language constructs and not proper objects of scientific inquiry. Indeed, Chomsky himself has found it easy to see the Subset Principle as an E-language principle, and he says (1987: 29): "Conceivably, there might be some significance to some notion of E-language in the theory of learnability, if [the] 'subset principle' plays a role in this theory as has been plausibly argued."

Taking Safir's concerns first, it is surely obvious that the computations required by the Subset Principle do not involve *sentences* of, say, English and Icelandic. Transparently, there is no sense in which a set of English sentences is a subset of a set of Icelandic sentences; rather, what must be intended is that the computations take place over structural *types*. To illustrate, the structural type in (42a) below is wellformed with both an English anaphor and the Icelandic anaphor *sig* in the anaphor position, but the structural type in (42b) is only wellformed in the case of the latter:[25]

(42)   a. [... [SUBJ$_i$ ... anaphor$_i$]]
        b. [SUBJ$_i$ ... [SUBJ ... [-finite]T ... anaphor$_i$]]

Now, as soon as we move to (42), we also engage, at least partially, Kapur et al.'s concern; the representations in (42) are not sentences, but I-language constructs, so it seems that we are justified in setting the bogeyman of extensionality aside.

From a different perspective, Wexler himself has maintained that the reference to sets of sentences in the original presentations of the Subset

Principle was no more than a convenient expository device. He suggests that it is straightforward to replace the well-known formulations with an alternative which is patently intensional and in Wexler (1993: 219), he offers a differently worded Subset Principle, along the lines of (43):[26]

(43) Suppose parameter p_i has two values, v_i^m and v_i^n, such that for all derivations D, if D is grammatical under setting v_i^m then D is grammatical under setting v_i^n. Then value v_i^m is unmarked with respect to value v_i^n and if the input is consistent with value v_i^m the learner selects this value.

Clearly, a *derivation* is an I-language concept, and it is easy to see that (43) has the same consequences as the earlier (5) and (6). Wexler goes on to note that (43) violates the spirit of Chomsky's rejection of E-language since it relies on there being a privileged set of *grammatical* derivations. These, in turn, can be identified with a set of grammatical sentences, which amounts to the very notion of E-language which Chomsky has rejected. Accordingly, he goes on to offer a further version of the Subset Principle, similar to (44):[27]

(44) Suppose that principle X allows for two values, v_i^m and v_i^n, of a parameter p_i. Suppose that for all derivations D, if $D(v_i^n)$ violates X, then $D(v_i^m)$ violates X. Then value v_i^m of parameter p_i is unmarked with respect to value v_i^n and if the input is consistent with value v_i^m the learner selects this value.

Here, there is no implicit reference to any set of grammatical sentences, and it appears that Wexler is right to maintain that it is possible to formulate a version of the Subset Principle which (a) is intensional, and (b) captures the spirit of Chomsky's rejection of sets of sentences as proper objects of scientific study.

There is perhaps more cause for concern when we turn to the scope of the Subset Principle. Above, we have outlined how it might be a necessary component of a learning theory for two parameters in the Binding Theory. Of course, there is nothing incoherent about these two parameters exhausting the principle's domain of application, but such a situation would be somewhat odd and is unlikely to increase our confidence in the need for the principle. The question we pose then is: are there other parameters in PPT which give rise to Subset Problems?

Above, in exercise 2.3, readers were asked to informally consider four parameters from this perspective. Of these, it seems clear that the Head–Complement Parameter does *not* call for the Subset Principle, since the sets of structures characterized by the different values of that parameter are disjoint. The three other examples, however, constitute *prima facie* cases for being subset parameters. Here, we shall focus on the Null Subject Parameter (for discussion suggesting that the Bounding Nodes Parameter does not form an obvious domain of application for the Subset Principle, see MacLaughlin, 1995: 155ff.).

The *prima facie* case that the Null Subject Parameter yields a Subset Problem is that languages which require overt pronominal subjects (such as English) are, in the relevant respect, a subset of those (such as Italian) which provide the option of expressing such a subject or not.[28] From this perspective, the English value of the parameter constitutes the unmarked option. However, this view neglects to take account of the consequences of setting the Null Subject Parameter one way or the other, consequences which, even in early formulations such as that appearing in Hyams (1986), were thought to extend beyond the licensing of null subjects. For instance, overt expletive subjects (tokens of *there* and *it*) are licensed in English, but there is nothing overt corresponding to such subjects in Italian. So, indicating the nonovert pronominal subject by *pro*, we can maintain that in Italian we find both structural types (45), whereas in English we find only (45a):

(45)   a. SUBJ–V ...
         b. *pro*–V ...

However, we must also observe that in English, we find the structural type in (46a), where in Italian, we see (46b):

(46)   a. Exp–V ...
         b. *pro*$_{Exp}$–V ...

This means that in the relevant respects, the two languages are intersecting. In principle, there are sentences to move the learner from a wrong parameter setting in both cases – sentences with null pronominal subjects if the target is Italian, and sentences with overt expletives if the target is English.[29]

Overall, it appears that, as soon as we move away from the Binding Theory, there is no compelling case of a classic PPT parameter which requires the Subset Principle. One of the difficulties in investigating this issue is that the formulation and consequences of specific parameters have been subject to fairly frequent revision. However, recent work in the Minimalist Program (Chomsky, 1995) has adopted a rather stable view on some major parameters, and, particularly in the light of Wexler's reformulation of the Subset Principle in (44), it is of interest to consider whether this principle has any role to play in the core derivations of this system.

The central source of parameterization in derivations in the Minimalist Program is the notion of *strength* associated with features, the idea being that a strong feature must be "checked" before the derivation branches to the interface levels of Phonetic Form (PF) and Logical Form (LF), since such features are assumed to be "visible" at PF, causing a derivation which still contains such a feature to crash at that interface. A corresponding weak feature can (and must, for economy reasons) be "checked" after the derivation branches in the mapping to LF.[30] Plausibly, weak features are unmarked, in one sense of this notion, relative to strong features, since the latter necessitate costly overt movement of constituents in order to be "checked."

If we consider an extensional formulation of the Subset Principle as in (5), it is apparent that it will not find a role in such derivations. Strong features require overt movement of constituents, whereas weak features do not. Thus, we find well-known contrasts like that in (47) between French and English, indicating that V-raising (to "check" a feature in TNS or AGR) is overt in French, but not in English:[31]

(47)   a. Jean embrasse souvent Marie
        b. *Jean souvent embrasse Marie
        c. John often kisses Mary
        d. *John kisses often Mary

Alternatively, we can consider contrasts between English and Chinese, such as that illustrated in (48), showing that English has obligatory WH-raising (to "check" a strong Q feature in C), whereas Chinese requires a question word to remain *in situ*:[32]

(48)   a. What will John eat?
        b. *John will eat what
        c. Zhang hui chi shenme?
           Zhang will eat what
           "What will Zhang eat?"
        d. *Shenme hui Zhang chi / *Shenme Zhang hui chi

In both these cases, and in many others, it is clear that the sets of sentences resulting from different values of feature strength are disjoint. What if we turn to the intensional formulation of the Subset Principle in (44)?

Interpretation in this case is not straightforward, since the parameters we are considering from the Minimalist Program do not occur in parameterized principles. There are nonetheless two principles which we can involve in assessing the properties of derivations. Most obvious among these are Procrastinate, which requires that overt movement should be avoided if possible, and Full Interpretation (FI), which stipulates that interface representations should contain only elements which are interpretable at that interface. With these two principles in mind, consider derivations containing tokens of a feature F which might be strong or weak.

The relevant part of (44) is reproduced here as (49), where we are supposing that i is unmarked relative to j:

(49)   For all derivations D if $D(v_i^m)$ violates X, then $D(v_i^n)$ violates X. Supposing that X can vary over FI and Procrastinate to take account of the fact that we lack parameterized principles, we can consider three relevantly distinct derivations, depending on whether F is not checked at all (D_0), is checked nonovertly (D_1) or is checked overtly (D_2).

For each of these derivations, for F strong or weak, it is possible to determine whether Procrastinate or FI are violated in that derivation. Conducting this exercise yields (50):

(50)   a. In D_0, both strong F and weak F yield violations of FI.

b. In D_1, strong F yields a violation of FI at PF; weak F yields no violations.

c. In D_2, both strong F and weak F yield violations of Procrastinate; in the case of the former, this is forced for convergence.

What does this reveal? Probably not a great deal, but it is worth noting that (50b) is sufficient on the adopted construal to show that strong F is *not* marked relative to weak F, a counter-intuitive outcome. In so far as we can make headway on this issue, it seems that no version of the Subset Principle has an application to the core derivations of the Minimalist Program.

Finally in this section, we should return briefly to the Binding Theory itself. Not surprisingly, there have been substantial advances in this field since Wexler and Manzini's seminal contributions appeared, and the general tenor of some of these has been that when the Binding Theory is properly articulated, it too does *not* give rise to Subset Problems. This view, if adopted, would move us towards seeing the Subset Principle's value as being a sharpening of our understanding of one of the properties human grammars do *not* have. We might even be attracted by the suggestion that here we have a respect in which human languages *are* well-designed – logically, children could have been presented with Subset Problems, but in point of fact, they are not.

There is not the space to pursue a comprehensive review of Binding Theory developments here, but one or two observations on the very influential proposals developed by Reinhart and Reuland (1991, 1993) should give some indication of the direction this research has taken.[33] First, there has been retrenchment as far as pronouns go. While Reinhart and Reuland, because they regard the thematic grids of predicates as crucially involved in binding, present their binding principles in a way which is very different to the familiar one, the upshot is that pronouns must be free in a local domain. More importantly, they distinguish only *two* major classes of anaphors in terms of three correlated properties: (a) their morphology; (b) the structural domain in which they must be bound; and (c) their subject-orientation. Simplifying considerably, there are SELF-anaphors, such as the English reflexives, which are morphologically complex, must be locally bound and are indifferent to the grammatical function of their antecedent; and there are SE-anaphors (based on the Italian anaphor *sè*) which are morphologically simple, can be bound within the domain of an INFL and are subject-oriented. The most crucial part of Reinhart and Reuland's approach from the current perspective is that both the domain properties and the proper antecedent properties follow from the morphosyntactic characteristics of the two classes of anaphors; extending and considerably modifying the movement account of Pica (1987), it is maintained that SELF-anaphors move to adjoin to the predicate of the clause in which they occur for theta-theoretic reasons, whereas SE-anaphors, lacking ϑ features, must move to adjoin to AGR in INFL so that they can inherit such features and be interpreted as arguments. It is important in this account that, in principle, the learner is provided with a clear indication in the morphological make-up of an anaphor as to its domain and proper antecedent properties, and questions of the learner having available a set of hypotheses for each anaphor simply do not arise.

Finally, cases of binding which have motivated binding domains beyond INFL are treated as *logophoric*, involving discourse mechanisms which fall outside the structural Binding Theory. To directly illustrate the need for *some* way of accounting for anaphor distributions which is independent of the Binding Theory, we can consider an English example such as (51), from Reinhart and Reuland (1991: 289):

(51)   Bismark$_i$'s impulsiveness had, as so often, rebounded against himself$_i$

In (51), the antecedent does not even c-command the anaphor, so such examples cannot be accommodated in any version of the Binding Theory. To the extent that an approach such as that of Reinhart and Reuland is adequate, it does not sit comfortably with Wexler's (1993:233) view that as different versions of the Binding Theory have to deal with the same range of variation, "[this] variation will have to be stated some place in the grammar, and there is reason to believe that the Subset Principle might turn out to be relevant in those cases." We can tentatively conclude, then, with Frank and Kapur (1996:629), that "there may be no true subset parameters." Such a conclusion does not suggest an exciting future for the Subset Principle; it should not, however, detract from the importance of its recent past.

2.4   Non-subset parameters

In the previous section, we took it for granted that the set-theoretic scenarios sketched in (4a) and (4b) are not immediately problematic. It is, however, readily conceivable that the situation represented there is damagingly simplified, and that as soon as we begin to consider realistic numbers of parameters generating large numbers of languages and *interacting* in complex and unpredictable ways, complications will arise. That this is indeed the case will be the theme of the rest of the discussion in this chapter.

The general tenor of the possibilities we shall be concerned with can be informally illustrated in a straightforward way. Suppose that a learner is trying to figure out the order of heads and complements in the ambient language and is presented with an SVO string. If the environment happens to be English, it would be appropriate to take this as indicative of heads preceding complements; however, if our learner is surrounded by German, this would be an unhelpful move, since German is a V2 language requiring that tensed verbs move to second position in matrix clauses from their underlying final position. In other words, the SVO string is a reliable indicator of head–complement order only if assumptions are made about other parametric options. Now, of course, there is no indication in this simple example of an insoluble problem; if the V2 property can be established independently via encounters with additional data, then our SVO string will have clear consequences for the learner, but now consider a slightly more complex case, elegantly described in Clark (1992).

As is well-known, the grammar of English is unusual in licensing Exceptional Case Marking (ECM) constructions such as (52):

(52)   John considers [us to be dangerous]

The difficulty created for theories of Case marking by such examples is that an infinitival INFL does not assign Case (or, as suggested in Chomsky and Lasnik (1995), it assigns NULL Case to PRO), but here we have a pronominal marked with objective Case occurring as subject of the infinitival clause. The "solution" to this dilemma in PPT was to allow verbs like *consider* to *exceptionally* govern and Case-mark the subject position of infinitivals, thereby providing a source of Case for the infinitival subject which is external to the clause in which the subject appears. A consequence of this is that the GC for the infinitival subject extends to the matrix clause, and this accounts for the examples in (53):

(53)   a. John$_i$ considers [himself$_i$ to be dangerous]
         b. *John$_i$ considers [him$_i$ to be dangerous]

Now, as Clark points out, it is also possible for overt subjects to appear in infinitival clauses in Irish. For Irish, however, there is no "extension" of the government domain, suggesting that Irish has a mechanism for Case marking such subjects from *within* the infinitival clause. Clark refers to such a mechanism as Structural Case Marking (SCM), and a consequence of this difference between Irish and English is that a sentence of Irish corresponding to (53a) is ill-formed; the subject position is not governed from outside the infinitival clause, so the governing category for this subject position does not extend beyond this clause.

With these assumptions, suppose a learner is presented with (52). One option is to conclude (correctly) that the language has ECM. However, if SCM is a possibility made available by UG, the learner might (incorrectly) suppose that adoption of this is the appropriate move. Next, the learner is presented with (53a). If ECM has already been chosen, there is no problem. However, if the learner has selected SCM, this will not allow for an analysis of (53a), and we might conclude, therefore, that the sequence of data in (52) and (53a) will inevitably lead the learner to the conclusion that English has an ECM grammar. But this would be premature, because, as we have seen in section 2.3, anaphors have the option of being long-distance bound. Therefore, with the hypothesis that English has an SCM grammar and confronted with (53a), the learner could retain the SCM assumption and conclude that *himself* is a long-distance anaphor. Here, then, we see three putative parameters interacting to ensure that an apparently helpful sequence of data cannot be regarded as infallibly diagnostic for the learner.

A formalization of situations such as the above and the consequences of that formalization are the subject matter of Gibson and Wexler (1994), and this section begins by considering how the Triggering Learning Algorithm (TLA) has been applied to learning situations which have some linguistic interest.

2.4.1   Applications of the TLA

Before we consider how the TLA performs in a simple parameter space, it is important to have access to two definitions which will play an important role in the subsequent discussion. Sentences which are diagnostic of a target are known as triggers and Gibson and Wexler (1994:409) distinguish between *global* and *local triggers*. Their definitions of these notions are reproduced in (54) and (55):[34]

(54)   A *global trigger* for value v_i^n of parameter p_i, $p_i(v_i^n)$, is a sentence S from the target grammar L such that S is grammatical if and only if the value for p_i is v_i^n, no matter what the values of parameters other than p_i are.[35]

A global trigger, according to this definition, does its work in guiding the learner to the correct hypothesis, irrespective of whatever other values parameters may have.

(55)   Given values for all parameters but one, parameter p_i, a *local trigger* for value v_i^n of parameter p_i, $p_i(v_i^n)$, is a sentence S from the target grammar L such that S is grammatical if and only if the value for p_i is v_i^n.[36]

Unlike a global trigger, a local trigger is only guaranteed to work in a situation where other parameter values are fixed in a specific way. In the light of the previous section, we should note in passing that there can never be triggers, global or local, for subset languages, since any sentence belonging to such a language will also belong to one or more superset languages. Thus, something like the Subset Principle remains a necessary component of the learning function, so long as subset parameters exist.[37]

In their Triggering Learning Algorithm (TLA) the learner chooses randomly a possible parameter setting as its starting hypothesis and waits for data from the environment to take actions that improve on it. Specifically, upon detection of an error (that is upon encountering a sentence that cannot be parsed with the current parameter setting) the learner's conjecture is modified by

(i) selecting randomly a single parameter p_i (the Single Value Constraint),
(ii) selecting randomly an alternative value for p_i, and
(iii) adopting the resulting new conjecture only if it parses successfully the sentence on which the previous conjecture was in error (the Greediness Constraint).

A class of languages can then be proved to be unlearnable if there is at least a possible starting hypothesis P_s from which the target hypothesis P_t cannot be reached by means of the mechanism described above. This happens when, for every neighbor P_n of P_s (that is for every hypothesis that differs from P_s in the value of exactly one parameter)

$$L(P_n) \cap L(P_t) - L(P_s) \neq \varnothing$$

In Gibson and Wexler's terminology, such a P_s would be called a *local maximum* with respect to the target P_t.

There are two ways for a P_s to be a local maximum with respect to a P_t: either P_s is a superset of P_t (in which case, assuming only positive evidence is available, no error will ever be detected) or P_s is such that on every sentence from $L(P_t)$ it is just as successful as any of the neighboring conjectures.

Conversely, it is possible to show that if there are no local maxima in the parameter space then the probability of the learner identifying the correct target becomes 1 in the limit, regardless of the starting conjecture.

Since we know that the space does not have local maxima, it follows that *triggers* (linguistic data that could prompt the learner to adopt correct values of at least some parameters) exist for every target and every incorrect conjecture. This in turn means that there is a lower bound $b > 0$ on the probability of such triggers appearing in the learner's environment (b could be thought of as the probability of the occurrence of the least frequently occurring triggering sentence with respect to any possible target and any intermediate conjecture).

Now, according to the TLA, the learner has no knowledge of which parameter value to reset in circumstances where the existing grammar does not produce an analysis. However, assuming a flat probability distribution over the set of k parameters, each will be selected with probability $1/k$. Suppose also, for simplicity, that all parameters are binary, a consequence of this being that the resetting of an incorrectly set parameter necessarily leads to it being correctly set. Then, the probability that a trigger S (which we are assuming to exist) will lead to a parameter being reset to its target value is bounded below by $b/k = q$.

Suppose next that P_s and P_t differ by two parameter mis-settings. If the learner hypothesizes P_s at time t, then the probability of the learner hypothesizing (correctly) P_t at time $t + 2$ (i.e. 2 "sentences" later) is bounded below by q^2. Generalizing, since we are supposing k parameters in total, the worst case we need to consider is one where the "distance" between P_s and P_t is k mis-set parameters. If P_s is the hypothesis at t, the probability of P_t being the hypothesis at $t + k$ (k "sentences" later) is bounded below by $q^k = r(> 0)$. Thus, we can conclude at this point that for any grammar, P_s, the probability of moving from it to the target via encounters with k sentences is greater than or equal to r.

Assume, then, that we allow the process above to run its course. After k sentences, the probability that the learner has achieved P_t is greater than or equal to r. If the learner has not achieved P_t by this point, it will be achieved in the next k sentences with probability greater than r. In other words, the probability of achieving P_t after $2k$ sentences is greater than or equal to $r + (1 - r)r$, the second factor here being reduced by the multiplier $(1 - r)$ in acknowledgment that there is a finite probability that convergence has occurred on the first k sentences. Iterating this process, we can see that after $3k$ sentences this probability is greater than or equal to $r + (1 - r)r + (1 - r)^2 r$. After i sets of k sentences, this probability can be expressed as the sum

$$r \sum_{j=0}^{i-1} (1 - r)^j$$

In order to show that, as the number of sentences presented to the learner goes to infinity, the probability of achieving the correct target tends to 1 all we have to do is to show that, as i goes to ∞, $\sum_{j=0}^{i-1}(1 - r)^j$ tends to $1/1 - (1 - r)$. In fact, if this is true, then $r\sum_{j=0}^{i-1}(1 - r)^j$ tends to

$$r \frac{1}{1 - (1 - r)} = \frac{r}{1 - (1 - r)} = \frac{r}{1 - 1 + r} = \frac{r}{r} = 1$$

To show that, as j goes to ∞, $\sum_{j=0}^{i-1}(1 - r)^j$ tends to $1/1 - (1 - r)$ we first observe that $0 < (1 - r) < 1$ (this follows from the fact that $0 < r < 1$) and then we show that, in general, for every m such that $0 < m < 1$ the sum below tends to $1/1 - m$ as n goes to ∞.

$$\sum_{j=0}^{n} m^j$$

This can be expanded as

$$1 + m + m^2 + \cdots + m^n$$

Multiplying every term by $(1 - m)/(1 - m) = 1$ we get

$$\frac{1 - m}{1 - m} + \frac{m(1 - m)}{1 - m} + \cdots \frac{m^n(1 - m)}{1 - m}$$

which yields

$$\frac{1 - m + m - m^2 + m^2 + \cdots - m^n + m^n - m^{n+1}}{1 - m}$$

and so, simplifying:

$$\frac{1 - m^{n+1}}{1 - m}$$

Now, since, by hypothesis, $0 < m < 1$, as n goes to ∞, m^{n+1} tends to 0. Therefore, $\sum_{j=0}^{n} m^j$ tends to

$$\frac{1 - 0}{1 - m} = \frac{1}{1 - m}$$

This completes the proof.[38]

The linguistically substantive part of Gibson and Wexler's discussion is devoted to demonstrating examples of parameter spaces where triggers do, or, more revealingly, do not exist. For the former, they consider the simplified scenario of the well-known X-bar parameters. Restricting ourselves simply to base word order, and assuming the four values generated by assigning order to the unordered parameters in (56), yields (57) (adapted from Gibson and Wexler, 1994: 416):

(56)   XP = Spec, X$'$
(57)   X$'$ = Comp, X

Spec-Head	Comp-Head	Data-types
Spec-final	Comp-final	VOS, VS
Spec-final	Comp-first	OVS, VS
Spec-first	Comp-final	SVO, SV
Spec-first	Comp-first	SOV, SV

A number of additional assumptions are made in connection with this simple example. Specifically, it is supposed that the learner gets no exposure to noncanonical word orders, as might, for example, occur in interrogatives, that objects do not appear without overt subjects, i.e.

there are no null subject sentences, and that representations of word-order and grammatical functions can be derived by preanalysis, i.e. data encounter the child's system already in the form indicated in the right-hand column of (57).[39]

It is then easy to see that the sentence type SV is a global trigger for the parameter value Spec-first and VS has similar properties for the value Spec-final – these structures each identify the appropriate parameter value irrespective of how the Comp–Head parameter is set. However, there are no global triggers for the relative ordering of head and complement, since the data yielded by different values of this parameter depend upon the value of the Spec–Head parameter. Taking values of the latter into account, however, there are obviously local triggers for Comp–Head.

Exercise

2.7   For each possible pair of source state and target state in (57), describe triggering routes consistent with the TLA which will move the learner from source to target, indicating the status of triggers as global or local.

A more complex case is provided by adding to the above set of parameters an additional one to distinguish between V2 languages, such as Dutch and German, and non-V2 languages such as English and French. It is not possible to consider the complete argument from Gibson and Wexler here, but it is straightforward enough to illustrate the major aspect of their conclusion. First, we need to do some simple sums. Adding a V2 parameter to the X-bar parameters of (56) yields eight possible language types. At any point at which learning is necessary, the learner can be in a state corresponding to one of these languages, with any of the other seven language types as the target. There are thus 56 (= 8 × 7) possible routes, each one defined by a possible (source, target) pair, which the learner must be guaranteed to be able to traverse if this set of languages is to be identified by the TLA. It turns out that, of these routes, there are six for which no triggers exist (see section 2.4.3 for a more careful assessment of this claim). We shall informally illustrate this for one case.

Suppose that the target is the grammar (Spec-first, Comp-final, −V2), i.e. a language with basic SVO order and no V2. Further, suppose that the learner currently has the grammar (Spec-final, Comp-final, +V2), i.e. a VOS grammar with V2. For the purposes of this parameter space, the data available to the learner are extended to include sentences which include auxiliaries, second objects and initial adverbs, as +V2 grammars all yield exactly the same set of well-formed structures if we restrict ourselves to S, V and O. The sentence types defined by the target grammar can then be listed as in (58) – remember that this is just a familiar SVO grammar:

(58)   a. SV, SVO, SVO1O2, SAuxV, SAuxVO, SAuxVO1O2
        b. AdvSVO, AdvSVO1O2, AdvSAuxV, AdvSAuxVO,
           AdvSAuxVO1O2

Of these example structures, all of those in (58a) belong to the current grammar. The sentence types of the current grammar appear in (59).

(59)   a. SV, SVO, SVO1O2, SAuxV, SAuxVO, SAuxVO1O2
        b. OVS,   O1VO2S,   O2VO1S,   OAuxVS,   O1AuxVO2S,
           O2AuxVO1S, AdvVS, AdvVOS, AdvVO1O2S AdvAuxVS,
           AdvAuxVOS, AdvAuxVO1O2S

So, although none of the patterns in (58a) is defined by the X-bar settings of the current grammar, +V2 ensures that we end up with each member of this list. Therefore, occurrence of any of these types will not occasion a change in the learner's grammar, as learning is error-driven. This is not the case for the structures in (58b) – none of these patterns displays V2 – so on encountering one of these, the learner will attempt to reset a parameter. The difficulty here is that in each case, such resetting of a *single* parameter (the Single Value Constraint) will result in a grammar in which the troublesome sentence-type (from (58b)) remains ungrammatical. Thus, because of the Greediness Constraint, no change will occur. Change of a single parameter value for our current state (Spec-final, Comp-final, +V2), yields the three candidates in (60):

(60)   a. (Spec-final, Comp-final, −V2)
        b. (Spec-final, Comp-first, +V2)
        c. (Spec-first, Comp-final, +V2)

Now consider the sentence type AdvSVO from the target. This cannot be analyzed in (60b,c), both of which are +V2; nor can it be analyzed in (60a), the comparable sentence type in this grammar being AdvVOS. The TLA, then, will leave the learner stuck in (Spec-final, Comp-final, +V2). Gibson and Wexler refer to a grammar from which there is no triggering route to a target grammar as a *local maximum* (page 53), and we will say that (Spec-final, Comp-final, +V2) constitutes a local maximum for (Spec-first, Comp-final, −V2).

Exercises

2.8   For each of the remaining sentence types in (58b), show that change of one parameter value in the current grammar cannot yield a grammar which analyzes the structure.

2.9   Show informally that for the TLA each of the left-hand grammars below is a local maximum for each of the right-hand grammars:

(Spec-final, Comp-first, +V2)(Spec-first, Comp-final, −V2)

(Spec-final, Comp-final, +V2)(Spec-first, Comp-first, −V2)

(Spec-init, Comp-first, +V2)(Spec-final, Comp-first, −V2)

Now, it might be felt that the existence of local maxima is sufficient to confound the triggering account leading to the TLA. However, such a conclusion would be premature for a number of reasons. Not least among these are the assumptions of the Single Value Constraint and the Greediness Constraint, assumptions which Gibson and Wexler characterize as subscribing to *conservatism*, and we shall briefly consider these in section 2.4.3. In the next section, however, I wish to focus on a response to the dilemma created by the existence of local maxima which the authors themselves favor.

2.4.2   Dealing with local maxima

In the preceding section, it was assumed that all three parameters in the space were available for resetting throughout the learning period. Alternatively, we might suppose that the three parameters under discussion are *ordered*; specifically, let us consider the consequences of the V2 parameter being set at the default −V2 until after a certain time has elapsed. No such restriction applies to the Spec–Head and Comp–Head parameters.

In fact, all the six grammars which are local maxima, including the one used above to illustrate the problem, are +V2. Furthermore, they are all local maxima for −V2 grammars. With the V2 parameter "off-line," suppose first that the target grammar is any which is −V2. In this case, the default setting for this parameter is correct, and the learner's exposure to data from the target grammar will eventually allow the Spec–Head and Comp–Head parameters to be correctly set; during this period, the possibility of resetting −V2 to +V2 is not available for the learner. At some point, of course, the +V2 option becomes available, but since by assumption the target is −V2 and the other two parameters are correctly set by this point, again the option will not be considered. Thus, supposing we can ensure that +V2 is not available for the time it takes the learner to set the X-bar parameters, whenever the target is −V2, the learner will converge on the correct grammar.

Now, suppose that the target is +V2. Throughout the period during which this value is not available, the learner will have an incorrect grammar which the TLA will seek to move towards the target. Of course, it cannot succeed, so now consider the point at which +V2 becomes available. Since for any +V2 grammar, there are no local maxima, the TLA will now be able to guarantee convergence during this second period of learning. Thus, for all possibilities, convergence is assured.

Exercise

2.10 Consider another parameter ordering where the V2 parameter is initially set at the default −V2, and the Spec–Head parameter has its value fixed before Comp–Head and V2, which become subject to resetting together at some later point. Investigate whether this ordering can deal with the local maxima introduced above.

As it stands, there is something which looks entirely stipulative about the ordering manoeuvre. What is needed is a story for underwriting the late emergence of +V2, and it is of interest that such stories, while remaining controversial in many details, do exist. For example, it has been maintained that at early stages of language acquisition, functional category projections, including the head C, which is standardly regarded as the target of V-movement in V2 languages, are simply not available by virtue of maturational constraints (Radford, 1990). If this is so, there is no legitimate target for the V2 effect, and the verb must remain *in situ*. This "discontinuous" view of grammatical development, with the possibility of functional categories maturing and thereby making available new grammatical options is currently not very fashionable (see, for example, Poeppel and Wexler, 1993; Harris and Wexler, 1996; Hyams, 1996, for vigorous defense of the Continuity Hypothesis as far as emerging grammatical structures are concerned). However, given the very uneven standard of data we have from the earliest stages of acquisition, it would be unreasonable to discount some version of a maturational account at this point (see Atkinson, 1996, for arguments in favor of keeping options open). It is perhaps worth noting that insistence on the early (or, indeed, late) appearance of functional categories is not readily intelligible in systems where categories are just feature sets. Here, the interesting questions focus on the development and projection of features, and one idea worth pursuing is that there is a maturational process whereby those features which are – Interpretable as this notion is understood by Chomsky (1995) are relatively late to emerge. Now, it is not implausible to suppose that whatever features are responsible for V2 are – Interpretable, and on these grounds, we might contemplate embedding the late setting of the V2 parameter within a broader developmental picture.

More generally, we might simply seek to exploit the view that movement represents a marked option in grammar, and is only adopted as a last resort. This sort of proposal might be regarded as consistent with Chomsky's Minimalist Program (1995), although it should be observed that deviations from canonical order of the verb and its arguments (accommodated in Gibson and Wexler's account by variation in the value of X-bar parameters) would also not be expected from this perspective (see Platzack, 1996, for relevant discussion). In short, it appears that there may well be value in taking seriously the ordered parameters option, and it is of interest that Gibson and Wexler see it as the most attractive way of dealing with the problem their formulation of the TLA has revealed.[40]

Missing in this discussion up to now has been any indication of whether children acquiring a V2 language pass through a stage at which they do not have V2. Accepting the orthodox view that the base word order of German is SOV, this suggests that German-acquiring children might pass through a stage of producing V-final matrix clauses. Now, it is well-known that German-acquiring children do indeed produce some utterances of this type, but unfortunately the verbs occurring in this context are fairly reliably identified as infinitive in form. By contrast, verb forms which are morphologically finite seem to appear in second position from a very early stage, suggesting that German children's acquisition of +V2 is not delayed. For now, we can only agree with Gibson and Wexler's conclusion (1994: 434–5) that "there does not seem to be much evidence for ... a [pre–V2] stage."[41]

2.4.3   *Further developments*

The ideas we have just considered represent an important first step in our understanding of how the notion of trigger might be formalized and also present us with interesting and somewhat surprising problems. In fact, there is an inadequacy in the Gibson and Wexler formalization, and in formulating it, Berwick and Niyogi (1996) have raised some new perspectives on the triggering problem.

As far as the inadequacy goes, it is best approached via an example. We have already noted the claim that there are precisely six (source, target) pairs for which triggers do not exist and which will lead the TLA into a local maximum. We also noted that all sources in this set of pairs were +V2, with all targets being −V2, an important observation in the context of the "maturational solution" to the local maxima problem. Now consider the situation where the source is (Spec-final, Comp-first, −V2), i.e. OVS, and the target is (Spec-first, Comp-final, −V2), i.e. SVO.

It is easy to outline a triggering path between this source and target, although since source and target differ by two parameter values, this will have to be a two-step process in the context of the Single Value Constraint. So, suppose that the learner receives the target datum SV; with a nonzero probability, this will lead the learner to shift to (Spec-first, Comp-first, −V2), i.e. SOV. Then suppose that the learner receives target datum SVO. Again, with nonzero probability, this will produce a shift to (Spec-first, Comp-final, −V2), the target. However, we must note that at the first step in this process, the same datum SV *could* have led the learner to shift, with nonzero probability, to (Spec-final, Comp-first, +V2), i.e. OVS +V2 – note that this shift satisfies the Single Value Constraint. Then, SVO *could* have led to a second shift to (Spec-final, Comp-final, +V2), i.e. VOS +V2. But now recall that VOS +V2 is a local maximum for simple SVO – this was the pair we used as illustration of the local maximum problem above. Accordingly, once the TLA has taken the learner into this state, there is no triggering route from there to the target.

Berwick and Niyogi show that as well as the six local maxima, there are a further six states in the Gibson and Wexler parameter space which are *connected* to local maxima in the manner we have outlined above for one such case. While there is a route that the TLA learner can follow from these states to any target, there are also routes from these states to local maxima, so the Gibson and Wexler claim that, setting local maxima aside, TLA learners converge on targets with probability 1 is not justified.

Exercise

2.11   Show that for each of the following (source, target) pairs, it is possible for the TLA to take the learner into a local maximum:

Source	Target
(Spec-first, Comp-final, −V2)	(Spec-final, Comp-first, −V2)
(Spec-first, Comp-first, −V2)	(Spec-final, Comp-first, −V2)
(Spec-final, Comp-first, −V2)	(Spec-first, Comp-first, −V2)

Now, it is important to be clear that the ordering account which Gibson and Wexler offer for dealing with the local maxima problem is not rendered incoherent by these conclusions. To maintain that +V2 is inaccessible in the early stages of acquisition also removes the problematic status of the states which are connected to local maxima; thus, the proposal that the X-bar parameters can be set first can be retained in the context of Berwick and Niyogi's observations. We might, however, wonder whether there are alternative ways of finessing the local maxima problem. Berwick and Niyogi themselves suggest that the Greediness Constraint is not well-founded.

Taking just one aspect of their concern about this principle, they challenge Gibson and Wexler's claim that Greediness contributes to conservatism, where conservatism itself is regarded as desirable. Recall that what Greediness requires of a newly favored hypothesis is an analysis of the current datum where the existing hypothesis fails. But, in itself, this is no recipe for conservatism, as Greediness will tolerate massive shifts in parameter settings, so long as an analysis results. It is the Single Value Constraint which guarantees conservatism, and Greediness plays no contribution in accounting for the gradualness of real-time acquisition which is what makes conservatism attractive. Dropping the Greediness Constraint has the immediate consequence of dealing with the local maxima problem, as a learner can now pass from states which do not analyze the current datum to other states with the same failing.

Exercise

2.12   Show how a non-greedy TLA learner can move between the following (source, target) pairs:

Source	Target
(Spec-first, Comp-final, +V2)	(Spec-final, Comp-first, −V2)
(Spec-final, Comp-final, +V2)	(Spec-first, Comp-final, −V2)
(Spec-final, Comp-first, +V2)	(Spec-first, Comp-first, −V2)

Finally, a development introduced by Berwick and Niyogi, is to compute and utilize the probabilities associated with a TLA learner moving from one state to another.[42] This enables them to quantify the amount of data a TLA learner must receive in order to converge on a particular target. Bertolo (1995b) has shown how this analysis can be used to produce estimates of "time" (measured in data presentations) that the +V2 parameter must be inaccessible if the maturational solution to the local maxima problem is to be solved in this way.

We noted earlier that the proof of convergence for the TLA only establishes that the presence of triggers (global or local) is a sufficient condition for learnability, and an issue raised by Gibson and Wexler's formalization of the TLA is the extensional relationship between the classes of parameter spaces which, on the one hand, can be shown to contain triggers, somehow defined, and on the other, can be learned by the TLA.

Frank and Kapur (1996) have begun investigation of these issues by formalizing a number of distinct definitions of different types of trigger, seeking to establish necessary and sufficient conditions for convergence. There is not space to go into all their conclusions here, but what is worth pointing out is that (a) the existence of global triggers does *not* provide a necessary condition for convergence under the TLA; and (b) the existence of local triggers also does not have this property. For (a), we may simply refer back to the simple X-bar parameter space from Gibson and Wexler. This does not have global triggers for all parameter values, but is nonetheless learnable by the TLA. For (b), readers are invited to try exercise 2.13. A necessary condition for TLA-convergence can be formulated, but it relies on the existence of a class of what Frank and Kapur refer to as *weak local triggers*, the existence of which merely guarantees that in any non-target state, there is a datum from the target which is inconsistent with this state and which will enable the TLA to change a parameter value, although not necessarily in the direction of the target. By constructing examples, Frank and Kapur are able to demonstrate that parameter spaces which are weakly locally triggered are a proper superset of the TLA-convergent spaces and they thus succeed in formulating a trigger-based necessary condition for TLA-convergence. It is not, however, a sufficient condition.

Exercise

2.13   Consider the abstract parameter space defined by two parameters which can each take the values + and −, such that the "languages" corresponding to the four possible parameter settings are as follows:

$$L(+,+) = a, d$$
$$L(+,-) = a, b$$
$$L(-,+) = c, e$$
$$L(-,-) = b, c$$

Show (a) that there is no local trigger for the + value of the second parameter; (b) that the TLA can take a learner from any source to any target.

Of more immediate linguistic interest is the possibility of *re-parameterizing* a parametric space and investigating the consequences of this operation for learnability. That such re-parameterization can be significant is readily illustrated (Frank and Kapur, 1996: 643f.). So, consider again the simple X-bar space of Gibson and Wexler from (56), and recall that all parameter values in this space are either globally or locally triggered. Suppose, now, that the space is re-parameterized in the following way. The Comp–Head parameter is as before, but we introduce a new parameter with the values "same" and "different." The value "same" is appropriate when Spec–Head order matches Comp–Head order, and the value "different" appears when these two orders diverge. In comparison with (56), this parameterization yields (61):

(61)

Same/Different	Comp–Head	Data-types
same	Comp-final	VS, VOS
different	Comp-final	SV, SVO
same	Comp-first	SV, SOV
different	Comp-first	VS, OVS

It is easy to see that under this re-parameterization, the word-order space has a local maximum. Suppose that the source grammar is (different, Comp-first) and the target is (same, Comp-final). Inspection of (61) shows that the only datum from the target not analyzed by the source is VOS. But, since VOS is not analyzable by either (same, Comp-first) or (different, Comp-final), the Single Value Constraint will require the TLA to remain with the source for evermore. Despite the triviality of the example, this is an extremely important observation, as it shows that in principle learnability considerations could be brought to bear in choosing between alternative parameterizations of a single set of data.

Exercise

2.14   Consider a parameterization for the Gibson and Wexler set of eight languages which has the following form. The second parameter is simply Comp-first or Comp-final as in the original parameterization. The first parameter is "same" or "different" as introduced above for the simple X-bar space. The third parameter (replacing V2) has the following two values (a) ("same" +V2) or ("different" −V2); (b) ("different" +V2) or ("same" −V2). For instance, the Gibson and Wexler language VOS +V2 has value (a) for this parameter, as does SVO; SVO +V2 has value (b), as does VOS.

(a) show that SVO is a local maximum for SOV under this parameterization;

(b) take the (source, target) pairs from exercise 2.9 and show that under this parameterization none of these sources is a local maximum for its paired target.

What message should we take away from this brief discussion of re-parameterization? We have already noted (with some reservation) Wexler's view that changes in Binding Theory will still need to account for variation and his belief that such variation will probably encounter Subset Problems in that domain. At the very least, we now have a demonstration that different "theories" of the Gibson and Wexler word-order space, while still accounting for the variation which exists in that space, lead to substantially different outcomes in terms of the problems they raise for a TLA-learner.[43] In these circumstances, it is important to be aware of the fact that theories of word-order radically different to those associated with the familiar X-bar principles have been proposed (Kayne, 1994; Chomsky, 1995; Phillips, 1996), and it would be premature to speculate on how the approaches to variation outlined in these theories might confront learnability questions.

2.4.4   Genetic algorithms and accounting for historical change

Above, we have considered a specific algorithm in some detail, drawing attention to its error-driven character and its reliance on the Single Value Constraint and the Greediness Constraint. We have also seen suspicions aired about the Greediness Constraint (Niyogi and Berwick,

1996), and noted that local maxima problems disappear if this constraint is not observed by the learner. In this section, we shall briefly consider a radically different kind of algorithm which is not error-driven and does not operate according to either of these constraints. This is the Genetic Algorithm of Clark (1992), and having sketched the main features of this approach, we will go on to get an idea of how it has been applied in understanding the nature of historical change, a problem which is generally accepted as being linked to language acquisition by children. Historical change has recently been approached from the perspective of cue-based learning and we shall conclude by examining the difference between this approach and that based on a Genetic Algorithm (see chapter 3 for more detailed discussion of historical change).

Clark's (1992) point of departure is the observation that learning algorithms that set parameters *deductively*, that is by exploring the effects of each possible combination of parameter values, in response to parametrically ambiguous data would have to examine a number of interactions as great as the total number of hypotheses made available by the parameter space.

Clark's response to this and other problems is to propose an account of a learner who simultaneously entertains a *set* of hypotheses, each of which confronts the data to which the learner is exposed. The initial set of hypotheses is chosen at random, but modifications in the pool of current hypotheses are determined by how well a hypothesis performs in analyzing the data and a number of operations on hypotheses which constitute the equivalent of hypotheses "mating" or "mutating." I shall first describe the system in a little more detail before coming back to emphasize how different it is to the TLA. For Clark, it is notationally appropriate for hypotheses to be represented as strings of binary digits. Thus, given an eight-parameter system, a typical hypothesis considered by a learner will be (1 0 0 1 1 0 1 0). Here, the 1 in first position might indicate that the grammar has long-distance anaphora, the 0 in second position, that it does not have ECM, the 0 in third position that it does not have head-initial constituents, etc.[44]

The initial set of hypotheses is presented with a datum and the learner attempts to analyze the datum in terms of each hypothesis. This procedure returns an indication of the extent to which each hypothesis succeeds in terms of the number of violations of UG principles which the analysis incurs. Obviously, if the datum can be interpreted, there are no such violations. Additionally, each hypothesis is evaluated with respect to whether it yields supersets of other hypotheses and in terms of relative "elegance," where this is assessed in terms of total number

of nodes, length of movement chains, etc. As a result of these procedures, each hypothesis in the candidate set is assessed for its *fitness*
relative to other hypotheses. Quite simply, a hypothesis which can
analyze a datum without violating UG principles, does not yield a
superset language with respect to other hypotheses and is more
"elegant" than other hypotheses will receive a high fitness score. The
converse situation will produce a low fitness score. The three factors
entering the computation of fitness are weighted to ensure that success
in analyzing the data is the most important element. It might be hoped
that the weights themselves would ultimately emerge from empirical
study; for the purposes of his discussion, Clark simply assumes specific
values.

What are the benefits of being fit? You get to breed, of course, and
Clark's model includes a "crossing over" operator which can take a
subset of parameter values from one hypothesis (e.g., the first four
values in the example above) and combine them with an appropriate
subset of values from another hypothesis (e.g., the last four values
from some hypothesis). The hypotheses which are given access to this
operation are those which are fit, so successful parameter settings in
terms of the target get propagated to new hypotheses. Additionally, fit
hypotheses are permitted to mutate, where mutation involves changing
just one value. By contrast, unfit hypotheses are removed from the set
of hypotheses at random intervals. Convergence, for Clark's model, is
understood in terms of the space of hypotheses eventually being
populated by one hypothesis; for successful learning, this hypothesis
will be correct for the target.

Even at this level of description, we can discern characteristics of this
approach which make it quite unlike the TLA. First, as the learner is
operating with a set of hypotheses, there is no simple sense in which
learning can be construed as error-driven. Of the current hypotheses,
some will succeed in analyzing an input sentence with favorable consequences for their future; others will fail to a greater or lesser extent,
with this extent being taken account of in the next step of the learning
procedure. Second, there is no straightforward interpretation of the
Greediness Constraint in this system. This is true in two senses: first, as
we have just seen, learning is not error-driven, so the presence of a
successful hypothesis in the current parameter space does not entail
that nothing changes; second, there is no guarantee that any new
hypothesis entering the procedure will be able to analyze the current
datum, although, *ceteris paribus*, new hypotheses should be *relatively*
successful. Third, the Single Value Constraint has no role to play in
this system. The mutation operator briefly mentioned above changes

only single values, but this can apply to a hypothesis which has successfully analyzed the previous datum as well as to one which has failed in some way or another. For the "crossing over" operator, of course, there is no affinity of any kind with the Single Value Constraint. Finally, it is worth noting that by building a subset factor into his measure of fitness, Clark is able to dispense with the Subset Principle as an explicit condition on the learning module. To see this, suppose that the learner's hypothesis space contains a subset and a superset hypothesis, with the target corresponding to the subset. In terms of analysis of data, the two hypotheses will be equally fit, but, as noted above, the superset hypothesis will be judged less fit than the subset hypothesis by virtue of the subset factor in the computation of fitness. As a consequence, over a period, the subset hypothesis will have additional opportunities to breed and mutate and eventually the superset grammar will be removed from the hypothesis set. Of course, this is not quite the same process as *retreat* from a superset to a subset, as both hypotheses are present in the hypothesis space.

In order to get a sense of how Clark and Roberts (1993) apply Clark's Genetic Algorithm to a specific historical change in French, it is necessary to introduce one piece of notation. Clark (1992) is concerned with the extent to which a single datum *expresses* one or more parameter values. For instance, consider a simple tensed clause in English such as (62):

(62)   John chases sheep

In order for this sentence to be successfully analyzed, the grammar must contain parameters set to specific values. In particular, harking back to Gibson and Wexler's word-order space, we might propose that the grammar should have the Spec–Head parameter set to Spec-first (0), the Head–Comp parameter set to Comp-final (1) and V2 set to −V2 (0). But other parameters, e.g. the Bounding Nodes Parameter, are irrelevant to a simple example like this. So, supposing that the word-order parameters occupy the first three positions in a vector of parameter values, with the next three concerning the status of NP, IP and CP as bounding nodes, we can maintain that (62) *expresses* the object in (63):[45]

(63)   (0 1 0 * * *)

Here, the asterisks indicate that this particular datum is silent on the value of the parameter in this position.

As should be clear from our discussion of the TLA, (62) can also be analyzed by a quite different grammar. Specifically, (62) *can* also express any of the objects in (64), with the verb having been raised to C and the subject appearing in (Spec, CP):

(64)   a. (0 1 1 * * *)
         b. (0 0 1 * * *)
         c. (1 0 1 * * *)
         d. (1 1 1 * * *)

In these circumstances, (62) expresses all of (63) and (64) *ambiguously*.

We now turn to the history of French and particularly the disappearance from French in the 16th century of (a) "simple inversion" in interrogatives; (b) null subjects; and (c) V2. To keep the discussion brief, I shall here focus just on the loss of V2, since this adequately illustrates the explanatory value Clark and Roberts see in the Genetic Algorithm. They also argue that the other two changes can be seen as directly contingent on the loss of V2.

Although we shall only be concerned with three of them, the five parameters involved in the overall analysis appear in (65):

(65)   a. Nominative Case is assigned (by I) under agreement
         b. Nominative Case is assigned (by I) under government[46]
         c. The language has clitic nominative pronouns
         d. Null subjects are licensed canonically
         e. The language has V2

Old French is reported as including the example in (66) (Clark and Roberts, 1993: 327):

(66)   (Et) lors demande Galaad ses armes
         (and) then asks Galahad (for) his arms

This is a V2 structure – the conjunction is standardly regarded as irrelevant for V2 – so, with the finite verb in C, the relevant part of the structure is (67):

(67)   [$_{CP}$ lors [$_{C'}$ [$_C$ demande - I][Galaad ...

In (67), the only option for Case marking of the subject is via government – finite I and the subject are not in a Spec–Head agreement configuration – so (67) unambiguously expresses the positive value of (65a). Additionally, of course, it provides an unambiguous indication of the operation of V2, so, with reference to the five parameters of (65), it expresses (68):

(68)   (* 1 * * 1)

Old French also contained SVX strings with X a complement of V, and the example cited by Clark and Roberts (1993) is (69):

(69)   Aucassin ala par le foret
         "Aucassin went through the forest"

In (69), we might propose a standard analysis with the subject in [Spec, IP] and Nominative Case assigned by finite I under Spec–Head agreement. Alternatively, we could suggest a V2 structure with the verb and its inflection raised to C and the subject in [Spec, CP] to fulfill V2 requirements. Under these analyses, (69) ambiguously expresses (70a,b):

(70)   a. (1 * * * 0)
         b. (* 1 * * 1)

How does Clark's Genetic Algorithm respond to this situation? Three observations are relevant. First, in (66) we have an *unambiguous* expression of V2; second, for the hypothesis space to continue to contain hypotheses based on both (70a) and (70b) would, as far as the first two parameters are concerned, raise the specter of supersets – a grammar with 1 in each of the first two positions will, *ceteris paribus*, generate a language which is a superset of both grammars which have a 1 and a 0 (in either order) in these positions. There will, therefore, be pressure from the superset factor in the computation of fitness to resolve the ambiguity of expression in one way or another. Third, structures of the type illustrated in (66) were *frequent* in Old French; Clark and Roberts cite 58 percent of matrix declaratives in representative texts having the form (X)VS whereas only 34 percent exhibit SV(X). Together, then, these factors conspire to favor (70b) over (70a) and lead to a characterization of Old French as a V2 language.[47]

Now, consider Middle French. As far as the data go, there are three key observations. First, examples which are unambiguously V2 continue to occur. Second, the relative frequencies of V2 structures and SV(X) structures changes quite dramatically, with texts containing only 10 percent V2 but 60 percent SV(X) (Clark and Roberts, 1993: 334). Third, a novel structure of XSV appears, which, unlike SV(X), *cannot* be viewed as expressing Case-assignment under government and V2, i.e. this structure *unambiguously* expresses (70a). What might the impact of these changes be for the Genetic Algorithm?

Focusing on V2, the unambiguous expression of the positive value of this parameter is now relatively infrequent. Furthermore, there is also now unambiguous expression of the negative value of the parameter in XSV structures. There is still pressure from the superset factor to resolve the ambiguity in the two analyses in (70), but now we can see how that pressure might lead to a different resolution to that we saw for Old French. Note also that the minor role we have identified for the elegance factor in the calculation of fitness now works in the direction of the preferred outcome. The upshot of all of this is that the Genetic Algorithm is viewed as providing a plausible account of the loss of V2 in 16th century French.[48]

What is presented as a very different approach to explaining historical change appears in Lightfoot (1997), although, as we shall see, this difference is somewhat nuanced. As we have seen throughout our discussion of the TLA, success is defined in terms of converging on a grammar for a target set of sentences and this emphasis on the role of E-language could be seen as at odds with the I-language approach supported by Chomsky and his associates throughout the recent development of generative grammar. From the orthodox Chomskyan point of view, then, a more "internalist" approach to acquisition is to be expected, and Lightfoot's proposals could be seen as a response to this pressure.

In the context of our discussion of Clark and Roberts' account of the loss of V2 in French, it is of interest that one of the cases Lightfoot uses to develop his ideas is the loss of V2 in English. Of course, this can alternatively be construed as the acquisition of V2 by a child acquiring a V2 language, in which case we are concerned with the nature of the change which led to V2 no longer being acquired.

In a V2 language, a consequence of the finite verb always appearing in second position is that *something* else must appear in first position. Of course, this may be a subject, as in the German example in (71a), but it does not have to be, as (71b,c) show.

(71)   a. Hans hat das Buch gekauft
          Hans has the book bought
          "Hans has bought the book"
       b. Das Buch hat Hans gekauft
       c. Gestern hat Hans das Buch gekauft
          yesterday has Hans the book bought
          "Hans bought the book yesterday"

In (71b), the direct object precedes the verb in second position and in (71c) an adverbial adjunct performs this function.

The standard analysis of V2 thus has the finite verb moving to C and an XP moving to the [Spec, CP] position. From this, it follows that finding an XP which is *arbitrary* with respect to its grammatical function appearing in the specifier of C can count as a *cue* for the +V2 value of the relevant parameter. Lightfoot schematizes this as (1997: 177):

(72) $_{SpecCP}$ [XP]

Why does Lightfoot wish to insist that the XP must be arbitrary in grammatical function? Because *subjects* appearing in initial position may simply be in [Spec, IP], and it would be inappropriate to allow such subjects to activate the cue in (72); obviously, subjects occurring in [Spec, CP] could activate the cue, but a child who is trying to figure out how to set the V2-parameter doesn't yet know how such subjects should be analyzed.[49] Additionally, we should note that children being exposed to Modern English will meet nonsubject XPs in initial position in topicalized structures. Lightfoot observes that in these structures, the nonsubjects will not be followed by finite verb forms, which suggests that (72) should perhaps be extended to (73):

(73) $_{\text{SpecCP}}$ [XP]C [Vfinite]

Whatever the details, the idea is that (72) or (73) is an *I-language representation* which is supplied with the relevant parameter; it can then be viewed as a signal to the child as to what to look out for in the linguistic environment as far as the setting of this parameter is concerned.

Turning, then, to the loss of V2 in the history of English, Lightfoot maintains that there is a traditional view that Old English/Middle English appeared to have *optional* V2. If this were true, it would be difficult to accommodate to his account, which seeks to explain the *obligatoriness* of V2 in German, Dutch and other V2 languages. However, he maintains that it is not true, and that in fact there were two dialects in Middle English. The Middle English of the north had a V2 grammar, but the southern variety did not have the option of raising V to C. Now, suppose that what happened in the crucial period was that children from northern England were increasingly exposed to southern English. A consequence of this would be that the cue in (73) would be activated less frequently. Suppose, further, that there is some threshold (Lightfoot speculates on the figure of 30 percent of degree-0 indicative clauses, based on statistical analyses of contemporary Dutch, German, etc.) for (73) to be activated sufficiently to set the linked parameter. The northern English children, whose linguistic environment we are considering, now find themselves in circumstances where the threshold is not reached. The consequence is that the V2 parameter is not set at +V2, and the V2 phenomenon vanishes in a generation.

Now, it is important to be clear about the sense in which this account differs from one which is externally driven and where the learner is seen as striving to match a grammar to a target. Our northern English children, if they were trying to develop a grammar which accurately mirrored their linguistic environment, would receive numerous instances of sentences displaying V2. Yet, if Lightfoot is correct, they effectively *ignored* these and developed grammars which excluded these structures. Lightfoot's subsequent discussion seeks to account for the loss of V-raising in English in similar terms and he also speculates about the emergence of creoles. However, the example I have briefly described here will serve the comparative purposes I now wish to pursue.

First, we should acknowledge that there are substantial similarities between Clark and Roberts' account of the loss of V2 in French and what Lightfoot has to say about the history of English. Recall that Clark and Roberts inferred a statistical shift in the probable make-up of a corpus of primary linguistic data between Old French and Middle French. The former contained large numbers of examples which un-ambiguously expressed +V2, relatively small numbers of examples which were ambiguous in this respect and no examples which un-ambiguously expressed −V2. For Middle French, there were relatively few unambiguous expressions of +V2, relatively many ambiguous cases and a new class of sentences unambiguously expressing −V2. For Lightfoot, a period in which at least 30 percent of the simple indicative clauses in a corpus were unambiguously V2 was followed by a period during which this figure fell below 30 percent. Lightfoot appears to perceive a fundamental distinction here with the Clark and Roberts learner "tracking input data" and being "forced to a new grammar which fits the new data better" (Lightfoot, 1997: 184). However, apart from the fact that in Lightfoot's account, the cue somehow comes with the parameter, I find it difficult to perceive any material difference between these positions. Lightfoot continues by noting that the Clark and Roberts account depends on non-V2 forms being introduced into Middle French, and to the extent that this is correct, it does appear to see the grammar as being shaped by an external set of sentences. As we have noted, the emergence of XSV forms in Middle French, as un-ambiguous expressions of −V2, was one factor which Clark and Roberts took account of. However, it is conceivable that the changes in the statistical distribution of (X)VS and SV(X) structures to which they refer would be sufficient to lead to the loss of V2 and if this is so, I believe that the accounts are near identical in this respect. Both offer an explanation of a historical change, and both do it on a very similar basis.[50]

A second point of some importance in the context of this book is that Lightfoot's claim to be relying on cue-based learning, while intuitively clear enough, raises the question as to whether his speculations can be properly linked to the framework of Dresher and Kaye (1990). His belief that thresholds will be associated with his cues is clearly vital to his account, and this does not amount to (72) or (73) immediately cueing the learner with the +V2 value of the relevant parameter.

The suggestion that there are striking similarities between these two attempts to link acquisition and historical change should not disguise the fact that there are potentially important differences between them. There is nothing explicitly corresponding to a cue linked to a specific parameter value in Clark and Roberts' framework; nor does Lightfoot's account include anything like a GA. Indeed, Lightfoot does not seek to present any kind of algorithm, but there is no reason in principle why formalizations of cue-based learners which have recently been developed by Bertolo et al. (1997a,b) should not be extended to incorporate something akin to his notion of a cue threshold. Then, a theory of cues would enable the development of a complete model. However, as Lightfoot himself acknowledges, he does not have a theory of cues. More worryingly, perhaps, he also suggests (1997: 190) that "we also have no very substantive theory of parameters." Even if this skepticism is justified, it need not impinge on the value of the work we have considered in this chapter. Much of this has depended only on parameter spaces having rather abstract properties. If Lightfoot's call for an adequate theory of parameters is answered, it will or will not instantiate these abstract properties. To the extent that it does, the learnability work of the past decade will engage it; to the extent that it doesn't, new conceptualizations will be necessary.

NOTES

1 In fact, this class of languages is identical with the set of primitive recursive languages, itself a proper subset of the set of recursively enumerable languages.

2 Marcus also briefly considers the concept of *partial feedback* where a signal could be regarded as providing a sufficient but not a necessary condition for grammaticality or its converse. Like complete feedback, there is no reason to believe that this exists.

3 Of course, in proceeding with this assumption, we are not bound to assert that children's grammars *never* change on the basis of exposure to negative data; but we are supposing that normal acquisition can occur without such incidents and that therefore such incidents do not impinge on our conceptualization of the learning problem.

4 This is because, on the assumption that *à qui* moves to the specifier of the subordinate CP in (1), it will not cross the intermediate CP boundary. It will, however, cross the intermediate IP boundary, as indicated in (i):

(i) ... [$_{CP}$ à qui [$_{IP}$ je crois ...

5 For further examples of this type of argument and responses to it, see Lightfoot (1989, 1991) and the commentaries on the 1989 article. In fact, Lightfoot has to modify his degree-0 claim so as to deal with Exceptional Case Marking constructions like (i):

> (i) They believe him to have left

In (i), *him* is Case-marked by *believe* "exceptionally" across a clause boundary, a phenomenon which occurs in English, but not many other languages. If Exceptional Case Marking is the result of setting a parameter, the child needs evidence to set this parameter, and Lightfoot is unable to identify any sentence type simpler than (i) which will supply this evidence. Accordingly, he concludes that parameters must be settable on the basis of degree-0-plus-a-bit, where the extension is intended to include no more than the "front" of an embedded clause. For alternative suggestions on how the domain for fixing parameters might be constrained, see Rizzi (1989).

6 Note further that the mere existence of order will not change the character of the learning problem unless the learner is in a position to exploit this order. As the simple formal example described in the text shows, this depends on the learner having access to the rule which determines the order. There is currently no justification for taking such a possibility seriously.

7 A formal version appears in Manzini and Wexler (1987: 425). It is here rephrased to keep our notation consistent:

Let p_i be a parameter with values $v_i^1 \dots v_i^n$, ϕ a learning function, and D a set of data. Then for every v_i^m, $1 \leq m \leq n$, $\phi(D) = \overline{Pv_i^m}$ if and only if

> (i) $D \subset L(\overline{Pv_i^m})$ and
> (ii) for every v_i^j, $1 \leq j \leq n$, if $D \subset L(\overline{Pv_i^j})$, then $L(\overline{Pv_i^m}) \subset L(\overline{Pv_i^j})$.

8 If we can stipulate that parameters must be fixed in a specific order, then it is easy to see how to avoid the superset problem in this case. So long as the learner sets p_j first, it will be possible to rely on either (7a) or (7b) depending on the value assigned to p_j. However, independent evidence would be needed to justify such a manoeuvre, with its attendant complications. Furthermore, in these circumstances, it would not be possible to link set-theoretic statements to markedness considerations. In the example in the text, v_i^1 would be marked or unmarked relative to v_i^2 depending on the value of p_j.

9 If dependent parameters are a likely source of trouble in learnability models, it is useful to have some sense of how common they might be. A surprising result, established by Bertolo (1995a), is that in parametric models where all parameters are binary, there can be a maximum of only *three* dependent parameters. Whether it is likely that empirically justified parametric systems will satisfy this constraint is, of course, questionable. In the next subsection, for example, we shall be meeting a nonbinary parameter.

10 For detailed discussion of the binding properties of Icelandic *sig*, including observations which vary in detail from Wexler and Manzini's account, see Thráinsson (1991) and Sigurjónsdóttir and Hyams (1992).

11 Manzini and Wexler (1987: 421) have a slightly more complex statement of
    this parameter to take account of the role of accessible subjects in distin-
    guishing pronominal and anaphoric GCs. Since these complexities will not
    play a role in our subsequent discussion, we shall operate with the simpler
    version.

12 In fact, the data in (12a,b) do not distinguish between (14c) and (14d).
    However, *sig* can be bound from outside a subjunctive clause in which it
    appears, as in (i) from Thráinsson (1991: 55):

    (i) Jón$_i$ sagði [að ég hefði svikið sig$_i$]
        "Jon said that I had (subj) betrayed self"

    This indicates that it is an indicative TNS, or "referential" TNS to use
    Manzini and Wexler's term, which defines the binding domain for this ana-
    phor.

13 For an alternative view on how to account for the distribution of Icelandic
    hann, see Sigurjónsdóttir and Hyams (1992).

14 We have already noted that Manzini and Wexler maintain that the
    Icelandic anaphor *sig* takes (14d) as its GC. However, as (19a) and (19b)
    show, the distribution of *hann* is indifferent to mood. If these conclusions
    are correct, it means that GC parameters are not set for *grammars* but for
    individual anaphors and pronouns. Wexler and Manzini explicitly accept
    this conclusion and formulate it as the Lexical Parameterization Hypothesis
    (Wexler and Manzini, 1987: 55).

15 The Subset Condition is simply a condition which requires parameters to
    determine nested sets of languages. As Wexler and Manzini are aware of
    the fact that there are parameters which do not satisfy this condition, the
    role of the Subset Condition has always been a mystery to me (Atkinson,
    1992: 146f.). Accordingly, I do not see the fact that (27) fails to satisfy the
    Subset Condition as a reason for rejecting it. Parity of reasoning would sug-
    gest rejection of the parameter determining the relative order of heads and
    complements, and it is clear that Wexler and Manzini would not advocate
    such a move.

16 Alongside (30), Manzini and Wexler offer a corresponding clause for pro-
    nouns. MacLaughlin (1995: 166) considers this unintelligible, and I think
    that she's right about this. However, as I am not at all certain that her pro-
    posed reformulation achieves intelligibility, I shall not discuss the pronom-
    inal case at all (see also Kapur et al. (1993: 213) for what seem to me to be
    legitimate concerns about the pronoun analogue to (30)).

17 Here, I use the gloss that Manzini and Wexler put on their formulation of
    the Spanning Hypothesis rather than that formulation itself. In my view,
    the gloss captures the nature of the hypothesis more clearly.

18 If we recall the Lexical Parameterization Hypothesis we can see that an impor-
    tant question is begged by this account. Are we to suppose that a binding
    domain associated with one anaphor will affect the binding domain of all pro-
    nouns, pushing them to the maximally marked value of (14a)? Or should we
    be considering pronouns and anaphors in matched sets, with an anaphor only
    affecting its mate? For discussion of this matter, see Newson (1990).

19 MacLaughlin (1995: 169) contains an important error, where she suggests that reliance on the Spanning Hypothesis could obviate the need for the Subset Principle. She maintains that "evidence that a pronoun selects a marked GCPa could be used to change an anaphor from a marked Governing Category Parameter to an unmarked GCPa, in order to span the space." Again her concern is that such a process would reduce the motivation for the Subset Principle. However, as (31b) shows, the Spanning Hypothesis is entirely consistent with an anaphor retaining a marked value even when the pronominal domain is minimal.

20 I guess everyone is allowed a change of mind. In Manzini and Wexler (1987: 439), we find: "English *he*, Italian *lui* and Japanese *kare* are all associated with value (a)." MacLaughlin (1995: 182) has additional observations on *kare*.

21 MacLaughlin (1995: 171) formulates three developmental predictions; however, it seems to me that they are not independent and all follow from (37).

22 Naturally, similar predictions can be made for values of the Proper Antecedent Parameter, but here I will focus exclusively on Governing Categories.

23 For more comprehensive summaries and evaluations, see Atkinson (1992: chapter 6), Kapur et al. (1993: 199ff.) and MacLaughlin (1995: 172ff.). Wexler (1993: 226ff.) is a response to some of the issues raised by Kapur et al.

24 In a recent study, Matsuoka (1997) has shown that some children in the age range 3;10 to 6;0 will interpret an English pronoun as a bound variable when it occurs in a conjoined structure such as (i):

(i) Every mermaid scratched the frog and her

Matsuoka interprets these results as supporting the approach to Binding Theory developed by Reinhart and Reuland (1993), which we shall consider briefly below.

25 Here is an appropriate point to note that in order to operate with representations like (42), it will be necessary for the learner to perform some rather sophisticated *preanalysis*. All learnability models in linguistics incur a considerable debt in the amount of preanalysis that they assume, a feature which is also true of, and made perfectly explicit in, the classic study of Wexler and Culicover (1980).

26 Here, I run together two separate statements from Wexler (1993), the first of which defines markedness, with the second giving the content of the Subset Principle. As usual, the notation has been altered for consistency.

27 Wexler gives only a definition of markedness in these terms and the last conjunct (44) formulates the Subset Principle. The notation has been altered for consistency.

28 As far as the optionality of pronominal subjects in Italian, Spanish, etc. is concerned, they are usually omitted unless required for discourse-related reasons.

29 Note that the view that the non-null subject setting of the parameter is unmarked must immediately confront the observation that children, including those acquiring nonnull subject languages such as English, go through

an early stage of acquisition at which subjects are not obligatory, i.e. they appear to adopt the parameter setting which gives them a superset language. This, along with observations about overt expletives and inverted auxiliaries, leads Hyams (1986) to reject the application of the Subset Principle to this parameter. For an alternative view, relying on the unavailability of functional categories and their projections in the earliest stages of acquisition, see Cinque (1989). MacLaughlin (1995) provides a discussion of the Null Subject Parameter, taking account of more recent views of Hyams (1994a), and suggesting that "there may not be [such a] parameter at all." This is not quite correct in that grammars are still assumed to vary in the licensing mechanisms they have available for null subjects: it is, however, correct in that null pronomials introducing clauses are no longer seen as a reliable diagnostic for a single parameter set in a specific way – they may be null topics, licensed via a discourse mechanism. Whatever the details, MacLaughlin's conclusion that the Null Subject Parameter should not be cited as a parameter clearly requiring the Subset Principle appears to be justified.

30 Economy is invoked here on the grounds that nonovert movement to check a feature is less costly than overt movement, this principle being known as Procrastinate. Different accounts of *why* nonovert movement is preferred appear in chapters 3 and 4 of Chomsky (1995), but these differences are of no concern in the present context. I assume here the account of feature strength which appears in chapter 3, since it is more likely to be familiar to readers. I do not believe that the version developed in chapter 4 of the same work materially changes the argument in the text. I use scare quotes with "checked" in acknowledgment of the detailed analysis of the notion contained in chapter 4. Again, I do not believe that this analysis affects the points I make.

31 I am, of course, here ignoring details of precisely which features get "checked" and what their locations are. The important point for our present purposes is simply that the French verb is required to raise.

32 Of course, (48b) is well-formed as an echo question. The asterisk here indicates that it cannot, however, be a well-formed WH-question.

33 Safir (1996) is an articulate representative of the "universalist approach" to the cross-linguistic study of pronouns and anaphors. The slogan of this approach could be: there is nothing special about pronouns and anaphors beyond the fact that they are pronouns and anaphors. This emphasis rules out the possibility of such items being associated with a *lexically* specific GC.

34 As usual, the notation has been altered for consistency.

35 In other words, if $L(\bar{P})$ is the target and the i-th value of $\bar{P}$ is v_i^n, a global trigger for v_i^n is a sentence in

$$L(\bar{P}) - \bigcup_{\overline{P'} \in \mathbf{P}^{\{(p_i, v_i^n)\}}} L(\overline{P'})$$

36 To paraphrase, let A be a partial assignment such that, for every $p_j \neq p_i$, $\langle p_j, v_j^m \rangle$ for some v_j^m. Then, if $L(\bar{P})$ (with $\bar{P} \in \mathbf{P}^A$) is the target and the i-th

value of $\bar{P}$ is v_i^n, a local trigger for v_i^n is a sentence in

$$L(\bar{P}) - \bigcup_{\overline{P'} \in \mathbf{P}^{A \cup \{\langle p_i v_i^n \rangle\}}} L(\overline{P'})$$

37 For this reason, Gibson and Wexler set subset parameters aside when discussing the TLA. As the previous section has indicated, this may not involve any serious loss of generality.

38 Strictly speaking, it is necessary to distinguish here between global and local triggers and between different ways in which parameter values are selected for modification (Frank and Kapur, 1996). Note also that in this proof we only established *sufficiency*, i.e. this proof leaves open the possibility that parameter spaces might be learned by the TLA even when there are *no* triggering data. We shall briefly consider this matter in section 2.4.3.

39 It is perhaps worth being explicit on the numerical consequences of this. Quite simply, it entails that the cardinality of each of the data sets to which the learner might be exposed is exactly 2! These data sets are indicated exhaustively in the right-hand column of (57).

40 For a formalization of parameter sequences consistent with the suggestion that parameters are subject to maturational constraints, see Bertolo (1995a,b).

41 It is of some interest that Wexler, as well as being responsible for the TLA, is probably the most outspoken supporter of the Continuity Hypothesis and the view that parameters are set very early. It is perhaps not surprising, then, that he prefers to remain noncommittal in a context where he is looking for a parameter to be set (relatively) late.

42 In fact, Berwick and Niyogi present Gibson and Wexler's learning problems as Markov chains with the probabilities in question just being the transition probabilities in a Markov network and local maxima having the characteristics of absorbing states.

43 It is noteworthy that modifications suggested by Frank and Kapur, which go beyond what we have considered here, produce systems which contain no local maxima. Specifically, they discuss the empirical generalization that V2 appears not to co-occur with VOS and OVS word orders, and one proposal for dealing with this is to allow VOS + V2 and OVS + V2 membership of the space, while supposing that V2 has *no effect* in these cases, i.e. VOS + V2 and VOS − V2 are extensionally identical, as are OVS + V2 and VOS − V2. With the Gibson and Wexler parameterization of the resultant space, there are no local maxima.

44 Obviously, it is necessary that any nonbinary parameters are recast as binary for this procedure. While this is formally possible, replacement of an n-value parameter by n binary parameters might have unfortunate consequences. For instance, the five-value GC Parameter of section 2.3.3 ensures that binding domains are "continuous," i.e. in (i), where GC(I), GC(II) and GC(III) are successively larger binding domains, it is not possible for an anaphor α to be bound from β and from δ, but not from γ:

(i) ... [GC(III) ... β ... [GC(II) ... γ ... [GC(I) ... δ ... α ...]]] ...

If the five values of the GC Parameter are replaced by five binary parameters (e.g. 0 and 1 corresponding to the statements: the domain of a finite TNS is/is not a GC), it would be necessary to stipulate that certain combinations of binary digits were not allowed. As current orthodoxy has it that parameters are binary and, as we have seen, there are versions of Binding Theory which entirely avoid parameterization, I shall not pursue this matter further.

45 Of course, (62) also expresses a variety of other parameter settings on common assumptions, e.g. those concerning the assignment of Case and θ-roles. Equally, it fails to express a range of additional parameters, e.g. those related to the Binding Theory. In a complete account, the vector in (63) would have positions corresponding to every parameter.

46 These two mechanisms for Nominative Case assignment have been proposed by Koopman and Sportiche (1991), the most direct motivation of (65b) being the necessity to Case-mark subjects in VSO languages, where the subject remains in situ in [Spec, VP]. It is of some interest that in their discussion of early stages in the acquisition of English, Déprez and Pierce (1993) suggest that children operate with *both* Case-marking mechanisms; they do not consider how the child deals with the obvious Subset Problem this raises.

47 Of course, if we suppose that the "elegance" factor in the calculation of fitness takes account of chain length, this will disfavor V2 analyses when compared to nonmovement analyses. For the argument in the text to go through, then, we need to assume that this factor is weighted in such a way in the calculation of fitness that its contribution is insignificant when compared to that coming from successful analyses of unambiguous cases and aversion to supersets.

48 An interesting consequence of this account is that if learners of Middle French did go through a process like that described by Clark and Roberts, it was necessary for them to effectively "ignore" tokens of V2 in their linguistic environments. We shall return to this. An obvious issue raised by my abbreviated account of Clark and Roberts' ideas is that a complete account would require an explanation for the emergence of XSV and the sharp drop in frequency of (X)VS. Obviously the former could well contribute to the latter, and Clark and Roberts speculate that the former could itself be due to morphological changes in subject pronouns.

49 Note that the reasoning here is entirely analogous to that which led Clark and Roberts to conclude that SV(X) sentences in French are ambiguous as far as their expression of parameter values goes.

50 There is, of course, the difference that Clark and Roberts are operating with a specific algorithm, whereas Lightfoot is speculating about the role of threshold frequencies. I do not see this as affecting the point made in the text.

3   Language change and learnability

Ian Roberts

3.1   Introduction and general hypotheses

For the study of language change to be relevant to learnability theory, a number of assumptions must be made both about language change and about the synchronic form of grammars. The principal assumption is the standard one from principles-and-parameters theory, namely that the grammar of a language L consists of UG principles with the values of the parameters which modulate those fixed principles. This point of view is succinctly stated by Chomsky as follows: "A particular language L is an instantiation of the initial state of the cognitive system of the language faculty with options specified" (Chomsky, 1995: 219). A simple example of this concerns the relative order of a verb and its direct object. In some languages (English, Romance, Bantu, etc.), verbs precede their objects. In other languages (Japanese, Korean, Turkish, Indic, etc.), verbs follow their objects. In terms of principles-and-parameters theory, we say that the existence and characterization of the verb, the direct object and the verb–object relation are to be stated as (or, at the relevant level of theoretical abstraction, derived from) UG principles, while the ordering of the verb and the object are attributable to a parametric choice (this parameter has been referred to as the Head Parameter; see for example, Travis, 1984; Koopman, 1984).

The options in question vary along both the synchronic and the diachronic dimensions. The conception of parametric options was developed to account for synchronic variation, but a moment's reflection shows that it must also apply in the diachronic dimension. In other words, parameter values can change as a function of time. We can in fact observe this very easily by comparing the Modern Romance languages with Latin in regard to word order. Latin word order was rather free, but object–verb order clearly predominated; on the other hand, as just mentioned, the Modern Romance languages are all verb–object. The contrast is illustrated in (74), with Italian representing Modern Romance:

(74) a. Ego apros tres et quidem pulcherrimos cepi. (Pliny the
Younger)
I boars three and indeed very-beautiful have-taken
(Object) (Verb)
b. Io ho preso dei cinghiali, tre e anche bellissimi.
I have-taken boars, three and indeed very-beautiful
(Verb) (Object)

Thus, if there is a parameter determining the relative order of verb and
direct object, its value has changed in the development of Latin into
Romance. The central issue for diachronic syntax in the context of
principles-and-parameters theory is accounting for how and why this
can happen. How do parameter values change over time? This is
arguably *the* fundamental question for comparative syntax, since it is
quite reasonable to view the existence of a variety of different grammatical systems (i.e. languages, at the relevant level of idealization)
as a result of language change; we know from the history of very
well-known language families such as Romance that a parent language can give rise to many distinct daughter languages over time.
Moreover, the existence of very large language families whose parent
language is unattested but amenable to some form of "reconstruction" is an accepted result of comparative and historical linguistics.
Given this, the study of language change may lead us to an understanding of why grammatical systems vary at all, and may also lead
to an account of the patterns of variation among grammatical
systems, i.e. language typology. In other words, it is possible that
the theory of language change will exhaust the theory of language
variation. I return to this point below.

Following a view that has been developed in terms of recent linguistic theory primarily by Lightfoot (1979, 1991), I assume that parameter
change is an aspect of the process of parameter setting. A change is
initiated when (a population of) learners converge on a grammatical
system which differs in at least one parameter value from the system
internalized by the speakers whose linguistic behavior provides the
input to the learners. As the younger generation replaces the older one,
the change is carried through the speech community. Of course, many
social, historical and cultural factors influence speech communities, and
hence the transmission of changes (see Labov, 1972, 1994). From the
perspective of linguistic theory, though, we must abstract away from
these factors and attempt – as far as the historical record permits – to
focus on change purely as a relation between grammatical systems. It is
very difficult to see any other way of accounting for language change

which will allow for the kinds of diachronic changes we can observe (e.g. that shown in (74)).

The assumption that parameter change is an aspect of the process of parameter fixation raises an important issue for language acquisition. The issue is summed up in the following quotation from Niyogi and Berwick (1995): "it is generally assumed that children acquire their target ... grammars without error. However, if this were always true ... grammatical changes within a population would seemingly never occur, since generation after generation of children would have successfully acquired the grammar of their parents" (Niyogi and Berwick, 1995: 1). Thus the standard paradigm for language acquisition is not immediately compatible with the observation that grammatical systems change over time. Clark and Roberts (1993, 1997) refer to this issue as the logical problem of language change, and sum it up as follows: "if the trigger experience of one generation, say G_1, permits members of G_1 to set parameter p_i to value v_k^i, why is the trigger experience produced by G_1 insufficient to cause the next generation to set p_i to v_k^i?" (Clark and Roberts, in progress: 12).[1] The simple answer to this question (which again goes back to Lightfoot, 1979) is that v_k^i is unlearnable. This is where learnability considerations connect to diachronic linguistics (and, indeed, to comparative linguistics if the above comments are right). Fleshing this idea out requires us to develop an account of the relation between the learner and the trigger; it also requires us to be very precise – much more precise than has often been the case in work in principles-and-parameters theory – about the nature and format of parameters. Our theory of the learner, the trigger and the nature of parameters is tested against the evidence from language change (gathering and interpreting this evidence is in itself a nontrivial task; however, I will gloss over this matter here). The result of this enterprise is an integrated theory of comparative and historical linguistics, which situates this discipline in its rightful place within modern cognitive science. In what follows, I will try to sketch how we can embark on this enterprise.

The general approach that I adopt attributes the possibility of language change to the interaction of the parameter-setting algorithm, the trigger and the nature of parameters. The relation between the trigger and parameter values is indirect, being "filtered" by the parameter-setting algorithm. In this way, we can solve the logical problem of language change. This relation between the trigger and parameter values is chaotic in that (a) we cannot predict a change, even if all the conditions for a change to take place are satisfied (here we are in the same situation as evolutionary biologists); (b) a very small change in some aspect of the trigger can lead to dramatic changes in the parametric system.

This approach has a very interesting general consequence. As mentioned above, the existence of language families shows us that a great deal of synchronic variation is the result of language change: we integrate this with what was said above by simply adding that the transmission of certain changes through a speech community is interrupted by some historical contingency (e.g. the break-up of the Western Roman Empire in the case of the Romance languages). It may be that all synchronic variation can be accounted for in this way; this amounts to the claim that there was once a Proto-World, a single language from which all languages historically derive. Establishing Proto-World is probably not feasible using the traditional techniques of comparative reconstruction, but the conceptual point is enough for our purposes (it is in any case likely given the single-origin theory of the origin of modern humans, currently the best-supported theory of the origin of this species). It implies that the parameter-setting algorithm is logically and chronologically prior to the parameters themselves; recent work by Clark (1994, 1996) has shown that plausible assumptions about the learner impose heavy constraints on the format for parameters, and in fact are compatible with the abandonment of this notion in favor of induction over tree fragments. We can thus think that the existence of parameters themselves is attributable to properties of the learning algorithm interacting with UG; parametric variation might then be an emergent property of this interaction. UG itself would then contain no "statement" of parameters at all. I will not explore this view in detail here, but it is compatible with everything that I have to say; it is also in the spirit of a minimalist linguistic theory.

Here I will sketch some assumptions about the nature of parameters and an associated markedness theory (section 3.2), and apply these to three cases of language change that I take to be typical (section 3.3): the loss of a movement dependency, grammaticalization, and change in verb–object order.

3.2   The nature of parameters

3.2.1   *General considerations*

Following Chomsky (1995), I assume that parameters reduce to the activation (or not) of a property P of functional heads. Here are some examples:

(75)   a. Does AgrS attract the (main, finite) verb?
          English: no; French: yes
       b. Does AgrS attract DP to its Spec?
          English, French: yes; Celtic: no
       c. Does (root) C attract V?
          German: yes; English, French: no
       d. Does AgrS license pro?
          Italian: yes; English, French: no
       e. Does WH move overtly?
          English: yes; Chinese: no

These parameters are all well-established in the literature on comparative syntax, and I will not discuss their motivation here.

Now, since parameters can be seen as binary properties, it is possible to code parameter values with the set $\{1,0\}$. Thus, if we impose an arbitrary order on the sequence of parameter values, we can give the index (or parameter assignment) of each grammatical system. Here are some plausible partial indices for well-known languages taking the parameters in (75) in the order given there:

(76)   English   01001
       French   11001
       Italian   11011
       Chinese   01010
       German   11101
       Welsh   10011

Exercise

3.1   Try to deduce what each parameter assignment tells us about the properties of each language. What are the predicted word orders of these languages? Try to verify these predictions with native speakers.

We can now see acquisition as the search for i, the index of the grammatical system presented to the learner, and change as the situation where generation G_1 has i, but G_2 has $j \neq i$.

Our approach makes it possible to see how many parameters there might be, at least in principle. Let us suppose that P is the property of attracting another category (or feature, in terms of Chomsky, 1995, chapter 4; there are technical points here that I'll gloss over – cf. the discussion of Roberts and Roussou, 1997, in the next section). Suppose further that each functional head can attract at most one head X and one maximal projection XP (this restriction follows from the theory of phrase structure proposed by Kayne, 1994). Then, for $n = |F|$, the cardinality of the set of functional heads, the cardinality of the set of parameters $|P|$ is $2n$ and the cardinality of the set of grammatical systems, $|G|$ is 2^{2n}. So, once we figure out how many functional heads there are, we can calculate how many grammatical systems there are. Doing this can tell us what constraints must be imposed on the learning device, as Clark (1992) has shown.

Functional heads abound in the recent literature on comparative syntax. In the most detailed discussion of clause structure across languages that I am aware of in recent research, Cinque (1997) gives the following structure of "IP" (I give only the labels of the categories; from left to right, each takes the maximal projection of the next as its immediate structural complement):

(77)

Mood$_{\text{Speech Act}}$	Mood$_{\text{Evaluative}}$	Mood$_{\text{Evidential}}$
Mod$_{\text{Epistemic}}$	T(Past)	T(Future)
Mood$_{\text{Irrealis}}$	Mod$_{\text{Necessity}}$	Mod$_{\text{Possibility}}$
Mod$_{\text{Volitional}}$	Mod$_{\text{Obligation}}$	Mod$_{\text{Ability/permission}}$
Asp$_{\text{Habitual}}$	Asp$_{\text{Repetitive(I)}}$	Asp$_{\text{Frequentative(I)}}$
Asp$_{\text{Celerative(I)}}$	T(Anterior)	Asp$_{\text{Terminative}}$
Asp$_{\text{Continuative}}$	Asp$_{\text{Perfect(?)}}$	Asp$_{\text{Retrospective}}$
Asp$_{\text{Proximative}}$	Asp$_{\text{Durative}}$	Asp$_{\text{Generic/progressive}}$
Asp$_{\text{Prospective}}$	Asp$_{\text{SgCompletive(I)}}$	Asp$_{\text{PlCompletive}}$
Voice	Asp$_{\text{Celerative(II)}}$	Asp$_{\text{SgCompletive(II)}}$
Asp$_{\text{Repetitive(II)}}$	Asp$_{\text{Frequentative(II)}}$	...

The total number of heads in this structure, as Cinque stresses, is a conservative estimate of the number of functional heads in "IP." No account is taken here of NegPs or AgrPs, for example. Moreover, "DP" and "CP" both have a complex structure (Rizzi, 1997, argues for splitting "CP" into Force, Topic, Focus and Finiteness, again with the possibility of interspersed AgrPs). Cinque postulates the clause structure in (77) on the basis of careful cross-linguistic argumentation, showing that adverbs, auxiliaries/particles and affixes are consistently ordered in the same way across languages. We can see this from the relative orders of English adverbs, for example:

(78)   *frankly* (Speech Act) ≻ *fortunately* (Evaluative) ≻ *allegedly* (Evidential) ≻ *probably* (Epistemic) ≻ *once* (Past) ≻ *then* (Future) ≻ *perhaps* (Irrealis) ≻ *necessarily* (Necessity) ≻ *possibly* (Possibility) ≻ *willingly* (Volition) ≻ *inevitably* (Obligation) ≻ *cleverly* (Ability/permission) ≻ *usually* (Habitual) ≻ *again*

(Repetitive(I)) ≻ *often* (Frequentative(I)) ≻ *quickly* (Celerative(I)) ≻ *already* (Anterior) ≻ *no longer* (Terminative) ≻ *still* (Continuative) ≻ *always* (Perfect(?)) ≻ *just* (Retrospective) ≻ *soon* (Proximative) ≻ *briefly* (Durative) ≻ *characteristically* (Generic/Progressive) ≻ *almost* (Prospective) ≻ *completely* (SgCompletive(I)) ≻ *tutto* (PlCompletive)^2 ≻ *well* (Voice) ≻ *fast/early* (Celerative(II)) ≻ *completely* (SgCompletive(II)) ≻ *again* (Repetitive(II)) ≻ *often* (Frequentative(II)) ...

Exercise

3.2   If you are a native speaker of English, construct sentences illustrating these orders of adverbs, and ungrammatical examples which violate the orders. You may find that you do not fully concur with the judgments reported by Cinque. If you are not a native speaker of English, translate the adverbs and try to see what the ordering is in your native language.

Cinque argues that the adverbs of each class occupy the specifier of the relevant functional head. In this way, the order of adverbs is dictated by the order of functional categories. This idea is strongly supported by the fact that preverbal particles and auxiliaries follow the same ordering, as a detailed discussion of a range of creoles, West African, Celtic and Tibeto-Burman languages shows. This ordering is partially instantiated by the English auxiliary system (with the proviso that modals and tense are morphologically combined), as examples like (79) show:

(79)   Dinner must have been being cooked (when we got there).

Moreover, suffixes show exactly the mirror-image order. Thus, in a system where $F_1 \ldots F_n$ are free, we find $F_1 F_2 F_3 F_4$ etc., while where $F_1 \ldots F_n$ are bound, we find $F_4 F_3 F_2 F_1$. This is a consequence of the universal order of functional heads combined with successive left-adjunction of heads. Thus, in Korean, we find verb forms like that in (80), where the order of the verbal suffixes is Voice–Aspect–Tense–Mood, exactly the opposite of the ordering found with the English auxiliaries in (79) (still retaining the proviso regarding the syncretism of tense with modal auxiliaries in English):

(80)   cap-hi - si - ess - ess - keyss - sup - ti - kka
         V– Passive Agr Ant Past Epistemic Agr Evid Q
         "Did you feel that (unspecified argument) had been caught?"

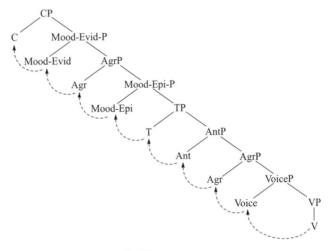

Figure 3.1 Structure of (80)

(80) can be derived by successive head movement of the verb as illustrated in figure 3.1. Assuming that the verb left-adjoins to each head, we derive the mirror-image ordering of suffixes from the *same* clause structure as that of English. We do not have to assume that the suffixes are syntactic affixes; it is possible to form the complex verb in the lexicon and then check features successively – on the ordering of checking and the order of affixes, cf. Chomsky (1995: 195–6).

Cinque surveys all of the Romance and Germanic languages, Hebrew, Bosnian/Serbo-Croatian, Chinese, Albanian, Hindi, Bantu, Hixkaryana, Lezgian, Mongolian, Malay, Zuni, Kammu, Nahuatl, Pawnee, Malayalam, Fula, Greek, Finnish, Mofu-Gudur, Evenki, Abkhaz, Ubykh, Arabic, Hungarian, Dagaare, Kom, Yoruba, Burmese, Garo, Kachin, Patani, Aleut, Tshangla, Central Alaskan Yup'ik, Thai, Kwaio, Ponapean, Kiribatese, Anejom, Samoan, Tokelau, Big Nambas, Walmadjari, Sanio-Hiowe, Fore, Menya, Tauya, Yreaba, Wahgi, Navajo, Canela-Crahô, Diegueño, Hidatsa, Ika, Macushi, Ute, Yavapai, Waorani and Basque, in addition to the languages mentioned above. Such striking cross-linguistic correlations strongly support the conclusion that a clause structure of the kind shown in (77) is made available by UG. It is of course always possible to encode the properties attributed to functional heads in terms of something else (feature structures, lexical items, semantics, etc.), but the complexity, the cross-linguistic similarities and the variation must be captured somehow.

Now let us calculate, on the assumption that (77) is the correct UG clause structure, how many parameters of clause structure there are. In (77), $n = 32$. Then $|P| = 64$ and $|G| = 2^{64}$. This is a very large space indeed, and bear in mind that this is the number of possible variants of "IP" alone. Once we take into account the full functional structures of "CP" and "DP," the space will grow still bigger. In a discussion of a 30-parameter system, giving 1,073,741,824 grammars, Clark (1990) points out that a learner which checks one grammar per second from birth would in the worst case take 34 years to converge if this is the number of possible grammars. Hence there must be a learning device which facilitates the search in this space.

We can, I think, make a similar argument on the basis of diachronic considerations. Two assumptions are generally made in all comparative and historical linguistics (in fact, they really make historical linguistics possible, and have done since the beginnings of the discipline). These are articulated by Croft (1994) as follows:[3]

(81)   a. Uniformitarianism: "the languages of the past are not different in nature from those of the present" (Croft, 1994: 204)

        b. Connectivity: "within a set of attested language states defined by a given typological classification, a language can ... shift from any state to any other state" (Croft, 1994: 205)

We can reformulate these assumptions in terms of principles-and-parameters theory as follows:

(82)   a. Uniformitarianism: the languages of the past conform to the same UG as those of the present

        b. Connectivity: a grammatical system can change into any other grammatical system given enough time (i.e. all parameters are equally variable)

Put this way, both assumptions seem entirely reasonable. To deny uniformitarianism would be to assert that speakers of languages of the past were cognitively different from speakers of currently existing languages. Presumably, though, at least as far back as the origin of modern *homo sapiens*, we do not want to say this. Effectively, (82a) is the null hypothesis regarding the relation of UG to language change. Denying (82b) would imply "privileging" certain parameters, a conceptually highly dubious move for which there seems to be no empirical motivation: (82b) is the null hypothesis regarding the role of parameters in language change. So we want to maintain the assumptions in (82). As I mentioned above, these are facilitating assumptions, in that they make it possible to start out towards an answer to the question of how parameters can change over time. Now, at present approximately 5,000 languages are spoken (Ruhlen, 1987). Suppose that this figure is constant throughout human history (back to the emergence of *homo sapiens*), and that every language changes with every generation, so if we have a new generation every 25 years, we have 20,000 languages per century. If the total number of grammatical systems is 2^{30} (following Clark's (1990) discussion), it would take 18,000 centuries for each type to be realized once. At present, the usual reckoning is that humans have been around for about 2000 centuries (i.e. 200,000 years – see for example Bickerton, 1991). Of course, the figures given here are rather arbitrary, but the point should be clear: given the kind of parameter space we seem to have, on the basis of the empirical examination of existing languages, there simply has not been enough time since the emergence of the species (and therefore, I am assuming, of UG) for anything like the total range of possibilities offered by UG to be realized. This conclusion effectively empties uniformitarianism and connectivity of content. In theory, we simply couldn't know whether a language of the past corresponded to the UG of the present or not, since the over-whelming likelihood is that such a language is typologically different from any language that existed before or since.

One might conclude that 30 parameters define too big a parametric space, but, as we have seen, comparative data leads us to postulate at least this big a space. Here we are faced – in a different context – with the familiar tension between the exigencies of empirical description, which lead us to postulate ever more entities, and the need for explanation, which requires us to eliminate as many entities as possible. Chomsky (1995: 4–5) notes that the principles-and-parameters model resolved this tension for synchronic comparative syntax, but we see that the problem re-emerges at a higher level.

It seems then that the parameter space is too big for the assumptions of uniformity and connectivity to have any empirical consequences. Since uniformity represents the null hypothesis about the relation of UG to change, and connectivity the null hypothesis about parametric change, this conclusion appears to cast doubt on the entire enterprise of looking at syntactic change from the point of view of principles-and-parameters theory. This is the conceptual problem caused by the size of the parameter space.

The size of the parameter space also raises an empirical issue: the fact that on the basis of a small subset of currently existing languages we can clearly observe language types, and note diachronic drift from one type to another, is simply astonishing. The view presented above implies that, as far as the history of humanity up to now is concerned, languages should appear to vary unpredictably and without assignable limits, even if we have a UG containing just 30 or so parameters. Obviously, we need to find ways to reduce the range of parametric possibilities while retaining (at least) 30 parameters. In the next paragraphs, I will consider two ways to do this.

First, we can suppose that something is causing grammatical systems to "clump" in the parametric space, rather like galaxies in the physical universe. What is the parameter-space equivalent of the forces that cause stars to bunch together into galaxies, etc.? To answer this question, I want to briefly introduce some of the concepts and terminology used in Kauffman (1995), some of which is based on dynamical-systems theory. Following Kauffman, my presentation will be informal throughout. We can think of a parametric system as a network of switches (cf. Chomsky, 1986), which can assume a number of possible states corresponding to the states of each switch (i.e. each parameter). Each possible state is a grammatical system, i.e. a language. Suppose that the switches are binary and are connected to other switches in Boolean relations (forming what Kauffman calls a Boolean network), as is often proposed regarding implicational and other relations among parameter values. Suppose, then, we have a network consisting of just three parameters, each of which receives "inputs" from the other two. I now quote Kauffman at length (in this quotation, read "parameter" for "bulb"):

Since each bulb can have only two values, on or off, which we can represent as 1 and 0, then it is easy to see that there are four possible input patterns it can receive from its two neighbors. Both inputs can be off (00), one or the other input can be on (01 or 10), or both inputs can be on (11) … For example, bulb 1 might be active only if both of its inputs were active the moment before … bulb 1 is an AND gate … Say I assign the AND function to bulb 1 and the OR function to bulbs 2 and 3. At each tick of the clock, each bulb examines the activities of its two inputs and adopts state 1 or 0 specified by its Boolean function …

As we can see, the system can be in a finite number of states, here eight. If started in one state, over time the system will flow through some sequence of states. This sequence is called a trajectory … Since there is a finite number of states, the system must eventually hit a state it has previously encountered. Then the trajectory will repeat. Since the system is deterministic, it will cycle forever around a recurrent loop of states called a state cycle. (Kauffman, 1995: 76–7)

Note that Kauffman views the state cycle in the temporal dimension – variables change their values with the ticking of a clock – but it is entirely possible to view the state cycle in a spatial dimension, as with synchronic parametric variation. A state cycle can consist of a single state (as with Kauffman's example network with one AND-bulb and two OR-bulbs if started at 111). It is also possible for a state cycle to include all possible states of the system. Most relevant to the present discussion is the case where the state cycle only includes a subpart of the overall state space. When this happens, we say that a given state cycle is an attractor (or forms a "basin of attraction"). It is in this sense that attractors can cause parametric systems to "clump together" in parametric space, i.e. to occupy only a small part of the space.[4]

I would like to suggest that the traditional linguistic concept of markedness creates basins of attraction in parameter space. In other words, unmarked values of parameters can effectively reduce the possible space that grammatical systems occupy, and so reduce the hyperastronomical range of possibilities (2^{30}, 2^{64}, etc.) to a sufficiently small state cycle for language types and diachronic drift to be discernible. Of course, this begs the question of the nature of markedness; I will return to this point in Section 3.2.3. Given the general considerations about the relation between language types, language acquisition and language change raised in the previous section, the attractors – markedness – must be introduced by the learning algorithm. Here again we see the consequences of assumptions regarding the nature of the learner for historical and comparative linguistics.

A second way to manage the size of the parameter space emerges from Kauffman's (1995) study of Boolean networks. Boolean networks, like any network of binary variables, have 2^n possible states for n variables. Applying this to principles-and-parameters theory, each such state is a grammatical system, as we saw above. Kauffman then defines the state cycle, which is some natural repetition of states. As I mentioned above, the state cycle can be very short, or it can correspond to the total number of possible states. Kauffman shows that there are various ways of restricting the state cycle, and thus of effectively making a system occupy just a part of its overall state space (in principles-and-parameters theory, the state space corresponds to what we have been calling the parameter space). One way to do this is by limiting the number of Boolean connections. To do this, Kauffman defines the quantity K, which designates the number of inputs determining the value of each variable in the system (i.e, the density of the connections in a Boolean network). If $K = 1$, i.e. each variable has just one input, the system is static. If $K > 2$, the system is chaotic, and fluctuates wildly. Most interestingly, if $K = 2$ the system is prone to occasional state-changes, but is neither frozen nor chaotic. Kauffman claims that biological systems are typically of this type – the evidence from the existence of different linguistic systems falling into more or less discernible types is that the parametric system is of this type, too. Another very interesting aspect of Kauffman's system is that he shows that, where $K = 2$, the size of the state cycle is roughly the square root of n, the number of binary variables. In the 64-parameter system for "IP" that was outlined above, the state cycle would be of length 8, i.e. there would be 8 possible states. In turn, this would mean that grammatical systems cycle through eight different possible clause structures of the 2^{64} made available by UG. This may in fact seem rather few, but then recall that 64 may be a small number of parameters. In general, then, Kauffman's work on Boolean networks suggests a way of solving the problem caused by extremely large parameter spaces, and allows us to understand why language types and diachronic drift can be observed even on the basis of a tiny sample of languages.

In order to restrict the parameter space along Kauffman's lines, then, we need to ensure that each parameter has only two inputs. This can be achieved by giving all parameters the following form:[5]

(83)   a. Is there X?   Yes/No
        b. If there is X, is there Y?   Yes/No

(83) gives rise to a structure like (84) for parameters:

(84)

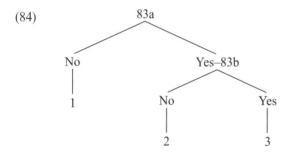

Each of these three values, 1, 2, 3, is a Boolean function of the other two, since the logical form of the parameter is $1 \lor (2 \lor 3)$, i.e. any system which chooses 1, 2 or 3 as the value of the parameter cannot choose either of the other two. Thus, each parameter value has exactly two inputs. In the next section, I will sketch an approach to parameters which has this property. Note that the deductive structure of parameters cannot be any "deeper" than that in (83), or the parametric system will become completely chaotic, if we apply Kauffman's conclusions to parameter spaces. This means that there are no complex networks of interactions among parameter values.[6] The variant properties of each functional feature F are fixed individually, rather than certain ones being "deduced" from others. The natural way to think of this is that parameter setting according to the schema in (84) is fairly directly connected to lexical acquisition (cf. Borer, 1984; Chomsky, 1995), with individual morphemes triggering the parameter values of each functional feature according to (84). This is very close to what is proposed in Chomsky (1995, chapter 4). In the next section I will present a refinement of Chomsky's system which corresponds exactly to (84).

We see then that the space of variation afforded by even a highly constrained system of parameters is very big, so big that in order to account for language acquisition and for simple historical and comparative observations (in fact, the actual existence of such observations in the first place, quite apart from their content), we must constrain the parameter space somehow. This can be done in two ways: either by positing attractors, i.e. a theory of markedness, or by constraining the inputs to parameter values. In the next section, I will outline a format for parameters which has both of these properties.

3.2.2   The form of parameters[7]

In the theory put forward in Chomsky (1995, chapter 4) movement is a consequence of the mechanism of feature checking which plays three principal roles. First, the requirement that features of a given type ("strong" features) be checked before Spell Out triggers overt movement, as such features are held to be uninterpretable at the PF interface. If they are not eliminated before the derivation reaches that interface, then, the basic principle of representational economy (Full Interpretation) is violated. For example, in English, subjects must raise from their merged VP-internal position to SpecAgrS because AgrS has a strong D-feature which must be checked against the subject.[8] In this way, the following configuration is obtained:

(85) $[_{AgrSP}$ DP[D] $[_{AgrS'}$ AgrS[D] ... [VP t_{DP} ...]]]

Here, since DP is in the checking domain of AgrS (the checking domain of a head H can be characterized approximately as the specifier of H or a head position adjoined to H – cf. Chomsky, 1995: 178–9, for a precise definition), its D-feature can be checked against that of AgrS. Both features are thus eliminated from the representation, and Full Interpretation is satisfied at PF. Since movement is held to be a last-resort operation, only applying when it has to, checking requirements of this sort are claimed to be the only motivation for movement. Indeed, Chomsky (1995: 269–70) builds this idea into the definition of movement in the following way:

(86)   a. F is an unchecked feature.

        b. F enters into a checking relation as a result of movement.

Here movement is seen as feature movement (Move-F), with movement of a category bearing the feature taking place only as a consequence of further requirements; I will gloss over this refinement here. Checking theory is thus the motor of movement.

Exercises

3.3   Construct checking-theoretic analyses for each of the cases of movement/attraction given in (75) in addition to DP-movement to SpecAgrSP, V-to-AgrS movement, V-to-C movement and WH-movement. What problems do you encounter?

3.4   Give a checking-theoretic analysis of the following paradigm for English interrogatives (you can decide for yourself about the grammaticality of (a)):

        a. ?John left?

        b. Has John left?

        c. *John saw who?

        d. Who did John see?

     What problems do you encounter?

The second function of checking theory in the system put forward in Chomsky (1995, chapter 4) is to account for cross-linguistic variation. The features associated with syntactic categories, such as the D-feature of AgrS mentioned in connection with (85), are free to vary from one grammatical system to another along the "strong–weak" dimension. Strong features trigger overt movement, as we saw above. Weak features, on the other hand, do not trigger overt movement. In fact, the Procrastinate principle has the effect that where a head has a weak feature, movement will be delayed until the post-Spell Out, covert part of the derivation. A strong feature overrides Procrastinate. In general, then, the strong–weak distinction, by differentially triggering overt movement, leads to overt word-order differences. This distinction is held to be the principal, if not the only, dimension of syntactic variation among grammatical systems.

Exercise

3.5   The following characteristics are found in null-subject languages:

A. Ability to "drop" pronominal subjects:
   a. Efighe (Greek)
      left-3sg
   b. È partito (Italian)
      Is-3sg left
      "He left"

B. In null-subject languages DP-subjects are free to appear in positions other than SpecAgrSP (subject to discourse conditions involving focus, topicalization, etc):
   a. I Maria (xthes) sinandise ton Yanni (Greek)
      the-nom Maria yesterday met-3s the-acc John
      "Mary met John (yesterday)"
   b. Sinandise i Maria ton Yanni
      met-3s the-nom Mary the-acc John

C. In null-subject languages, extraction of the subject of a finite clause over an overt complementizer is allowed:
   a. Chi hai detto che ha telefonato? (Italian)
      Who have-you said that has telephoned?
   b. *Who did you say that left?

Is there a way to unite these properties under a single checking-theoretic parameter?

Finally, checking theory can account for certain morphological relations among syntactic constituents, particularly relations of case and agreement. We can see this in the example of subject-raising to AgrS, illustrated in (85). Here the subject agrees with and checks for Nominative Case with AgrS. These operations – both of which can be seen as further instances of checking – correlate with the morphological form of the subject (a pronominal subject must be formally nominative in this position of a finite clause, and number is typically manifested in the form of the subject DP) and the verb (in the present tense only, where regular verbs bear an -*s* ending just where the subject is singular). In Chomsky (1995), these further instances of feature-checking are seen as "free riders" associated with the feature which gives rise to movement (the D-feature), and are checked as a kind of by-product of the fundamental D-feature-checking operation shown in (85). Furthermore, certain features are held to be interpretable, while others are not. For example, the categorial and person/number (ϕ-) features of DPs are interpretable, while those of AgrS are not. On the other hand, abstract case features are [−interpretable]. Interpretable features are not deleted by checking, but are merely "erased"; as such they remain available for interpretation at LF. The full picture of the checking relations involving the subject and AgrS in (85) is thus as in (87) (deleted features are underlined, erased ones are not):

(87) $[_{AgrSP}$ DP[<u>Nom</u>, D, $\phi]$ $[_{AgrS'}$AgrS[<u>D, Nom, ϕ</u>] $\ldots$ $[_{VP}$ t$_{DP}$ $\ldots]]]$

Thus checking theory, in part by means of the distinction between deletion and erasure, captures aspects of the morphological form of the categories involved in the checking relations. It is easy to see that in languages with richer inflectional morphology than English, checking theory would play a greater role in determining the morphological form of syntactic categories.[9]

Exercise

3.6   Give an account of the checking relations in the following Latin sentence:

Puer	bonus	puellam	pulchram	amat
boy	good	girl	beautiful	loves
masc, sg	masc, sg	fem, sg	fem, sg	present
nom	nom	acc	acc	indicative
				active, 3sg

"The good boy loves the beautiful girl"

The notion of feature-interpretability, combined with the distinction between deletion and erasure, captures the fact that the subject DP is interpreted as a DP (which may imply referentiality – Longobardi, 1994) with a given person/number specification, while AgrS has no interpretation but merely formally licenses the subject.

Although it clearly plays a central role in Chomsky's theory, the checking approach introduces a number of redundancies and conceptual problems. First, it requires the introduction into the derivation of features whose sole purpose is to be deleted: examples of this are the features of AgrS in (87).[10] Such features only exist internally to the syntactic component, C_{HL} in Chomsky's terminology. In minimalist theory, the properties of the syntax are held to be determined by the interfaces; purely syntax-internal properties, with the possible exception of economy constraints, play a minor or negligible role. In the context of such a theory the kind of proliferation of features with no syntax-external existence that checking theory leads to is undesirable, and should be avoided if possible. A theory which can achieve the same empirical results without postulating such a proliferation would, other things being equal, be preferable to checking theory. More importantly, the features which actually trigger movement, such as AgrS's D-feature in our example, are always uninterpretable features of functional heads which are consequently deleted before the interfaces. Indeed, the checking operation itself is what guarantees the deletion of these features, which are really only diacritics for movement (overt if strong, covert if weak). In effect, the notion of movement cannot be distinguished from the notion of such features (this is particularly clear in the definition of movement given in (86) above). This approach in fact leads to circularity: the idea is that noninterpretable features on the attractor are introduced so that F-checking will eliminate them, triggering Movement, but at the same time F-checking itself is introduced to eliminate these features. Thus F-checking and Movement are allowed to co-exist as primitives, while they are never seen independently: they are always seen in connection to each other. In a minimalist framework then, it would be desirable to eliminate at least one of them. Roberts and Roussou's proposal is that it is preferable to eliminate feature-checking. The question that remains open of course is how the empirical generalizations of the F-checking mechanism are captured. Roberts and Roussou (1997) suggest that this can be achieved on the basis of two primitives: Merge (of which Movement is really a subcase – see Chomsky, 1995) and interface interpretability.

Going back to feature-checking, the second problem that arises is the following: it is not clear how strong features, although they delete/erase because PF cannot tolerate them, may have a PF reflex. This can be seen with the nominative feature of the subject DP in (87). If this DP is a pronoun, the nominative feature has a reflex in PF in that the pronoun will be nominative (*I* rather than *me*, etc.). But the nominative feature is deleted prior to Spell Out and hence is not, and by Full Interpretation cannot be, visible to PF. This will be generally true of Case features, despite the fact that such features are abundantly realized in the morpho-phonology of many languages. Indeed Chomsky (1995: 385, n. 50) suggests that one possibility "would be to interpret overt erasure of F as meaning conversion of F to phonological properties, hence stripped away at Spell-Out". Thus in any case the morphophonological reflexes need to be considered, although it is not quite clear how this can be achieved in Chomsky's system with respect to strong features (but see Chomsky, 1996, for a rather different possibility).

Third, feature-checking requires the presence of the same feature twice, once on the attractor and once on the attractee. Again, this is clearly seen in (87), where D and Nom occur twice each. However, interpretable features only appear once at the LF interface. The mechanisms of deletion and erasure must be stipulated simply in order to guarantee this. An *a priori* simpler theory would contain only the interpretable occurrences of features, but such a theory would not be checking theory.

Fourth, as mentioned above, checking theory in fact imposes a ranking of principles in that a strong feature induces a tolerable violation of Procrastinate. This kind of principle-ranking is not found elsewhere in minimalist approaches (as opposed, for example, to optimality-theoretic approaches) and appears to be a conceptual anomaly induced by the use of checking theory to account for parametric variation. In effect, then, checking theory accounts for parametric variation at the price of introducing an unprecedented soft constraint: Procrastinate.

Fifth, Case features are unique in being uninterpretable for both the attractor and the attractee, a condition which casts doubt on their existence.[11] All other features are interpretable for the moved category (the attractee; cf. D and ϕ-features in (87)), but not for the attractor. At least one facet of the theory presented which should be rethought is the treatment of abstract Case. As it stands, checking theory provides no explanation of this anomaly, nor of the related point that only the features of attractees are interpretable. As such, then, the status of Case is uncertain in this theory: it is not fully unified with other types of feature-checking.

Finally, the distinction between deletion and erasure is stipulated, as is the inventory of interpretable features and the fact that such features are invariably associated with attractees. It is far from obvious that the notion of interpretability can in any natural way be reduced to semantics.

We see that checking theory accounts for movement by introducing essentially diacritic features on functional heads which trigger movement – features stipulated to be uninterpretable and hence required to delete. It accounts for parametric variation by introducing an unprecedented and undesirable (in this theory) soft constraint. And it cannot naturally account for morphophonological properties of agreement and particularly case, given other assumptions regarding interpretability and deletion. Hence it turns out that all three functions of checking theory are problematic.

Roberts and Roussou (1997) explore an alternative to checking theory in deriving the properties of Attract/Move, which avoids the above problems and has certain empirical advantages. In the present context, one major advantage of their alternative approach is that it permits the formulation of a theory of cross-linguistic variation which lends itself naturally to the diachronic domain, and which has the requisite properties for restricting the parameter space.

Roberts and Roussou's goal in reformulating checking theory is to give expression to the idea that movement, cross-linguistic variation and at least some morphophonological properties are reflexes of a single property of C_{HL}, and moreover that property of C_{HL} is driven by the interfaces. They take this property to be *interface interpretability*. Taking the standard view of the interfaces as PF and LF (i.e. the interfaces with the Articulatory–Perceptual and the Conceptual–Intentional systems respectively), they take interpretability to be the property of mapping a syntactic feature to a PF or LF expression. More precisely, they assume that all features have an LF-interpretation, i.e. there is a universal pool of substantive features, and that languages vary in which features are required to have a PF-interpretation (be overtly realized). A functional feature F which requires a PF-realization is notated F*. In a sense, then, Roberts and Roussou assume that all LF-features are interpretable in Chomsky's sense, and all PF-features are strong in his sense (in these terms, "strength" reduces to PF-realization and is cross-linguistically unpredictable because PF is cross-linguistically unpredictable).

Roberts and Roussou designate a functional feature F which requires a PF-realization as F*. The diacritic * is distributed randomly across the inventory of features in each language (here they assume that there is no selection by languages among the universal set of features; this seems to be the null hypothesis and is in principle open to falsification – Cinque's results (see previous section) suggest that the null hypothesis is correct. The overall conception of the lexicon, then, is that it contains the following elements:

(88)   a. lexical categories
        b. substantive universals encoded as features of functional heads
        c. * assigned in a language-particular fashion to (b)

F* must have a PF-realization, and this realization can be achieved in three ways: by Move, by Merge (lexical insertion) or by both together. Again, which option is taken depends on the lexicon, but the most economical is always preferred. For this reason, Merge is always preferred over Move. If the lexicon provides a phonological matrix for F*, then this matrix will be F*'s realization, and Move is unavailable.

Conversely, if the lexicon has no phonological matrix for F*, material from elsewhere must be moved to F (subject to the usual constraints on movement). Alternatively, we can view * as the phonological matrix for F; in this way, its cross-linguistic arbitrariness becomes completely natural. Categories triggering movement can be thought of as PF-parasites.

We thus see a further dimension of parametric variation along the Move vs. Merge axis. Since these are the only ways of associating lexical material with syntactic positions in minimalist theory, they represent natural options. Finally, F* may be associated with a phonological matrix which is a syntactic affix, and which hence triggers both Move and Merge, following the Stray Affix Filter (or whatever constraint this follows from). From an economy perspective, this option is equivalent to Move (on the assumption that Merge is costless – cf. Chomsky, 1995, and below).

So we have the following system of parametric variation:

(89)   a. F*? [Yes/No]
        b. If F*, is * satisfied by Move or Merge?

(89) clearly has the overall form of (83). We can also give (89) in a form comparable to (84), as follows:

(90)   89a

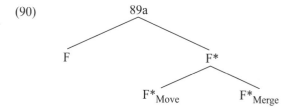

In other words, each value has just two inputs, as desired from the perspective of Kauffman's work on state spaces. Following his results, then, this format for parameters will lead to a dramatic restriction on the overall parameter space. Note that it is immediately obvious that the PF-realization of each feature of a functional head is quite independent of the PF-realization of any other functional head: that is, the connections among the variables are restricted to those illustrated in (84). In fact, the relation between F and F* and that between F*$_{Move}$ and F*$_{Merge}$ is AND-NOT. In the next section, I will discuss the markedness relations among these options.

Two points which further distinguish this approach from the "orthodox minimalism" of Chomsky (1995) should be noted. First, no feature can fail to have an interface realization. In Chomsky's system, abstract Case is uninterpretable and potentially weak; this suggests that this theoretical construct has no role to play in the approach developed here. I will not go into the consequences of abandoning abstract Case here, but this represents a natural move in the context of minimalism, and leads to an empirically useful reconsideration of grammatical-function changing operations, *for*-infinitives and other constructions.

Second, although Roberts and Roussou use the terminology of movement, and I will also do so here, nothing really depends on this. A theoretically more parsimonious and empirically equivalent position is to claim that movement dependencies are chains, or, more generally, dependencies between positions in a syntactic representation in the sense of Manzini (1995). We can define a dependency as follows:

(91)   a. (α, β) is a simple dependency iff:
           (i) (α, β) has a well-formed interpretation;
           (ii) α asymmetrically c-commands β, and there is no γ such
                that γ asymmetrically c-commands β but not α.
        b. If (α, β) and (β, γ) are dependencies, then (α, β, γ) is a
           composed dependency.

In fact, there is evidence from language change that Manzini's notion of dependency lends itself more naturally than the usual notion of chain to the computation of the simplicity of representations by the language learner.

Before returning to the diachronic discussion, let us briefly look at the implications of Roberts and Roussou's approach for synchronic cross-linguistic variation (the following analysis is developed in much more detail in Roberts and Roussou, 1997). Consider first the case of the feature which we take to be responsible for giving a clause the interpretation of a yes/no question: Q. Let us assume that, since being a yes/no question is a property of a clause, Q is associated with the head-position of the clause, namely C. We observe the following variation:

(92)   a. Did John see Mary?   (English: Q^*_{Move})
        b. A welodd John Mary?   (Welsh: Q^*_{Merge})
        c. Il a vu Marie?   (Colloquial French: Q is silent).

The PF-realization of Q varies as a function of what the lexicon makes available: English has no Q-particle and so movement (of T) is chosen. Welsh has a Q-particle, and so movement is blocked by the more economical Merge. In Colloquial French (92c), Q has no PF-realization.

In this case, interrogative force is not grammaticalized and is marked purely by intonation.

Consider next A′-dependencies. How is WH-movement to SpecCP triggered in familiar languages? WH-C is * in such languages, giving rise to T-to-C movement, but this movement alone does not suffice for a coherent interpretation where a WH-XP is present, as (93) shows:

(93)   a. Who did John see – ? (WH*$_{Move}$)
       b. *Did John see who?

In order to obtain a coherent interpretation, a WH-XP is attracted to the WH-C, creating a specifier. This takes place, Roberts and Roussou propose, owing to the following recoverability condition (a condition which connects the interpretative properties of the two interfaces):

(94)   PF-recoverability of chains: the highest F* in a chain must identify the LF-feature of that chain.

Identification is defined as follows:[12]

(95)   α identifies β for F where:
       a. α is (a projection of) F*$_{Merge}$
       b. β is not F*$_{Merge}$
       c. (α, β) is a simple dependency in the sense of (91a)

In the Spec–head configuration in CP, the WH-XP is able to identify the WH-C by forming a dependency with it. Note that identification really does mean that the two elements become a single entity, i.e. a single dependency.

Roberts and Roussou show that this approach correctly predicts that languages with dedicated WH-particles lack WH-XPs and WH-movement (Cheng, 1991: 30). This is because the WH-particles do not require, and therefore cannot have, identification of WH-C by the WH-XP. Where WH-C requires no PF realization, WH-movement takes place to license the operator, e.g. in Colloquial French.

With this admittedly sketchy overview of Roberts and Roussou's system in mind, we can return to the diachronic issues.

3.2.3   Markedness

Clark and Roberts (1993, 1997) propose that markedness (and hence the clustering of grammatical systems in parametric space that makes language acquisition and historical–comparative linguistics possible) is a consequence of the computationally conservative nature of the parameter-setting device, the learner. This device has a built-in preference for relatively simple representations. Now, if all movement operations are adjunctions (as proposed by Kayne, 1994), then movement always creates relatively complex representations, in the obvious sense that (96b) is a more complex structure than (96a):

(96)   a.   H

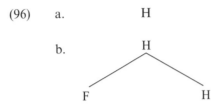

Thus movement will always be a marked option. Hence we see that F^*_{Move} is a marked option relative to F. Also, if no phonological matrix is simpler than the presence of a phonological matrix, F^*_{Merge} is relatively marked as compared to F^*_{Move}, as the following table illustrates:

(97)

F^*_{Move}	F^*_{Merge}	
1	0	Move
0	1	Merge
0	0	F is silent

In terms of the format in (90), the first three values are associated with 0 as the value for F, while the last one has 1. The total range of values for a functional feature are: 010, 001, 100.

Clark and Roberts (1993:317–18) introduce the notion of parameter expression (P-expression), which they define as follows:

(98)   Parameter expression: a sentence S expresses a parameter P if a grammar must fix P to a definite value in order to assign a well-formed representation to S.

As Clark and Roberts say (1993:317–18): "When a given datum expresses some parameter value, the learner will be under pressure to set that parameter to the value expressed by the datum …" The trigger can then be defined as in (99):

(99)   Trigger: a sentence S is a trigger for parameter P if S expresses P.

Given markedness, only marked values of parameters need to be expressed. P-expression then reduces to:

(100) a. expression of movement relations (via syntactic "displacement")[13]
       b. expression of free functional morphemes (via PF-realization)

More generally, acquirers are looking for overt realizations of functional heads. If they analyze a functional head as $[_F \; F \;]$, we have the F^*_{Merge} (001, in terms of (90)) option. If it is analyzed as $[_F \; L \; F \;]$, (where L stands for any lexical head), we have the F^*_{Move} (010) option. The crucial point, however, is that the conservative nature of the learner, since maximally simple representations are preferred, always favors the default option F (100). So, if the elements and relations which lead to one of the complex realizations of F are not robustly expressed in the trigger, the default option is chosen.

The above paragraphs describe the approach to markedness that I will assume (with one important modification to the notion of phonological markedness to be given below). However, before turning to the diachronic data, I would like to briefly compare my notion of markedness with recent proposals of Cinque's (1997). As part of his study of clause structure across languages, Cinque observes that functional heads seem to have both marked and unmarked values. A selection of these is given in (101):

(101)

	Unmarked	Marked
Mood$_{Speech \; Act}$	declarative	–declarative
Mood$_{Evaluative}$	–[–fortunate]	–fortunate
Mood$_{Evidential}$	direct evidence	–direct evidence
Mood$_{Epistemic}$	commitment	–commitment

The observations of marked and unmarked values are based on familiar criteria: marked features are "more restricted [in] application, less frequent, conceptually more complex, expressed by overt morphology" (Cinque, 1997: 214), while unmarked features are the opposite. Note in particular that marked features can thus be morphologically realized while unmarked features are not.

How does this kind of markedness (which I will refer to as "Jakobsonian") relate to the proposals I have just made? The two notions are quite distinct, in several important respects. First, Jakobsonian markedness refers to values of functional heads, while the one just sketched refers to realizations of those heads. Second, Jakobsonian markedness is not parameterized: the features are available in every language, and (presumably) stand in the same markedness relations in every language – Jakobsonian markedness is thus given by UG, while the one just sketched derives from a formal property of the learning algorithm. They are thus quite different kinds of thing. Third, Jakobsonian markedness is a substantive notion (note the reference to conceptual complexity in the above quotation from Cinque), while that just sketched is a formal notion.

So there are very good reasons to keep the two kinds of markedness distinct, as formal (the one sketched here) and substantive (Jakobsonian) notions with quite different cognitive status (the former deriving from the learning device, the latter from UG). However, two things lead us to say a little more than this. First, common to both notions is the idea that overt morphophonological realization is marked, while zero realization is unmarked. Second, there are very significant cross-linguistic generalizations in Cinque's version of substantive markedness that we would like to find an expression for, since we are trying to develop an overall system for accounting for cross-linguistic variation in functional heads (note that Cinque simply observes the correlations; he does not explain them).

Tentatively, I think that the two notions of markedness can be connected by taking a lead from Cinque (who takes it from Jakobson (see Cinque, 1997: 214)) in regarding unmarked values as, in a sense, underspecified. What is needed is a feature hierarchy. Functional heads, as features F, G, H ... , can come with various further feature specifications f, g, h ... (I will write the subfeatures with lower case and potentially autonomous functional features with upper case). We can then treat unmarked values of functional heads as simply the autonomous functional feature F, while the marked value will have a further subfeature, giving $F + f$. So $Mood_{Speech Act}$ means "declarative", while $Mood_{Speech Act}[-declarative]$ means nondeclarative. Of course, on this view, $[-declarative]$ doesn't exist (and neither does $[+declarative]$, this being the unmarked value of the category). What exist are other speech-act features: Q, Exclamative, Imperative, etc. These are all sub-features of $Mood_{Speech Act}$. In other words, instead of saying that we have $Mood_{Speech Act}$ with the two values $[\pm declarative]$, we can stipulate that $Mood_{Speech Act} = Declarative$ by default and consider $Mood_{Speech Act} = Imperative$, Interrogative, etc. as marked subfeatures. Now, if the parameterization operator of (88c) applies to all types of features, $F + f$ will have two chances of PF-realization, while F will only have one. Thus, marked feature values are more likely to be overtly realized than unmarked ones and we derive implicational statements of the form "If a language has a declarative particle, then it has an interrogative particle," etc., from the fact that where F* must be realized, so must all subfeatures of F*. Note that this idea carries over to the F^*_{Move} case, which seems right. In many languages, for example, marked illocutionary forces are associated with movement to $Mood_{Speech\ Act}$, while declaratives are not (this is approximately the situation in "residual V2" languages like Modern English). So we also derive the (correct) implicational universal "If a language has movement to $Mood_{Speech\ Act}$ in declaratives, then it has such movement in interrogatives, etc."[14]

Exercise

3.7   Construct a markedness system for agreement. The system doesn't have to be empirically adequate, but just able to illustrate the logic of markedness (see Corbett, 1983, for a typologically based account of the cross-linguistic facts).

Leaving aside these rather more speculative remarks, we can move on to the diachronic data.

3.3   Changes

Here we look first at a change involving the loss of a movement dependency and the associated loss of the phonological realization of a functional head (section 3.3.1). In section 3.3.2, we look at how new inflectional material may be created. We will see that this involves the loss of a movement dependency followed by the creation of a movement dependency as a side effect of a different parameter change. In 3.3.3, I will sketch an approach to word-order change. To the extent that the loss of movement dependencies plays a role in all the changes considered here, the assumption about the learning device which was entertained in the previous section is supported. It goes without saying that much of what is presented glosses over details both of interpretation and analysis of data. This is done in the interest of clarity of exposition.

3.3.1   The loss of verb movement in English

It is well-known that English has historically lost verb movement to Infl (cf., Pollock, 1989; Roberts, 1992; among others). More precisely, in finite clauses in Modern English only auxiliary verbs are able to appear in AgrS and C. The historical evidence from English prior to roughly 1600 shows that at this earlier period English verbs were able to move to T, AgrS and C (in this respect, earlier English patterned like Modern French – see Pollock, 1989). This can be shown by examples like the following:

(102) a. Negation:
Wepyng and teres counforteth not dissolute laghers
"Weeping and tears do not comfort dissolute laughers"
(1400–50; N. Love *The Myrour of the Blessyd Lyf of Jesu Christ*; Gray, 1985: 97)
  b. Adverbial positioning:
The Turks made anone redy a grete ordonnaunce
"The Turks soon prepared a large number of weapons"
(*c.* 1482; Kaye *The Delectable Newsse of the Glorious Victorye of the Rhodyans agaynest the Turkes*; Gray, 1985: 23)
  c. Floated Quantifiers:
In doleful wise they ended both their days
"Dolefully, they both ended their days" (1589; Marlowe *The Jew of Malta*, III, iii, 21)
  d. Inversion:
What menythe this pryste?
"What does this priest mean?" (1466–7; Anon., from J. Gairdner (ed.), 1876, *The Historical Collections of a London Citizen*; Gray, 1985: 11)

(102a–c) show that V has left VP, since material which it is assumed occupies a position left-peripheral to VP intervenes between the verb and the object. Note that these orders are ungrammatical in today's English. (102d) shows main-verb inversion over the subject. Standard assumptions imply that the verb must move first to AgrS to get to C (this is the Head Movement Constraint of Travis, 1984; Baker, 1988), the position it occupies in this example. So we conclude that AgrS attracted V at this period. In Roberts and Roussou's terms, English at this time had AgrS*$_{Move}$. According to most accounts (Kroch, 1989; Lightfoot, 1991; Roberts, 1992), verb movement of this type began to decline in the latter part of the 16th century and was lost from the colloquial language in the 17th century, although it remained in the literary language throughout the 17th century and perhaps slightly longer (see Jespersen, 1959, vol. VI, p. 502). Kroch (1989), reanalyzing the quantitative data in Ellegård (1953), shows that the crucial turning point in the change was 1575.

By eliminating a movement dependency from a large class of cases, the loss of main-verb movement in English clearly allowed a relatively more elegant grammatical system. The innovative grammar without verb movement contains simpler representations for large classes of simple examples than the older grammar which involves verb movement. This can be illustrated with a simple sentence like *John walks*. The structure of this sentence before and after the change is given in (103) (glossing over the functional structure between AgrS and VP):

(103)   a. Before

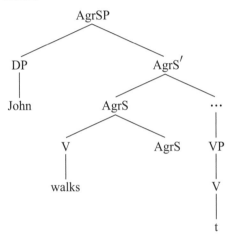

         b. After

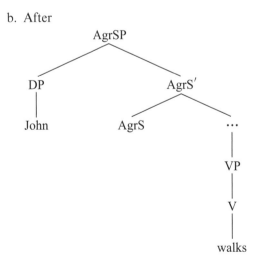

Inspection of the two structures shows the second to be simpler. In this sense, then, the change represents a reduction in complexity and therefore in markedness. This is directly captured by Roberts and Roussou's notation: $\text{AgrS*}_{\text{Move}} \succ \text{AgrS}$.[15] In order to see the role of the learning algorithm, we need to look more closely at the causes of this change.

Beginning with Roberts (1985), it has been argued that the loss of parts of the verbal conjugation in English is related to this change. There is little doubt that, as part of the general loss of inflectional morphology that took place during the Middle English period, a large number of verbal endings had disappeared by the end of the 15th century. In particular, Gray (1985: 495f.) gives the following paradigms for London-area English *c*. 1400 and *c*. 1500:

(104)   a. 1400: cast(e), cast-est, cast-eth, caste(n), caste(n), caste(n).
        b. 1500: cast, cast-est, cast-eth, cast(e), cast(e), cast(e)

Presumably these are caused by phonological erosion of final nasals and of unstressed vowels (cf. the suggestion above that the phonological realization of functional material – including therefore agreement marking – may be a marked property). In particular, in the 16th century there are only a very few attested survivals of any plural ending (Jespersen, 1909–49; Barber, 1976). It is therefore plausible to suppose that the presence of agreement morphology, particularly plural endings, was connected to the loss of AgrS's attractive property. There is good cross-linguistic evidence, recently summarized and analyzed by Vikner (1995), that the presence of an agreement paradigm distinct from tense marking correlates with the existence of a French- or ME-style verb movement operation. Vikner (1995) argues that the presence of person agreement in all simple tenses correlates with this kind of verb movement. French, Middle English and Icelandic have such agreement, while Modern English and the Mainland Scandinavian languages lack it (see Vikner, 1995, for detailed discussion and illustration). So there is a considerable amount of cross-linguistic evidence for a correlation between verbal agreement morphology and verb movement to AgrS.[16] We can formulate this as follows, adopting Vikner's generalization:

(105)   If V is marked with person agreement in all simple tenses, then AgrS is *(Move).

(105) states a natural correlation between the phonological realization of AgrS's ϕ-features, and in particular person, and the agreement marking on V. It is stated as a one-way implication in order to allow for other realizations of AgrS not involving verbal paradigms. Leaving these other realizations of AgrS aside, (105) states that V must be realized

in AgrS where it manifests sufficient ϕ-features. The sufficiency is stated in terms of person marking, one of the main categories of ϕ-features. Essentially, then, we claim that the existence of person marking across tenses will give AgrS*; in other words, the presence of person marking activates AgrS, which is spelled-out by means of verb movement.

Exercise

3.8   Consider the following paradigms:
(A) French: parle, parles, parle, parlons, parlez, parlent.
(B) Middle Scots: castis, castis, castis, castis, castis, castis.
(C) Faroese: kasti, kastar, kastar, kasta, kasta, kasta.

What predictions do the text proposals make about verb movement in these languages? Are they confirmed or not by the following data?

(a) French:
    1. Jean ne **fume** pas.
       Jean neg smokes neg
       "John doesn't smoke."
    2. *Jean ne pas **fume**.
       Jean neg neg smokes
(b) Middle Scots:
    1. Quhy **sing** ye nocht, for schame! (c. 1480s; Anon. The Unicornis Tale, 227)
    2. For then they **observit** not *Flowing* nor **eschewit** not *Ryming in termes* (1584: James VI. The Essays of a Prentice, Preface to the Reader)
(c) Faroese:
    1. Eg ikki **kendi**.
       I not know
       "I don't know"
    2. *Eg **kendi** ikki.
       "I know not."

Two ambiguous word orders, one of them extremely common in the 16th century, combined with the elegance condition in the learning algorithm and the loss of verbal agreement morphology, led to the parameter change. These were: (a) the introduction of large numbers of periphrastic constructions with auxiliaries, particularly *do*, and (b) stylistic fronting. A notable characteristic of 16th century English is the possibility of positive declarative *do*. The following quotation from a contemporary grammar illustrates the point:

(106)   *I do* is a verbe muche comenly used in our tonge to be before
other verbes, as, it is all one to say *I do speake* and such like
and *I speake* (1530; Palsgrave, *Eclaircissement de la langue
françoyse* 84, 380, 523; cited in Visser, 1960–63: 1419)

While it is unclear what caused the development of positive declarative
do-insertion and what caused the restriction in the distribution of *do* to
its modern contexts in the 17th century, there is no doubt that this construction existed in the 16th century (see Ellegård, 1953; Visser, 1960–
63; Denison, 1985; Roberts, 1992 for proposals). Another early 16th
century development was the introduction of a syntactic class of modal
auxiliaries (Lightfoot, 1979; Roberts, 1985, 1992). The importance of
the new constructions involving modals and *do* is that they were
indeterminate with respect to the parameter governing the movement
of lexical verbs. Since AgrS was filled by an auxiliary (and by this time,
modals and *do* were auxiliaries – i.e. realizations of functional heads
(probably T) – cf. Roberts, 1992), V could not, in any case, move
there. Also, AgrS's PF-realization requirement was satisfied by the
auxiliary. From early in the 16th century the number of such
constructions increased significantly, leading to a diminution of the
evidence for movement of lexical verbs.

Stylistic fronting is a process which is found in various
Scandinavian languages, notably Icelandic. It involves the fronting of
some light element, usually an adverb or participle, where there is a
subject gap:

(107)   þarna er konan *kosin* var forseti.
"There is the woman that elected was president" (Platzack,
1987: example (27), pp. 394–5)

Platzack (1994) gives evidence of the following kind, showing that
Middle English had stylistic fronting:

(108)   that ladyes … might se Who that beste were of dede
"that ladies … might see who best were of deed"

In sentences like the above, we have the order *adverb/participle–verb*.
As long as there is sufficient verbal agreement morphology, this construction must involve both verb fronting and stylistic fronting.
However, once verbal agreement marking is lost, such sentences are
compatible with the absence of verb movement and the absence of
stylistic fronting. This is a simpler structure, and so preferred by the
learner. The relevant parts of the two structures are illustrated in
(109):

(109)   a. Before:

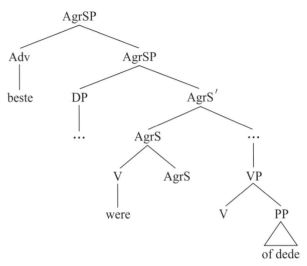

         b. After:

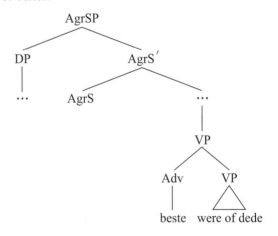

Three factors led to the parameter change. First, as we saw, was the loss of verbal agreement morphology. The second factor leading to the parametric change was that certain constructions in the input were compatible with grammars lacking verb movement. Again, this in itself does not guarantee the loss of verb movement. This kind of syntactic ambiguity is, however, a precondition for the loss of movement. Variation (in the form of ambiguity) is a precursor to selection. But, as in the case of natural selection, variation alone does not ensure selection. The crucial third factor is the sensitivity in the selection procedure to complexity.

The causal factor, then, is the sensitivity of the learning device to the complexity of representations. The older system generates representations which are systematically more complex than the competing innovative system, as illustrated above.

Of course, the drive to minimize complexity is balanced by the requirement to represent the input; thus, robust evidence for verb movement is unproblematic for learners since they will accept a slight increase in complexity in order to represent the input data. The situation for learners of English in the 16th century was one where the morphological and syntactic evidence for verb movement was no longer categorical. Hence, given the general drive to minimize complexity, the system which did not feature the option of verb movement was preferred. This meant that the parametric value of AgrS changed and verb movement to AgrS was lost.

3.3.2   *The development of the Romance future and conditional tenses*

Although functional features have an interpretation, this interpretation is special in various ways (von Fintel, 1995, observes that functional categories tend to be permutation-invariant and of high type).[17] Moreover, even when they are phonologically realized, the phonological realization is always "light," often lacking in stress, or failing to meet the criteria for minimal wordhood (see McCarthy and Prince, 1986), as is the case for monomoraic *the* and *a* in English. It may be, then, that functional elements are required to fall below certain threshold values for phonological and semantic content.[18] In general, functional categories lack θ-roles and metrical strength. In other words, members of functional categories are athematic and aprosodic.

The above observations give us a key to understanding the widespread process of grammaticalization. If a lexical item, l, of category L has the following three properties, it may be subject to reanalysis as a functional head:

(110)   a. l is in a category L which is always moved to a functional head F
         b. l is atonic
         c. l has a potentially athematic interpretation

Reanalysis of a lexical item as a functional item is caused by the elegance condition in the learning algorithm, since it will prefer a representation which lacks movement to one which contains movement.

Unlike the case discussed in the previous section, the elimination of movement in this case leaves the unmoved element in the former target position of movement.

At first sight, it might appear that this means that syntactic complexity outranks phonological complexity in terms of markedness, since the loss of movement and reanalysis of *habere* as a tense marker reduces syntactic markedness (by elimination of movement) but increases PF-markedness (by giving a realization to a feature-value of T (or some other functional head)). However, we can refine our notion of phonological markedness so that it relates to prosodic factors, so that functional elements (tend to) fall below the prosodic threshold for wordhood. This means that F^*_{Merge} is not intrinsically PF-marked, while F^*_{Move} might be, depending on the nature of the moved element. In the case at hand, then, reanalysing *habere* as a reduced particle rather than a moved full verb arguably led to a reduction of both syntactic and PF-markedness.

The case of reanalysis of a lexical item as a functional item that we will be concerned with involves the development of the future and conditional tenses of most of the modern Romance languages (not all of them, since southern Italian dialects and Sardinian don't have future tenses). Traditional manuals of Romance philology describe these forms as originating in a periphrastic construction in Latin formed by an infinitive followed by *habere* "to have." For example, the future tense of nearly all Modern French verbs quite transparently shows this development. Compare the endings attached to the infinite of *chanter* below, forming the future, with the present tense of *avoir* "to have":

(111)　　*chanter* (future tense): chanter-ai, chanter-as, chanter-a, chanter-ons, chanter-ez, chanter-ont

　　　　avoir (present tense): ai, as, a, avons, avez, ont

The full lexical Latin verb *habere* was reanalyzed as the future/conditional ending in the modern Romance languages in two stages. First, *habere* was reanalyzed as a future auxiliary comparable to *will* in Modern English. This was a change from no realization of the future/conditional by T to realization by an overt free morpheme, i.e. Move ≻ Merge. Second, the auxiliary *habere*, an autonomous word, was reanalyzed as a verbal affix associated with movement to T (i.e. *habere* "leaves behind" Fut* in T). This is a change from Merge to Move. The first change appears to have taken place once in late or post-imperial Latin and, hence, effected all the modern Romance standards. The second change arguably took place at different times in different languages.

The two changes can be schematized as follows:

(112) $[_{TP}$ $[_{VP}$ $[_{XP}$ amare] t_{habeo} $[_T$ habeo$]]]$ ≻ $[_{TP}$ $[_{XP}$ amare] $[_T$ habeo $]]$

(113) $[_{TP}$ $[_{XP}$ amare] $[_T$ habeo$]]$ ≻ $[_{TP}$ $[_{XP}$ $t_V]$ $[_T$ amar + FUT $]]$

In Classical Latin, *habere* was a full verb with the core meaning "to own" or "to possess". The following is an example of *habere* with a complement containing an infinitive where it is clear that *habere* is functioning as a verb of possession:

(114)   De re publica nihil habeo ad te scribere.
         of thing public nothing I-have to you to-write
         "I have nothing to write to you about the republic." (Cicero;
         cited in Tekavcic, 1980)

In this kind of example, there is no reason to treat *habere* any differently from a standard transitive verb: it is a V with a DP complement (in the above example, with a fairly complex internal structure) to which it assigns a θ-role.

The reanalysis of future/conditional *habere* gave rise to a lexical split, in that reflexes of *habere* in other contexts (essentially, where *habere* was not adjacent to an infinitive – see below) retain the possessive and related senses that are found in Classical Latin (this is true in Modern French and Italian, but possessive *habere* has been lost in contemporary Spanish and Portuguese). The reflexes of *habere* have also arguably been grammaticalized in other ways in other contexts: in existential constructions and in perfect tenses, although here again the Iberian languages have largely lost *habere*.

Benveniste (1968) clarifies a number of aspects of the developments in Late Latin. He points out that the periphrastic construction originates with "Christian writers and theologians starting with Tertullian", i.e. early in the 3rd century AD. The "overwhelming majority of examples", according to Benveniste, indicate that the periphrasis involved a passive infinitive, as in the following:

(115)   in nationibus a quibus magis suscipi habebat
         among nations-ABL by which-ABL most to-be-accepted had
         "Among nations by which the most was to be accepted"

The periphrasis "acts as the equivalent of the future passive participle" and "served to indicate the predestination of an object to follow a certain course of events." It seems clear that *habere* here has a modal interpretation that essentially involves the notion of futurity. The "thematic" interpretation of possession seems to be absent. In marking purely temporal content, *habere* is close to an auxiliary like Modern English *will*. In these constructions at least, then, *habere* was athematic from quite an early time.

Benveniste shows that between the third century and the sixth century the periphrasis spread to a wider range of verbs and contexts: active intransitives and deponents. By the end of the Imperial period the periphrasis clearly had a straightforward future meaning (cf. Benveniste, 1968; Bourciez, 1930; Tekavcic, 1980). The following example, from Tekavcic (1980: 237)), is a seventh-century case of clearly temporal *habere*:

(116) et quod sum, essere abetis
   and that I-am, to-be *habere*-2pl
   "and what I am, you will be"
   (seventh-century inscription)

The spelling has been Latinized in this example, and it is likely that it is somewhat distant from the contemporary pronunciation. The following is generally said to be the first example of the Romance synthetic future, and gives a clearer idea of the pronunciation:

(117) Iustinianus dicebat: "Daras."
   Iustinianus said "give + *habere* + 2sg"
   "Iustinianus said: You will give."
   (Fredegario, seventh century)

Here we see that the second singular of *habere* is reduced to -*as*. Tekavcic (1980: 236) gives the forms of *habere* in this context as:

(118) a(i)o, as, a(t), (av)emo, (av)ete(s), an(t)

These forms, particularly the elimination of the stem *av*- in the 1pl and 2pl, indicate that future *habere* was aprosodic at this time.

A third factor is relevant in the reanalysis of *habere*. In Late Latin, the system of clausal complementation underwent major changes. In Classical Latin finite indicative complements were rare; the standard forms of clausal complementation involved subjunctive complements, infinitivals or participials. After verbs of saying and believing, for example, the standard kind of complementation involved the accusative and infinitive construction. Complements which were the precursors of the standard Modern Romance finite clause involving the neuter singular relative pronoun *quod* existed but were somewhat marginal, being restricted to a fairly small class of verbs. However, in the Late Latin period this form of complementation became much more frequent; see Bourciez (1930: 122–3), Vincent (1991). I tentatively suggest on the basis of the morphological form of *quod* and the distribution of *quod* clauses in classical Latin that these were DPs containing clauses. The change in the complementation system entailed a categorial reanalysis of many complex DP complements as CPs (see also Kiparsky, 1994, for a similar proposal regarding proto-Germanic). Suppose further that infinitival complements were also categorially reanalyzed at the same time, becoming reduced IPs (possibly TPs) where previously they had had more structure. If this is correct, this created a structure where *habere*, a verb whose primary content was temporal/modal, appeared systematically in a functional head position with a TP complement (cf. (113), where XP = TP).

The three factors outlined above created sufficient ambiguity in strings containing infinitive + *habere* to make possible the reanalysis of *habere* as a functional element. The reanalysis was possible because *habere* had a nonthematic temporal/modal meaning and a prosodically reduced form and it always appeared with an adjacent bare infinitival complement. These factors in themselves did not cause the reanalysis, however. Rather, considerations of complexity led the learner to select grammars that reduced the complexity of the representations that covered infinitive + *habere*. The older representation involved a V position in which *habere* was generated and a head-movement relation between *habere* and some verbal functional projection (probably T), as shown in (112) above. The innovative representation involved direct generation of *habere* in the functional position. A structure created by adjoining one head to another is eliminated as well as an additional category.

The reanalysis of *habere* as an affix created a movement dependency. F^*_{Move} arguably only develops in "head-final" systems, where the functional head F is to the right of the lexical head L and no complement of L can intervene between L and F:

(119) $[_{FP} [_{LP} \text{ L }] \text{ F }] \succ [_{FP} [_{LP} t_L] \text{ L} + \text{F }]$

If adjunction is always to the left of the host (Kayne, 1994), the general preference for suffixal morphology in the world's languages is accounted for. In fact, in terms of the universal base hypothesis in Kayne (1994), (119) should be given as follows:

(120) $[_{FP} [_{LP} \text{ L }] \text{ F } t_{LP}] \succ [_{FP} \text{ L} + \text{F} [_{LP} t_L]]$

This change involves simplification, if we assume that pied-piping a maximal projection is more costly than simple head movement (which follows from the general elegance property if "movement" is copying).

In our case, we can see the development of the Move option for future/conditional *habere* as a side effect of a different change which was going on in Latin/Romance around the same time: the change from OV to VO word order. The OV-to-VO shift was accompanied by a shift from superficial *main verb – aux* order to *aux – main verb* order. In *main verb – aux* order, the infinitive preceded *habere*. When *main verb – aux* orders were lost as a part of the general word-order change, the sequence *infinitive + habere* was reanalyzed as a case of syntactic affixation and so the auxiliary became an affix. So the creation of movement of the infinitive to *habere* was a side effect of the word-order change (at least in Gallo- and most of Italo-Romance; in Ibero-Romance the situation is more complex, as there is evidence that the Medieval reflexes of *habere* were clitics – I will not go into this here, however).

The above sketch of how new inflectional material may be introduced can potentially handle many cases of "grammaticalization," a pervasive kind of change much discussed in the typological literature on diachronic syntax (cf. Lehmann, 1985; Heine, Claudi and Hünnemeyer, 1991; Traugott and Heine, 1991).

Exercise

3.9   Here are the facts of Old Spanish, alluded to but not discussed in the text. Old Spanish futures occur in three different forms, distinguished by the relative order of the infinitive (INFIN), the reflex of *habere* (AUX) and pronominal clitics (CL), as follows:

   a. INFIN–CL–AUX
      dezir lo hedes al rey?
      tell it you.will to.the king
      "Will you tell it to the king?" (Zif 124; Lema and Rivero, 1991)

   b. CL–INFIN–AUX
      a quien **nos dar edes** por cabdiello?
      to who us give you.will as leader
      "Who will you give us as leader?" (Zif 163; *ibid.*)

   c. INFIN–AUX–CL
      escalentar an se uno a otro
      warm will SE one to other
      "They will warm each other" (Ecl 4:11; *ibid.*)

How might these alternations be analyzed? What do they tell us about the grammaticalization of *habere* in Old Spanish?

I turn next to a brief consideration of word-order change.

3.3.3   Word-order change

Here I am mainly concerned with the loss of OV orders, as seen in the history of Romance and English. I will sketch an account which could apply to both languages. The loss of VSO (as in various dialects of Modern Arabic, and Modern Hebrew) is presumably analogous to the loss of verb movement in English, in a system where the subject is throughout in a position different from that of English (on VSO order, see McCloskey, 1996; Shlonsky, 1997, and various papers in Borsley and Roberts, 1996). The development of VSO order is an intriguing and difficult matter (see Watkins, 1963, 1964) which I leave aside. For reasons that will emerge below, I take the development of OV to be linked to the development of morphological case.

I will follow Kayne's (1994) idea that all languages are underlyingly head-initial. In a system like Kayne's, superficial OV patterns, or, more generally, head-final typologies, must be derived by leftward-movement processes. Chomsky (1995) adopts a similar position. Zwart (1994) has shown that this approach yields positive results in the analysis of Dutch. The purpose of this section is to explore the consequences of what we will call the Zwart/Kayne view for word-order changes. Given these assumptions, Clark and Roberts' assumptions about the learning device can be used to derive an explanatory account of the cause of these word-order changes.

What changes in a shift from OV to VO is leftward-movement possibilities of complements, as follows:

(121)   a. O [$_{VP}$ V t] (OV order)
         b. [$_{VP}$ V O] (VO order)

So word-order change can be seen as a type of change that is already very familiar: the loss of a movement dependency. It thus falls into the same general category of changes as those discussed above. Word-order change can thus be understood in terms of the theory of markedness sketched in 3.2.2.

At the same time as the change from OV to VO in early Middle English, two other important syntactic changes took place: the loss of complement clitics and the loss of scrambling. Van Kemenade (1987) argues at length that the cliticization of objects was dramatically reduced in the 12th century and completely extinct by 1400. On the other hand, subject cliticization was productive until $c.$ 1400, especially in southern texts. The loss of the subject clitics was connected to the loss of V2. However, our main interest here is in complement clitics. Scrambling, too, was lost at this time. This underlies the often-made observation that English word order was "rigidified" in ME, which is consistent with the typological generalization that scrambling is correlated with OV order.

Another change that takes place in early ME is the loss of the morphological case declensions. OE had a rich system of case morphology, with four cases distinguished in two numbers, and up to seven declension classes. Owing at least in part to phonological changes (the reduction of unstressed vowels to schwa and the loss of final nasals) and in part to standard processes of morphological "levelling" this system was reduced by early Middle English to one where nominative–accusative distinctions were essentially no longer made, and only the dative (-e) and genitive singular (-(e)s) survived. Of these, the former did not last long, and so we arrive at essentially the modern system.

The basic property which gives rise to OV order is complement fronting to SpecAgrO. So we have AgrO*$_{Move}$. Like AgrS (in nonnull-subject languages), AgrO* triggers DP-movement in order to "specify" its nonovert ϕ-features (see Roberts and Roussou, 1997, on AgrS and subject-movement). AgrO thus has the marked property of creating a movement dependency. This property is connected to morphological case marking on complements – this idea captures the typological generalization that morphological case marking is a property of OV languages (cf. Greenberg, 1996). As I mentioned above, OE had a rich morphological case system, which broke down in the early Middle English period. Once this happened, there was no morphological trigger for movement to SpecAgrO. However, this does not on its own change the value of the parameter. What was crucial was the existence of "extraposed" postverbal DPs, and a number of other postverbal constituents; some of these are illustrated in (122). (122a) and (122b) are instances of "Verb-Projection raising," where the complement verb and other VP-material belonging to it appear following the finite subordinate verb; (122c) is a straightforward case where a complement DP follows the finite verb:

(122)   a. hwær ænegu þeod at oþerre mehte [*frið begietan*]
where any people from other might peace obtain
"where any people might obtain peace from another"
(*Or* 31.14–15; Pintzuk, 1991: 113)

   b. ... þæt nan man ne mihte [*ða meniu geniman*]
that no man neg could the multitude count
"... that no man could count the multitude" (ÆLS 25.418;
Pintzuk, 1991: 33)

   c. ...þæt ænig mon atellan mæge [$_{DP}$ *ealne þone demm*]
that any man relate can all the misery
"... that any man can relate all the misery"
(*Or* 52.6-7; Pintzuk, 1991: 36)

Once the morphological trigger for DP-movement to SpecAgrOP was lost, VO and other verb–complement orders could be analyzed as not involving DP-movement. Nothing in UG or OE favors this kind of reanalysis, but we take a preference for maximally simple representations of the input to be a property of the learner. Hence the simplest system compatible with the input is chosen. In Early Modern English, this meant assuming that objects did not move to SpecAgrOP. Thus the AgrO parameter changed and the word order changed. In this way, the word-order change in English becomes an instance of a typical kind of change: the loss of an overt movement rule caused by the loss of the morphological trigger for a strong feature of a functional head.

It is very plausible that the same happened in the development from Latin to Romance. Latin was OV with scrambling and rich morphological case; Modern Romance languages are all VO, lack scrambling and have no morphological case (outside the pronominal system). Although essentially no records remain from the likely period of word-order change (the sixth century to the ninth century), it seems likely that an account of the sort sketched above would carry over.[19]

Exercise

3.10   Assume (i) that all languages have an underlying structure where subject and object both appear in VP, subject precedes verb and verb precedes object (i.e. [$_{VP}$ S V O]), (ii) that there are functional positions to the left of and structurally higher than VP which can license subject and object, and (iii) that all the logically possible mutations of S, V and O order exist in the world's languages (this is factually correct). Now construct derivations for each order. According to the proposals made in the text, what case and agreement properties are allowed/ required with each order?

3.4   Conclusion

In the foregoing, I have tried to argue that an understanding of the precise properties of the parameter-setting algorithm plays a central role in comparative and historical linguistics, once this discipline takes its rightful place within cognitive science. The case studies of language change (which are of necessity simplified and abbreviated to the point of sketchiness) support the existence of a conservative elegance property in the learner. From this we can derive a theory of markedness, and from the theory of markedness, accounts of language change and language typology.

The approach described here makes predictions about language acquisition. It implies that children learning a system where certain functional features have Move and/or Merge properties should go through a stage of trying to do without them. In Roberts (1998), I argued that one can understand the well-known root-infinitive phenomenon of language acquisition in these terms (see also Rizzi, 1994; Wexler, 1994).

NOTES

1 The notation has been altered for consistency.
2 The reader will note that *tutto* is not an English adverb. It is the Italian floating quantifier "all." Apparently, English has no adverb which is able to occupy this position.
3 The concept of uniformitarianism was first put forward by the 18th-century geologist James Hutton. Hutton's idea was that the features of the earth had evolved over long periods of time through processes of erosion, etc., rather than having been divinely created. The term became used thanks to Lyell (1830–33). See Ruhlen (1987: 25ff.).
4 Unfortunately, the term "attractor" will be used in a different sense in the next section, to refer to a category which triggers movement in syntax. To change either term would involve departing from standard usage, and so I hope the homonymy will not lead to confusion.
5 It may seem that we have two binary parameters here. I am assuming that there is just one because both of (83a–b) relate to a single functional feature F. If we take (83) to define two intrinsically connected binary parameters, the result is just the same.
6 This conclusion departs from what has often been claimed about parameters. See chapters 2 and 4 for further discussion of this.

7 This section is a summary of parts of Roberts and Roussou (1997). A number of theoretical points left open or glossed over here are dealt with more fully there. I am indebted to Anna Roussou's collaboration in developing these ideas. She should not be held responsible for the presentation given here, though, nor for the conclusions regarding markedness and learnability that I draw.

8 In Chomsky (1995:4.10) AgrSP is abandoned and subjects in a language like English are taken to occupy SpecTP. This does not materially affect the role of strong features in triggering subject raising out of VP, however. On why the object cannot usually raise to this position, see Chomsky (1995:182-6). On the possibility of an expletive subject in this position, see Chomsky (1995:4.9).

9 Although, of course, we don't mean to imply that checking theory determines all aspects of morphological form – see Halle and Marantz (1993, Appendix) on this.

10 Dropping Agr from the theory – as proposed in Chomsky (1995:4.10) (see note 8) – does not affect this point. In such an approach, the relevant features are syncretically encoded on other heads, e.g. T. The fact that the features enter the derivation only to be eliminated is unchanged.

11 Heloisa Salles (personal communication) points out that case morphology in languages like Latin is syncretic with interpretable ϕ-features, at least with number. The *-us* ending in a form like *dominus* ("master") encodes the following features: Singular, Masculine, Nominative, 2nd Declension. Of these, only the first is clearly interpretable, since Masculine relates to grammatical, not natural, gender. Overt case morphology may thus be associated with interpretable features, although it is by no means obvious that it always is. Abstract case in a language such as English is not associated with interpretable features, however.

12 (95b) is, strictly speaking, redundant, as it follows from the idea that movement is a last-resort operation.

13 "Displacement" refers to a perturbation of the expected order, which I take to be given by UG, along the lines of Kayne (1994).

14 One could extend this line of reasoning, following recent proposals by Giorgi and Pianesi (1998), and say that F can be entirely absent from the representation, but will be "read in" at LF by convention. On the other hand, F + f is parameterized, and so might be PF-realized. Cinque (1997:220) criticizes the Giorgi and Pianesi approach on the grounds that it leads to two ways of giving a default value for F: F is either present with the default value or absent and interpreted with a default value. In terms of the proposal being made here, though, we could think that F can only be present with a default value if PF-realized, and this is a case of formal markedness, as defined here, and so is distinct from the maximal default. The maximally unmarked case is then where F has no PF-realization and the default LF-interpretation. It is natural to think of this as the absence of F from the numeration. In fact, the assumption of computational conservativeness of the learner almost requires this: learners will not assign a structural representation to something that does not require one. What this idea does require, of course, is a theory of LF which can tell us how the defaults are filled in.

15 The subject moves to SpecAgrSP for different reasons, arguably connected to the Extended Projection Principle (whose nature I will not speculate on here).

16 Jonas (personal communication) argues that Faroese is a counterexample to Vikner's generalization. Jonas studies two dialects of Faroese, one which has V-to-AgrS movement (Faroese 1) and one which lacks it (Faroese 2). Neither dialect has person marking in all tenses. Vikner (personal communication) suggests that the survival of verb movement in Faroese 1 may be an archaism. Since we formulate the trigger for verb movement as a one-way implication (see below), we can accommodate this variety, along with those of Kronoby (a Swedish dialect spoken in Finland) and the Norwegian of Tromsø. We are, however, led to follow Vikner (1995: 20–1) in regarding the 2sg past-tense ending in early Modern English (e.g. *thou spakest*) as dying out in the 16th century in Standard English. Interestingly, the 2sg -*st* ending is sometimes written in the past tenses in Faroese, but usually not pronounced (Lockwood, 1977, cited by both Vikner and Jonas.) If we speculate that this was the case in late 16th- and early 17th-century English, then we have an exactly parallel situation in the two languages: sporadic person agreement and apparently optional verb movement. Although rather speculative, this conclusion supports Vikner's generalization and the formulation of it given below.

17 Permutation invariance refers to the fact that the meanings of functional categories do not vary under permutations of the universe of discourse. To quote von Fintel:

> The intuition is that logicality means being insensitive to specific facts about the world. For example, the quantifier *all* expresses a purely mathematical relationship between two sets of individuals (the subset relation). Its semantics would not be affected if we switched a couple of individuals while keeping the cardinality of the two sets constant. There couldn't be a logical item *all blonde* because it would be sensitive to more than numerical relations. (von Fintel, 1995: 179)

18 Note that, if this is true, the learner's task is simplified, in that the elements which are crucial for fixing parameter values are prosodically flagged. It may also contribute to an account of why grammatical systems vary and change, since the crucial PF information is presented in a "weak" form.

19 The obvious anomaly concerns clitics: why has Romance retained clitics while English has lost its clitics? I will leave this question open here, although it is worth pointing out that the Modern Romance clitic systems arguably postdate the word-order change.

4 Information theory, complexity and linguistic descriptions

Robin Clark

4.1 Introduction and motivation

What is a syntactic parameter? An initial response is that it is a unit of syntactic variation, but surely this is an unsatisfying answer. Syntactic variation is exactly what the theory of parameters seeks to explain. Furthermore, it is far from obvious that parameters are units in any primitive sense. An explanatory theory of language variation and language learnability should try to provide an account of the content of the notion of parameter. This chapter is an invitation to a branch of mathematics – information theory and, more specifically, Kolmogorov complexity – that may provide the foundations for a full-blown linguistic theory of parameters. The very nature of the topic requires that we cover a broad range of mathematics. We will start with a brief overview of probability theory and then turn to a discussion of some of the fundamental elements of information theory, along with applications to linguistics. We will then consider a computational approach to (linguistic) descriptions and introduce some computational mathematics needed for a complexity-theoretic approach to descriptions. Using some results from data compression, we will then combine probability and information theory, on the one hand, with computational mathematics on the other hand to give a theory of optimal descriptions. Finally, we will show how optimal descriptions are related to likely descriptions, a relationship of deep significance to studies of linguistic variation and typology.

Theoretical linguistics has not been much informed by developments in information theory since the early 1950s. Thus, most theoretical linguists and developmental psycholinguists will find the formal work presented in this chapter alien. Nevertheless, recent work has shown that there is much to be learned from the study of the statistical properties of natural language and I have tried to keep such work near at hand in writing this chapter. I have tried to keep the exposition as approachable as possible by including linguistic examples, exercises and simple applications of the mathematics under discussion. I have not bothered to give proofs of the main theorems, but have included citations to works where the proofs can be found. I hope that linguists will find useful and interesting material in this chapter and that they will be able to apply some of the mathematics to their own research. The recent increase in interest in statistical approaches to natural language underscores the fact that theoretical linguists must inform themselves of the theory and techniques of these approaches if they are to participate in the growing discussion on statistical learning in the cognitive science community. I particularly hope that the results reported in this chapter provide support for the view that statistical models must use linguistic theory as a guide, just as linguistic theory should inform itself from the results of the statistical models. The two approaches should be fused into a coherent theoretical world view.

A linguist trained in the generative tradition might find it strange to appeal to information theory to provide the formal foundations for linguistic variation. Information theory is grounded in the mathematics of probability and statistics while generative grammar has as its antecedents logic and the theory of formal languages and automata. Indeed, generative linguists long ago eschewed information theory and statistics as useless for the scientific study of language. It is important to recall that early approaches to the study of syntax that were grounded in information theory and statistics were woefully inadequate, as Chomsky (1956) brilliantly showed. In particular, such theories assumed that co-occurrence restrictions between words were local in the string and that these restrictions could be captured using *digrams* (transition probabilities between pairs of words in the string) or *trigrams* (word triples). If this approach were correct, then syntactic structures could be adequately captured using regular grammars (and their associated class of automata, the finite state machines). Chomsky (1956) showed that this could not be the case using the following simple construction; consider the relationship between *both* and *and* or *either* and *or*:

(123)   both S_1 and S_2
        either S_1 or S_2

If the first member of the pair appears in a sentence, then the second member *must* appear. The relationship between these pairs, however, is unbounded; in fact, the constructions are isomorphic to the language $a^n b^n$ (any number of *a*s followed by the same number of *b*s) which is known to be context free. The structure in (123) is a successful application of the pumping lemma for context-free languages.[1]

Chomsky concludes his discussion of early information-theoretic approaches to natural language syntax with a general dismissal of statistical approaches in general:

Whatever the other interest of statistical approximation in this sense may be, it is clear that it can shed no light on the problems of grammar... As *n* increases, an nth order approximation to English will exclude (as more and more improbable) an ever-increasing number of grammatical sentences while it still contains vast numbers of completely ungrammatical strings. We are forced to conclude that there is apparently no significant approach to the problems of grammar in this direction. (1956: 116)

Indeed, as his discussion makes clear, the example in (124) was intended to demonstrate that any approach based on word digrams was doomed to failure:

(124)   Colorless green ideas sleep furiously.

Each adjacent pair of words in (124) would have a vanishingly small probability of occurrence in natural texts. Nevertheless, the string in (124) is read with sentence intonation by native speakers of English and easily recognized as a "syntactical," albeit nonsensical, string of English.

This early split between the information theorists and the generative grammarians has had a profound impact on the development of the field. While much of the work done on learning over the past five decades has concerned itself with mathematical, particularly statistical, models of learning,[2] linguistically sophisticated studies of language development have tended to ignore the possible role of statistical learning in the acquisition of grammar. Language acquisition has been taken as involving a separate mental component that is completely segregated from other learning algorithms; thus, linguists interested in child language development have generally not attempted to relate their observations to general learning algorithms. The idea that language is learned by a special mental device is quite consonant with nativism, although the two are not equivalent.

Empirically, however, languages are learned in the real world and in real time. Texts, the raw material of learning, will inevitably have statistical properties. It may be that real-world learners are oblivious to these statistical properties but it would be surprising if such a learner ignores a potentially useful source of information given the demanding constraints that the natural environment places on the learning problem. Furthermore, properties like noise resistance and indirect negative evidence have a clear statistical interpretation (Kapur, 1991).

The very fact that the learner will have to face some degree of uncertainty in distinguishing different candidate hypotheses suggests that statistical methods will be of great utility to learners (Clark, 1992). Finally, recent work in developmental psycholinguistics has indicated that children are sensitive to statistical properties of the environment. The time has come for linguists and developmental psycholinguists to reconsider the relationship between statistical learning and core grammar. This chapter is intended both as an introduction to information theory and as a discussion of the potential relevance of statistics and information theory to current linguistic theory.

4.2   The simplicity of the input to the learner

In this section, we will turn to an intuitive account of the relationship between texts and parameter setting. As discussed in section 1.1.5.1 above, the notion of *text* as conceived in the paradigm of identification in the limit is both too general and too restrictive. We might, as a result, consider constraining our texts to those that satisfy some complexity metric; intuitively, we would want texts containing examples that would plausibly be addressed to real learners. In this sense the definition of text is too general since it admits too broad a class of texts.

The definition is too narrow in the sense that it excludes sentence fragments, phrases, single words, intrusions from different dialects and languages, and so on, from the set of texts. A cursory glance at transcripts of parental speech to children quickly reveals that much of it consists of phrases and sentence fragments (see (126) below). These fragments may be of some benefit to the learner to the degree that they might aid in the isolation and identification of single lexical items, as well as exemplifying well-formed phrases. It is remarkable, too, that children are able to cope successfully with language variation. Virtually all children live in an environment where they are exposed to a variety of different dialects and many, if not most, of the world's children are exposed to texts drawn from distinct languages. Children, nevertheless, are able to sort out the different grammars that underlie the text they have been exposed to and successfully learn the distinct dialects and languages they were (consistently) exposed to. Furthermore, if the grammars contain "variable rules" – that is, rules that apply probabilistically – children are quite capable of matching the probabilities. The proper treatment of such variation is problematic and will not be treated here. Nevertheless, the existence of such language variation is of tremendous significance to theories of learning and a mature theory must be able to treat such variation. A rich theory of learning should account for the following kinds of facts:

(125) a. Learners are capable of sorting through language variation to converge to the grammars that they have been consistently exposed to.

   b. Learners are capable of frequency matching variable phenomena in their linguistic environment.

Both phenomena in (125) suggest that children are capable of acquiring sophisticated linguistic knowledge in the face of real-world variation. While a full treatment of the problems raised by (125) is well beyond the scope of the present work, it behooves the linguist to consider the kinds of algorithms that can identify grammars in environments that contain variation. Certainly, algorithms that can exploit statistical regularities in the linguistic environment will be useful; the present chapter is intended as an introduction to these techniques.

Turning to actual adult input to children, an immediately striking property of such input is its simplicity. One of the most compelling arguments for nativism flows from the very simplicity of the input; in particular, the argument from the poverty of the stimulus is related to the "impoverished" nature of the adult input to children. In its simplest form, the thesis of the poverty of the stimulus simply notes that the evidence available to the learner massively underdetermines the knowledge state that the learner ultimately achieves. In general, the learner receives simple grammatical input from the environment. For example, the following utterances were addressed to Adam by various adults in his environment:[3]

(126) it's a movie camera.
   no, it takes movies, then you show them later on.
   we had a Halloween party.
   you want to put that on the floor?
   what does he have?
   fishing rod?
   would you ask Cromer if he would like some coffee?
   the man on the radio.

For the most part, these utterances to children consist of simple sentences without much embedding, although there are a few noun phrases, echo questions, repetitions and expansions. Indeed, as Gleitman and Wanner (1982) observe, speech to young learners is "propositionally simple, limited in vocabulary, slowly and carefully enunciated, repetitive, deictic, and usually referring to the here and now" (p. 15).[4]

The input to the learner is so simple that one might well ask how something so complex as an adult grammar could be accurately acquired from it. One problem is that the learner's final state is very rich, capable in principle of detecting and characterizing ambiguities, paraphrases, synonymy, antonymy and so on. If the input is so simple, how can the learner learn something so complex?[5] Supposing that, in general, speech addressed to children is simpler than speech between adults, how do children learn to speak like adults? An appropriate response to this question consists of two intimately related parts:

(127)   a. In its relevant respects, adult speech to children contains just enough information to allow them to accomplish the task of learning the adult grammar.

   b. Children are able to carry out their task on such input because they are structured to do so; they know what to look for.

Most, if not all, observable language variation must have been acquired by children. Although some variation may be the result of learning after the critical period, all of it is learnable by children. But if children are capable of learning these variable properties, then they must have learned it from a text. All that is variable in language must be such that it can be learned by children from (adult) speech to children. Thus, if anything, the relative simplicity of adult speech to children increases the need for some sort of innate learning device. In particular, those properties of the target grammar which must be learned from experience must be of sufficient simplicity to be "witnessed" in the input text. If a grammatical theory is to have the learnability property, then, it must be able to guarantee a connection between those parts of the grammar which are to be learned and the evidence available to the learner, whether the learning is done by pure induction or by some method of parameter setting. This requirement puts very strong constraints on the grammatical theory:

(128)   Any linguistic theory must be such that the properties it posits as varying cross-linguistically must have a "witness" (a structure that exemplifies it) in an appropriately simple input text.

Another way to state the problem is that all relevant linguistic variation must be "projectable" from input texts of the type normally encountered by children. However much languages may vary one from the other, it must be the case that children can learn these variant properties from texts consisting almost entirely of simple, grammatical utterances. Thus, even the most complex variant properties must have their roots in simple expressions. I will assume here a fairly standard principles and parameters (*P&P*) model.[6] According to this framework, grammars consist of a core set of principles whose behavior may be modulated by a finite set of parameters each of which may be fixed by only a finite set of (discrete) values. The learner's task is to discover the values of these parameters. The assumption that the learner discovers grammars on the basis of experience implies that, in order to fix the value of a parameter, the learner must be exposed to the effects of that particular parameter setting on the input text. In general, any theory of grammar must admit points of variation which the learner determines in the course of mastering a mother tongue. The *P&P* model conceives of these points of variation as "switches" which can be set in only a finite number of distinct ways. Other theories might conceive of them as elementary structures that must be induced from linguistic experience.[7] However we conceive of them, it must be the case that they can be acquired on the basis of the kind of linguistic experience that children generally have. Given this conception of the learning problem, grammarians should be concerned with some notion of the complexity of parameters. That is, there must be some general constraint on parameters such that the information they encode can be set on the basis of relatively simple texts. On the most general interpretation of the notion of parameter, however, the values that parameters may take on are not *informationally encapsulated*. Parameter settings would be informationally encapsulated if there were contexts where the setting did not interact with any other element of the grammar. These contexts would be "dead giveaways" in that they would tip the learner off as to the correct value for a given parameter. But this claim would be tantamount to saying that parameters are construction specific; such an approach would negate the theoretical value of adopting the *P&P* framework. Instead, parameter settings interact with grammatical principles, other parameter settings, lexical information and so on to generate a text.

Put tersely, linguistically variant properties that cannot be expressed on simple structures cannot be learned, given the computational bounds on the learner. Standard *P&P* theory, however, has had little to say about the relationship between variation and texts. We can easily imagine a parameter that could only "receive expression on" (alternatively, be witnessed by) structure of relatively great depth; for example, a structure involving multiple embeddings of a raising verb, a verb of propositional attitude, a verb of perceptual report and an indirect question might be accorded some special treatment in a grammar and, thus, count as a variant property. Presumably, this never happens since the kind of structure which witnesses this property virtually never occurs and, so, would be unlikely to influence learners. In other words, the theory of parameters must be supported by a theory that explicitly relates the complexity of structures over which a learner could detect the influence of particular parameter settings to the likelihood of such structures occurring in a real text and, thus, being detected by real learners. The remainder of this chapter will be devoted to developing this intuition and providing an explicit mathematical theory which can be used to generate testable predictions about the relationship between parameterized theories, texts and learning.

In order to firm up these intuitions, let us begin with a concrete example. Suppose that the learner has encountered a sentence which can, but need not, be analyzed as having the order SVO; the sentences in (129) show such examples drawn from two different languages, English and German:

(129)   a. John saw Bill.
         b. Peter kauft Brötchen
            "Peter buys bread"

The sentence in (129a) is drawn from a language that is genuinely SVO; the parameter settings that specify the grammar of English result in verb phrases that are genuinely head-initial. The sentence in (129b) is drawn from a language that is not SVO but is, rather, underlyingly SOV; the parameter settings that specify the grammar of German result in root V2 structures, creating the illusion, in this one example, that the language is SVO (until you know the rest of the grammar, of course). A learner encountering an apparent SVO structure for the first time has no prior information about the correct parameter settings. Thus, as far as the learner knows, (129b) might be drawn from a genuine SVO language like English and (129a) might be drawn from a language that is not underlyingly SVO, but has V2 phenomena.

Taken in isolation, the sentences in (129) are ambiguous as to the mechanisms which generated them. The problem here, of course, is that the learner must interpret the example encountered in the text relative to parameter settings; in particular, the learner must be able to assess the relative likelihood of a given parameter setting relative to a text. Thus, (129b) is *prima facie* support for VO order when taken in isolation; when it occurs in the context of the appropriate type of German text, however, it is consistent with the V2 analysis that ultimately wins out. Our first task is, then, to say what it means for an input text to be *appropriate*. In addition, the learner must be capable of weighing the evidence given its context in an input sequence; within the context of a German text, a root SVO sentence lends more support to a V2 analysis than a root SVO sentence within the context of an English text. The learner must be capable of computing these differences. We must say what it means for a particular parameter setting to be supported in a text. The following (adapted from Clark, 1994) attempts to formalize what it means for a particular parameter value to be expressed by a sentence in a text:

(130)   *Parameter Expression*
A string ω with representation τ expresses the value v_i of a parameter p in a grammar G just in case p must be set to v_i in order for G to represent ω with τ.

The definition in (130) relativizes the expression of a parameter value to a single grammar, G. We will assume that the learner comes equipped with at least one hypothesis about the target grammar.[8] When an input datum is encountered, in the form of a string, ω, the learner attempts to assign it a grammatical representation. If the learner succeeds in doing so using G, then it must be because some variable property (a parameter) in G was fixed to the correct value, v_i. In other words, had v_i been some other value, the learner's grammar would have failed to associate a well-formed representation with ω. This is what it means to express a parameter. The string ω might express several parameter values relative to G. Furthermore, ω might express different values relative to different grammars, G' and G''. This latter is the case with the examples in (129), above. The SVO strings expressed different values relative to different grammars.

In general, a set of parameter settings in a system of parameters $\mathcal{P}$ is learnable from a text just in case each setting in the system is expressed in that text; in other words:

(131)   *Parameter Expressibility*
For all parameters p_i in a system of parameters $\mathcal{P}$ and for each possible value v_j of p_i, there must exist a datum d_k in the input text such that a syntactic analysis τ of d_k express v_j.

Nothing in the definition in (130) requires parameter expression to be unambiguous relative to a single input datum. The examples in (129) are completely ambiguous as to their parameter expression. The text presented to a learner consists of a sequence of strings. Thus, each datum in the text can be ambiguous as to its parameter expression. The learner will only be able to set parameters gradually by considering a number of examples. The child exposed to German is driven to the hypothesis that the target is SOV on the basis of a number of different factors, including the presence of strings with OV order. A grammar with parameter settings that work for an underlyingly SVO word order will fail on such examples, while a grammar allowing for V2 structures with underlyingly SOV order will succeed. The learner will eventually be driven to the correct parameter settings even though any one input datum is ambiguous with respect to parameter expression.

This scenario suggests, in turn, that there is a statistical component to parameter setting. In order to specify the value of a parameter, the learner must consider classes of data which express parameter values ambiguously, preferring to set parameters to values that are expressed most frequently. On this view, the learner processes each new datum, keeping track of the (ambiguous) parameter expression it finds as a result of its processing; those values which are most often expressed are most likely to be selected by the learner.[9] Crucially, the learner cannot set a parameter on the basis of a single exposure to a datum. We can simulate this effect by setting thresholds on parameter setting as in (132). Given a particular parameter p_m which is to be set to a particular value v_n, there is some basic threshold frequency $\Phi_{(m,n)}$ that must be met in order to set p_m to v_n. Letting $f_{(m,n)}(s_i)$ be the actual frequency perceived in the input text, we can formalize this intuition as:[10]

(132)   *Frequency of Parameter Expression*
Given an input text σ_i, a target parameter sequence p_a and a learning system $\mathcal{L}$, $\lim_{T \to \infty} \bar{\mu}_0(\mathcal{L}, T) = 1$ if, for all parameter values v in positions m in the target p_a, $f_{(v,m)}(\sigma_i) \geq \Phi_{(v,m)}(p_a)$.

Here, I intend the threshold represented by $\Phi_{(v,m)}(p_a)$ to be the number of times the learner must encounter a construction which expresses the value v of parameter m in the input text in order to correctly set the parameter.

Parameters that are expressed in "simple" structures are likely to be expressed with fairly high frequency. As an empirical hypothesis we might suppose that a parameter which can be expressed on a simple structure can, likewise, be formulated relative to such a simple structure. In other words:

(133)   Complexity of linguistic expression is directly proportional to complexity of formulation.

A system of parameters will be learnable just in case each possible parameter value in the system can be expressed on a structure that is simple enough that the learner is likely to encounter that structure with a frequency that is greater than $\Phi_{(m,n)}(p_a)$, the threshold frequency for setting parameter m to value n given the target sequence p_a.

The Boundedness of Parameter Expression (Clark, 1992) captures this intuition:

(134)   *Boundedness of Parameter Expression (BPE)*
         For all parameter values v_i in a system of parameters $\mathcal{P}$, there exists a syntactic structure τ_j that express v_i where the complexity $C(\tau_j)$ is less than or equal to some constant U.

The BPE is conceptually related to the BDE of Wexler and Culicover (1980). Both the BPE and the BDE attempt to place an upper bound on the complexity of the data that the learner must see in order to converge on the target. If the constant U in (134) is sufficiently small, then each parameter value v_i in $\mathcal{P}$ is expressed on a structure that is simple enough that the learner is likely to encounter the relevant data with frequency greater than $\Phi_{(m,v_i)}(p_a)$ for the target p_a.

As we place tighter time bounds on the learner, the length of the texts on which the learner is required to converge become shorter; we would expect that the constant U in (134) would likewise decrease. This reflects the idea that the simpler a structure on which a parameter value is expressed, the likelier the learner is to encounter that structure when parsing the input sequence. This, in turn, implies that the hypothesis that the learner is computationally bounded will interact with the theory of linguistic variation and typology. If parameter values must be expressed on extremely compact structures, then the set of parameters we can incorporate in our theory of UG will be tightly constrained, thus placing a limit on the kind of linguistic variation we can observe in principle. If this is correct, then complexity limits on learning will translate to substantive constraints on linguistic theories. The bulk of this chapter is devoted to an exposition of the mathematics necessary to explore this intuition empirically.

Summarizing, a system has the learnability property just in case there is some learner that learns the languages determined by that system from any arbitrarily selected "fair" text, one where each parameter value is expressed above the learnability threshold. The complexity bound U established for the constraint in (134) should serve to limit the complexity of the input text; in particular, given U we can establish an upper bound on both the sample size and the time required by the learner. As we will show, as the complexity bound U grows, the sentences which express structures near the bound become less likely. It will take increasingly large samples to learn more complex parameter values. Assuming, as seems reasonable, that the time to converge is a function of the size of the text φ learns on, then the time-complexity of learning is also a function of U. But U is a bound on parameter expression: no parameter can contain more information than can be expressed by a phrase marker of complexity at most U. In other words, the information content of a parameter value is directly related to probabilities. Finally, since cross-linguistic variation is determined by the different parameter values, U also limits the amount of variation that is possible across languages. We turn now to the formalization of these intuitions.

4.3   Statistical and computational foundations

In this section, we will turn to a brief review of the statistical, information-theoretic and computational background required by a full-blown theory of parametric variation.

4.3.1   Probability and information theory

We will begin with the concept of a *sample space* for a random experiment. The sample space is the set of all possible outcomes for an experiment. For example, if the experiment is to select a letter of the English alphabet at random then the sample space consists of the 26 letters of the alphabet. Similarly, if the experiment is the roll of a die, then the sample space is the set of integers $\{1, 2, 3, 4, 5, 6\}$ corresponding to the number of dots of the uppermost face of the die. An event is a subset of the sample space that satisfies some predicate. For example, an event might be selecting a vowel from the sample space of the alphabet or rolling an even number from the sample space of rolling a die.

Events over a sample space can be quite complex and interesting things, although the examples in the preceding paragraph were quite trivial. A linguist might be interested in the event consisting of a pre-vocalic consonant cluster where the sample space is the set of words in a particular text. Similarly, one might be interested in the event of a noun immediately following the definite article *the* where the event space is a large sample of English texts. Notice that the role played by descriptions is crucial here. The notions of sample space and event will underlie our notion of probability which, in turn, is basic to information theory. A sample space, however, must be defined and, clearly, the events that are defined over a sample can only be individuated relative to predicates which may, themselves, be theoretical terms like *noun* or *inflection*. There is nothing ill-defined in talking about events like the occurrence of a VP in a sample space of texts, for example, so long as we have some independent means of identifying VPs.

Exercise

4.1   Reconsider Chomsky's discussion of statistical approaches to language on page 128. Are there events defined over the sample space of English texts that will undercut some of his arguments?

We turn now to the notion of the probability of an event. For present purposes, we can remain agnostic about the interpretation of *probability*; we need not commit ourselves to whether probabilities correspond to frequencies or expectations,[11] although we can always base our estimates of probabilities on empirically observed frequencies in texts. Thus, we can associate with each event A its probability $P[A]$ by calculating $\frac{n_A}{n}$ where n_A is the number of sample points that fall under event A and n is the total number of sample points. For example, consider a deck of 52 cards consisting of 4 suits of 13 cards each. The probability of drawing any one card is $\frac{1}{52}$; the probability of drawing an ace is $\frac{4}{52} = \frac{1}{13}$ since there are four aces in the deck. We must assume that a family of events $\mathcal{F}$ defined over a sample space Ω satisfy the following axioms:

(135)   **A1.** $\varnothing$ and Ω are elements of $\mathcal{F}$.
   A2. Let $\overline{A}$ denote the complement of event A. If $A \in \mathcal{F}$ then $\overline{A} \in \mathcal{F}$.
   A3. If $A_1, A_2, A_3 \ldots$ are elements of $\mathcal{F}$ then so is their union; that is $\bigcup_{n=1}^{\infty} A_n \in \mathcal{F}$.

Axiom **A1** guarantees that both $\varnothing$ (no event) and Ω (all events) are included in the family of events $\mathcal{F}$ while axiom **A2** guarantees that if an event is included in $\mathcal{F}$ then so is its complement. Finally, **A3** guarantees that $\mathcal{F}$ is closed under the operation of union. Taken together, the three axioms guarantee that $\mathcal{F}$ is closed under Boolean operations, a fact which greatly simplifies our computations over the event space.

A probability measure P is a function on $\mathcal{F}$ that satisfies the following axioms:

(136)   **P1.** $0 \leq P[A]$ for every event A.
   P2. $P[\Omega] = 1$.
   P3. $P[A \cup B] = P[A] + P[B]$ if the events A and B are mutually exclusive.

P4. If the events $A_1, A_2, A_3 \ldots$ are mutually exclusive $(A_i \cap A_j = \emptyset$ if $i \neq j)$ then:

$$P[\bigcup_{n=1}^{\infty} A_n] = \sum_{n=a}^{\infty} P[A_n]$$

Axiom *P1* guarantees that every event A has a measurable positive probability. Axiom *P2* says that some event has to happen; the probabilities in $\mathcal{F}$ sum to 1. Axioms *P3* and *P4* say that the probabilities of mutually exclusive events (for example, the event A of a single die coming up 2 after being rolled and the event B of the die coming up 5) are additive.

The axioms in (135) and (136) guarantee that the following statements hold (see Allen, 1990, for the proofs):

(137) Let P be a probability measure defined on the family $\mathcal{F}$ of events on sample space Ω. Then all of the following hold:
   a. $P[\emptyset] = 0$;
   b. $P[A] = 1 - P[\overline{A}]$ for every event A;
   c. $P[A \cup B] = (P[A] + P[B]) - P[A \cap B]$ for any events A and B;
   d. $A \subset B$ implies $P[A] \leq P[B]$ for any events A and B.

The properties in (137) provide useful computational principles for manipulating probabilities. Note that (137c) generalizes the principle that independent events are additive. The probability of either A or B is the probability of A added with the probability of B, while the probability of both A and B happening is subtracted out; since A happens and B happens if both A and B happen, we must subtract out the latter, lest we overestimate the probability of $A \cup B$.

Exercises

4.2   Consider rolling a pair of dice. Each die has six faces numbered one through six, so a pair of dice can come up as an integer from two to twelve. What are the probabilities associated with each outcome?

4.3   Use the probability measure from the preceding exercise to compute the probability that the dice come up either showing five or seven. What is the probability that the dice come up showing anything but five or seven? What is the probability that the dice come up showing a number between four and eight?

4.4   Select a page from this book and compute the probability of selecting a noun at random from that page. Likewise, compute the probability of selecting a verb and the probability of selecting a preposition. How would you compute the probability of selecting anything but a noun, verb or preposition from that page?

We now turn to one of the foundations of the theory of complexity, *entropy*, a measurement of the uncertainty in a system. Intuitively, we would like a way of measuring the average uncertainty of a system. Let us take *uncertainty* to mean, in this context, the number of yes/no questions it would take to specify the value of a random variable. In this case, *average uncertainty* would mean the average number of such questions. Clearly, the arithmetic average of the probabilities of the events associated with the random variable will not be very informative; for any given random variable, this measure will always return the same result since the probabilities will always sum to 1.

A more informative metric is given in (138). The calculation here corresponds to the geometric mean of the probabilities:

(138)   The entropy H of a random variable X is given by:

$$H(X) = -\sum_{x \in X} p(x) \log p(x)$$

As an illustration of entropy, consider a fair coin which turns up heads 50 percent of the time, tails 50 percent of the time and never lands on its edge. The random variable, in this case, is whether the coin landed heads or tails. In order to specify the outcome of an experiment, we would always need one bit of information. Notice that the entropy of this random variable is 1, corresponding to the one bit required to specify the outcome.

Compare the above example with the case of an unfair coin that lands heads 80 percent of the time and tails 20 percent of the time; thus, $P[x = H] = 0.8$ and $P[x = T] = 0.2$. The uncertainty in this case is much lower since heads turns up most of the time. The entropy of the random variable in this case is about 0.72. Finally, consider the case of a massively unfair coin that always lands heads. In this case, $P[x = H] = 1$ so that there is no uncertainty in the system and the entropy of the random variable is zero.

In itself, entropy might not appear to be of great interest to linguists. One can imagine, for example, defining a random variable to be the grammatical category of words in a text, calculating the probability that a noun or a verb would be selected at random from a text and then calculating the entropy of this random variable. It is far from evident what use the resulting number would be. Linguistics, however, is very interested in relations between linguistic elements. One can think of relations like agreement, subcategorization and case assignment as relations where one element determines properties of another element; in the current context, many linguistic relations reduce uncertainty. Thus, knowing properties of some linguistic elements can reduce uncertainty about properties of other linguistic elements. The following relation, *conditional entropy*, should be of great interest to linguists:

(139)   The conditional entropy of a random variable Y given another random variable X is defined as:

$$H(Y|X) = \sum_{x \in X} p(x) H(Y|X = x)$$

$$= -\sum_{x \in X} p(x) \sum_{y \in Y} p(y|x) \log p(y|x)$$

$$= -\sum_{x \in X} \sum_{y \in Y} p(x, y) \log p(y|x)$$

The conditional entropy of a random variable given another random variable shows how the second effects the uncertainty of the first.

Conditional entropy can have great linguistic interest. Consider, for example, how heads can influence the distribution of elements around them. In particular, knowledge of the properties of a head can yield knowledge about its environment. Consider, for example, the influence of verbal subcategorization and thematic relations as exemplified by the verb *hit*:

(140)   a. John hit the ball.
         b. John hit near the ball.
         c. #John hit the refusal.
         d. #John hit for the ball.
         e. *?John hit.

The contrast between (140a) and (140b), on the one hand, and (140e), on the other, shows that *hit* is likely to introduce an object (although the object may be a location, as shown in (140b)). Knowledge of the meaning of *hit* implies some knowledge of what can be an object of the verb. Thus, (140c) is peculiar since *the refusal* is not a concrete object and (140d) is similarly strange since *for the ball* does not denote a location. Thus, knowledge of the syntactic and semantic properties of heads can reduce the uncertainty of the kinds of items that can surround the head.

The above reasoning suggests that knowledge of heads can reduce the entropy of the area around the head. As a concrete illustration, consider the difference between clitic pronouns and free-standing pronouns. Clitic pronouns occur in very restricted syntactic environments; in French, for example, clitic pronouns can only occur in the verbal auxiliary system and are subject to a number of ordering constraints. Free-standing pronouns can occur in a wider variety of syntactic environments, including left and right dislocations. Thus, knowledge that a particular element is a clitic pronoun will reduce the entropy of positions around that pronoun while free-standing pronouns are less informative. Kapur and Clark (1996), using adult input found in the CHILDES database, report that this is indeed the case. Thus, computing the conditional entropy of pronouns should allow the learner to distinguish clitics from free-standing pronouns.

A highly suggestive result is reported in Brill and Kapur (1993). We reasoned above that heads should lower the uncertainty of their immediate environment since they select for semantic, syntactic and morphological properties of the elements that they govern. Knowledge that a particular element is a verb should, then, be highly informative, since verbs are good predictors of linguistic features of their environment. For example, if the learner knows that its language is VO and it has just seen a verb whose semantico-syntactic properties are known, then its uncertainty about what will follow should be significantly reduced. Consider, however, languages in which the verb does not occur in its base position in surface form. In this case, knowledge of the verb's properties may not be as informative a predictor since the verb may not be directly placing constraints on its immediate surface environment.

Verb-second languages like modern German are an interesting case in this respect. As mentioned above, modern German is underlyingly SOV although the root clause involves verb-second. Roughly, a constituent is moved to the initial position (presumably the Spec-CP) and the tensed verb is then attracted to the second position (presumably C^0). Some orders are given in (141):

(141)   a. Der Lehrer gibt den Kindern dieses Buch.
         the teacher (NOM) gives the children (DAT) this book (ACC)
      b. Dieses Buch gibt der Lehrer den Kindern.
         this book (ACC) gives the teacher (NOM) the children

(DAT)

"The teacher gives the children this book."

c. Gestern hat der Lehrer den Kindern dieses Buch gegeben.

yesterday has the teacher (NOM) the children (DAT) this book (ACC) given.

"Yesterday, the teacher gave the children this book."

Notice that verb need not place any direct constraint on the element immediately to its left, although the language is head-final. Thus, in root clauses, the tensed verb is not as good a predictor of the properties of its immediate environment as it is in embedded clauses.

Brill and Kapur (1993) studied the properties of adult utterances of a number of the languages in the CHILDES database in an attempt to see what kind of statistical information could be gleaned from adult speech to children. In particular, they calculated the conditional entropy of three positions preceding and three positions following the verb in adult utterances in Danish, Dutch, English, French, German, Italian, Polish, Tamil and Turkish. *Position* here refers to words and not to larger syntactic constituents. They noted that in Danish, Dutch and German – all verb-second languages – the conditional entropy of the position preceding the verb was relatively high compared to the other languages. Indeed, entropy conditioned on position near the verb could be used to accurately distinguish verb-second languages from other languages. This suggests that learners can use a straightforward calculation of entropy to detect fundamental word-order properties of the target language.

Exercise

4.5   Saffran, Aslin and Newport (1996) report on evidence that very young children track the conditional probabilities of linguistic elements. They constructed an artificial language consisting of four "words" of three syllables each. A spoken text was constructed by randomly concatenating the artificial words. The text itself did not contain breaks between words or intonational information that could be used to distinguish word breaks. Eight-month-old children were exposed to eight minutes of this text and then given a preferential listening task. In this task, children were presented with words from the artificial language and nonword sequences consisting of, for example, the last two syllables of one word and the first syllable of another word. Thus, the children were exposed to these nonword sequences during the experiment. Saffran, Aslin and Newport report that children were able to distinguish true words from the artificial language from nonword sequences. That is, if *bidaku* and *padoti* were "words" children differentiated them from nonword, but possible, sequences like *dakupa* and *dotibi*. In this exercise, we will construct an entropy-based model of this behavior.

We will use the following four "words" from their study: *tupiro*, *golabu*, *bidaku* and *padoti*. Divide the words into syllables and construct a table with each syllable labeling a row of the table and each syllable labeling a column of the table. For each entry in the table, compute the probability that the syllable labeling the row is followed by the syllable labeling the column in a text as described in the preceding paragraph.

Using the table you have constructed, compute the conditional entropy of one position preceding and one position following each syllable. How do the conditional entropy results distinguish between initial, middle and final syllables?

Do these results generalize? That is, how accurate do you think the technique would be for finding word boundaries in a large sample of English text? What would happen as the sample size (words of text) grows?

We turn now to a final information-theoretic measure, relative entropy. Relative entropy compares the difference between two probability mass functions:

(142)   The relative entropy between two probability mass functions $p(x)$ and $q(x)$ is defined as:

$$D(p\|q) = \sum_{x \in X} p(x) \log \frac{p(x)}{q(x)}$$

As always, one can take the output of relative entropy to be the number of bits needed to describe the difference between the two probability mass functions. Let us consider a linguistic application of relative entropy. As noted above, verbs tend to place a variety of morphological and semantic constraints on elements that they govern. As a result, for example, the positions around the verb tend to be associated with fairly low conditional entropy. Thus, verbs in a particular language have particular effects on the distribution of elements. Brill and Kapur (1993), again using adult utterances from the CHILDES database, created a "distributional fingerprint" for five

Language	Size (K-words)	Number Correct (20 total)
Dutch	41	19 (95%)
English	314	20 (100%)
French	46	16 (80%)
German	14	17 (85%)
Italian	24	18 (90%)

Figure 4.1 Verb Classes from Relative Entropy

representative verbs from a set of languages. The distributional fingerprint was a probability vector over words, indicating the probability of
a word w occurring before or after any of the five verbs. Having done
this, they computed the distributional fingerprints of all words in the
corpus and compared them to the five representative verbs using relative entropy. The 20 words that yielded the smallest relative entropy
were then taken to be verbs; the chart reproduced in figure 4.1 illustrates how accurate this procedure was. Thus, having discovered a
small set of verbs, new words that have a similar distributional fingerprint to the elements in this core set are also likely to be verbs. The
technique of computing distributional fingerprints is a useful heuristic
for finding possible word classes.

A further application is suggested by the work of Resnik (1993), who
uses relative entropy to distinguish word senses. For example, the word
grade has one sense that is related to words like *school* and another
that is related to words like *slope*. One sense or the other can be
primed by the local context. Let us denote one context by c_1 and the
other context by c_2. The probability that a given word sense occurs in
c_1 is denoted by $p(x|c_1)$ and the probability that it occurs in c_2 is
denoted by $p(x|c_2)$. The distance between the two senses would then be
given by:

(143)   The *distance* between probability distributions p_{c_1} and p_{c_2} is:

$$D(p_{c_1}||p_{c_2}) = \sum_x p(x|c_1) \log \frac{p(x|c_1)}{p(x|c_2)}$$

The metric in (143) is, of course, relative entropy – as comparison with
(142) immediately reveals. Thus, relative entropy can be used in
distinguishing word senses, given knowledge of the likelihood of a
word sense given a particular context.

In this section, we have reviewed some tools from probability theory
and information theory that have immediate linguistic applications.

The crucial property of all the linguistic analyses reviewed in this subsection is that they have assumed a linguistic model that underlies the generation of texts. Once these assumptions have been made, information-theoretic metrics can be used as analytic tools. Thus, information theory and statistical models are best viewed as a partner to symbolic analyses rather than as a genuine replacement. In the next section, we will turn to information-theoretic tools that will provide the theoretic basis for an explanatory theory of linguistic parameters.

4.3.2   The structure of descriptions

Our goal in this section is to formalize our intuitions about the relationship between the expression of a particular parameter value, the inherent complexity of the structures that express that particular parameter value and the likelihood of such structures actually occurring in the learner's input text. A fruitful approach has been to investigate the *inherent* descriptive complexity of an object. We will attempt to formalize this theory in the remainder of the chapter. We can begin by asking whether there is some general method for calculating the amount of information associated with an object. In general, the object can be a phrase marker, a linguistic derivation, a strand of DNA or a lump of coal. The theory we will discuss is general enough to cover such diverse cases.

Let us begin, at an informal level, by trying to develop an intuition about the relationship between probability and symbolic structure. To take a rather artificial example, let us suppose that we wish to transmit a description of an object to some receiver; the complexity of the object should correspond (roughly) to the effort we must go through in order to encode and transmit the description. The best measure of effort available is just the length of the description since it is likely to take less effort to transmit a short description than a long description. In general, we might wish to transmit some short sequence of instructions that would allow the receiver to reconstruct the description of the object. Notice that this is very similar to an axiomatic theory of the description: from some small set of axioms, we want to derive the description as a theorem after a finite number of steps. Consider, in the above light, the following three strings:

(144)   a. 0110110110110110110110110110110110110110011

b. 0110101000001001111001100110011111110011101111001100
100100001000

c. 1000001011001110111001100101111000001001010100

The string in (144a) appears to have a good deal of structure. Indeed, our description might be the program "Print the sequence *011* fifteen times," which would allow the receiver to completely reconstruct the string. Assuming that the print instruction can be encoded in two bits and the repeat instruction in two bits, the length of the description would be $2 + 2 + 4 + 3 = 11$ bits (that is, the bit length of the two instructions plus 4 for encoding 15 plus the length of "011") which is less than 45 bits (the length of the string). Thus, the program exploits the structure that we have discovered in the string to create a description that is shorter than the string itself.

Compare the string in (144a) with the one in (144b). The string in (144b) appears to have much less structure than the string in (144a); indeed, the string passes many of the tests for randomness (Cover and Thomas, 1991). In fact, the string in (144b) is the binary expansion of $\sqrt{2} - 1$. Thus, the transmitter could encode and transmit a set of instructions specifying the receiver to compute $\sqrt{2} - 1$ and again, transmit a message that is less complex than the original string. Thus, although the sequence appears complex at first glance, there is structure present that the transmitter can exploit.[12]

Consider, finally, the string in (144c). This string has little to no structure, having been generated by a series of coin tosses. There would seem to be no description of (144c) that is shorter than (144c) itself. Thus, the transmitter has little choice but to transmit all 45 bits of (144c). Notice the connection, made informally here, between the complexity of the description of an object, computation and *randomness*. This is an important intuition underlying descriptive complexity and we will rely heavily on this intuition throughout. These intuitions are summarized in (145):

(145)   a. Descriptions of objects can be shortened by using instructions to compute predictable structure.

   b. Random or unstructured objects have descriptions that cannot be shortened or compressed by computing such structure.

Objects with structure should have short descriptions because the description can rely on the structure of the object to tell the receiver how to compute the description. A random object has no discernible structure for the transmitter to exploit so the transmitter has no choice but to transmit the entire description. Thus, if an object is genuinely random, its description should be incompressible. A sequence of coin tosses or rolls of a die cannot be compressed because no element in the sequence can be predicted from the items that precede it; there is no causal relationship between the result of one coin toss and the one that follows it. The connection with information theory and statistics should now become, at least dimly, apparent. Recall that information theory is a metric of uncertainty that, intuitively, allows us to predict the average number of yes/no questions needed to encode the value of a random variable. The notion of predictability plays a role, then, in the metrics that make up information theory and the core theory of descriptive (or Kolmogorov) complexity. Languages, of course, have a great deal of structure, so we would expect them to have a relatively low descriptive complexity. Indeed, generative grammar rests on the foundation that languages can be described using axiomatic methods. These axiomatic systems can be thought of as compressed descriptions of the languages concerned.

Generally, given a description language D, the complexity of an object should correspond to the length of the shortest description of that object in D. Of course, since the descriptions can be thought of as a way of deriving a full description of the object from some set of instructions, our description language should be powerful enough to describe computations. In other words, D should be thought of as a programming language. For present purposes, we will use the Turing machine as our model of a computational framework and we will take as given a universal Turing machine U and that D is a programming language for U. We turn now to a brief discussion of Turing machines.

4.3.3   Machines, programs and descriptions

We turn, now, to some central notions of computation theory that will allow us to connect statistical properties like randomness and compressibility to symbolic descriptions. Basic to the work to be discussed below is the notion of a Turing machine. We can visualize a Turing machine as consisting of a read/write head (the *cursor*), positioned on an infinite paper tape, marked off into squares. Each square may be blank or may contain a symbol. A Turing machine has a single data structure, a string of symbols, and a very restricted set of operations. It may move a cursor left or right on the string, it can read the symbol of the string at the current cursor position and it may write a symbol at its current cursor position. The string acts both as a data structure and as a memory device for the Turing machine. Although the architecture is quite simple, Turing machines are powerful computational devices, capable of performing any algorithm and simulating any programming language; indeed, Turing machines can compute the *recursively enumerable* (r.e.) sets.[13] Since the r.e. sets properly contain both the context-sensitive and context-free languages, the computational model discussed here provides us with more than adequate power for computing linguistic structures.

Formally, a Turing machine consists of a quadruple $M = \langle K, \Sigma, \delta, s \rangle$ specified as follows:

- K is a finite set of states.
- $s \in K$ is a special state, called the *initial state*.
- Σ is a finite set of symbols, disjoint from K, called the *alphabet* of M. Σ must contain the following reserved special symbols:
  (i) $\sqcup$, corresponding to a blank on the tape.
  (ii) $\triangleright$, the *first symbol*.
- δ is a transition function that maps pairs from $K \times \Sigma$ to $(K \cup \{h, \text{"yes"}, \text{"no"}\}) \times \Sigma \times \{\leftarrow, \rightarrow, -\}$.
- h is the *halting state*.
- "yes" is the *accepting state*.
- "no" is the *rejecting state*.
- $\{\leftarrow, \rightarrow, -\} \notin K \cup \Sigma$ are cursor directions:
  (i) $\leftarrow$ for "left"
  (ii) $\rightarrow$ for "right"
  (iii) $-$ for "stay"

The function δ is the program of the Turing machine; it specifies the current state that the machine is in ($q_i \in K$), the current symbol being read by the cursor $\sigma \in \Sigma$ and a triple $\delta(q_i, \sigma) = \langle q_j, \rho, D \rangle$. The triple $\langle q_j, \rho, D \rangle$ specifies the state, q_j, that the Turing machine will enter upon reading σ, the new symbol ρ that the Turing machine will write over the old symbol σ, and D is a member of the set $\{\leftarrow, \rightarrow, -\}$ of cursor moves. For example, the following:

$$q_1, 1, \langle q_2, 0, \rightarrow \rangle$$

states that if the machine is in state q_1 and the cursor is reading 1 on the tape then the state of the machine changes to q_2, it writes a 0 over the 1 on the tape, and it moves one square to the right.

The machine starts at the symbol $\triangleright$ on the tape in the state s. From this initial configuration, the behavior of the Turing machine is fully specified by the function δ. It continues to move through its computations until one of the three halting states (h, "yes," "no") has been reached. If the machine halts in the "yes" state on string x then it accepts x, if it halts in the "no" state on x then it rejects x. Finally, if it halts in the state h leaving the string y on the tape, then we will say that y is the output of the machine on x.[14]

A final possibility is that the machine doesn't halt at all on x, but continues forever. In that case, we will write $M(x) = \nearrow$ for the Turing machine M does not halt on x. Let us note that there is no general method that will allow us to predict whether or not an arbitrary Turing machine will halt on a string. This is the famous *halting problem*. We refer the reader to Rogers (1967) for a proof and theoretical discussion. For our purposes, it is sufficient to note the existence of the halting problem. The proof, however, crucially relies on the ability of a Universal Turing machine to simulate other Turing machines. Since our discussion of complexity will rely on Universal Turing machines, let us briefly consider them. Intuitively, a Universal Turing machine may be thought of as being *programmable* in the same way that a personal computer is programmable. We can imagine that each δ function can be enumerated by an infinite list. The index of a Turing machine M will be the number associated with M's δ function on the list. A Universal Turing machine can be given a pair (i, x) where i is the index of a Turing machine and x is a string. It finds the δ function in the ith position on the list and simulates the Turing machine, M_i on the string x. We can define a Universal Turing machine, $M_{\mathcal{U}}$, as follows:

(146)   If $M_{\mathcal{U}}$ is a Universal Turing machine then:

$$M_{\mathcal{U}}(i, x) = M_i(x)$$

where M_i is the ith Turing machine in the enumeration.

Exercises

4.6   Write a Turing machine program for adding two numbers.

4.7   Write a Turing machine program which accepts any string consisting of only 1s but rejects any string containing one or more 0s.

4.8   Write a Turing machine program which accepts any string which contains an odd number of 1s and which rejects any string containing an even number of 1s.

4.9   Write a Turing machine program which accepts any string which contains more 1s than 0s.

We should note that the architecture for the Turing machine described above, with a single infinite tape and a read/write head, is not the only possible architecture for a Turing machine. Consider, for example, a k-string Turing machine, where $k \geq 1$ is an integer. As above, a k-string Turing machine $M = \langle K, \Sigma, \delta, s \rangle$ consists of a set K of states, an alphabet Σ, an initial state s and a set δ. Like the one-string machine above δ determines the next state, but unlike the one-string machine it also determines the symbol overwritten and the cursor movement by looking at the current state and symbol for each of the k strings. Thus, δ is a transition function that maps pairs from $K \times \Sigma^k$ to $(K \cup \{h, \quad \text{"yes"}, \quad \text{"no"}\}) \times (\Sigma \times \{\leftarrow, \rightarrow, -\})^k$. For example, $\delta(q_i, \sigma_1 \ldots \sigma_k) = (q_j, \rho_1, D_1 \ldots \rho_k, D_k)$ means that the machine M is in state q_i when it reads σ_1 in the first string, σ_2 in the second string and so on. It then enters state q_j, writes ρ_1 in the first string, moving the first cursor in direction D_1, writes ρ_2 in the second string, moving the second cursor in direction D_2 and so on. All the strings begin with the reserved symbol $\triangleright$. The output of the machine can be read from the kth string if the machine halts. Notice that the one-string Turing machine described above is just a special case of a k-string machine, so that this new characterization is a generalization of the old one.

As an example, consider the δ function for a two-string machine which decides palindromes. Intuitively, the machine starts by copying its input onto the second tape, positioning its first cursor at the start of the first string and its second cursor at the end of the second string. It then steps through the first string from left to right and the second string from right to left, comparing symbols as it does so. As long as the two symbols match, it continues.

(147) $\delta(s, 0, \sqcup) = (s, 0, \rightarrow, 0, \rightarrow)$
$\delta(s, 1, \sqcup) = (s, 1, \rightarrow, 1, \rightarrow)$
$\delta(s, \triangleright, \triangleright) = (s, \triangleright, \rightarrow, \triangleright, \rightarrow)$
$\delta(s, \sqcup, \sqcup) = (q, \sqcup, \leftarrow, \sqcup, -)$
$\delta(q, 0, \sqcup) = (q, 0, \leftarrow, \sqcup, -)$
$\delta(q, 1, \sqcup) = (q, 1, \leftarrow, \sqcup, -)$
$\delta(q, \triangleright, \sqcup) = (p, \triangleright, \leftarrow, \sqcup, \rightarrow)$
$\delta(p, 0, 0) = (p, 0, \leftarrow, \sqcup, \rightarrow)$
$\delta(p, 1, 1) = (p, 1, \leftarrow, \sqcup, \rightarrow)$
$\delta(p, 0, 1) = (\text{"no,"} \ 0, -, 1, -)$
$\delta(p, 1, 0) = (\text{"no,"} \ 1, -, 0, -)$
$\delta(p, \sqcup, \triangleright) = (\text{"yes,"} \ \sqcup, -, \triangleright, -)$

The structure of the program in (147) should be fairly easy to see. While the machine is in the s state, it copies the string on the first tape to the second tape. When it hits a blank on the first tape, it enters state q and repositions its first cursor to the beginning of the first string, leaving its second cursor at the end of the second string. When it reads $\triangleright$ in the first string, it has hit the beginning of that string and can now compare the two strings. It enters the p state and begins the comparison. If the two strings disagree at any point, it enters the "no" state and stops. If it reads ⊔ in the first string and ▷ in the second string, then it has gone through the entire string. It enters the "yes" state and halts. Otherwise, it simply continues the comparison.

It is interesting to note that adding strings does not change the set of functions computed by the Turing machine. A one-string machine accepts the same languages that a two-string machine accepts. Programming a two-string machine can be simpler than programming a one-string one, however. This fact will be relevant to our discussion of complexity below. In the palindrome example, a two-string machine is relatively easy to program since it can copy the input string and then compare the two strings point by point. A one-string machine is fairly laborious to program since it must move back and forth from the beginning to the end of the string, comparing symbols one by one. This requires a larger number of states as well as more instructions. It is important to note, however, that an n-string Universal Turing machine can simulate the output behavior of an m-string machine, where $m \neq n$, so that an external observer would be unable to guess whether the machine had m or n strings.

Although the structure of a Turing machine is quite simple, it is a powerful computational device. The palindrome language is context-free, for example. In fact, Turing machines can compute the r.e. sets. Although the exact character of the set of natural languages is as yet unknown, recent research indicates that it is likely to be mildly context-sensitive and the set of mildly context-sensitive languages lies well within the set of r.e. languages. Thus, a Turing machine has more than enough power to compute the representations for natural language sentences.

In this section, we have developed the notion of a "computational description" by invoking the formal architecture of a Turing machine. We will use this computational architecture to develop programs for computing linguistic descriptions. One way to think of linguistic theory is as a description of a Universal Turing machine, call it TM_{UG}, which has been optimized to compute linguistic descriptions. Particular grammars would be represented as the index of a Turing machine which would be given to TM_{UG} as a program. The learner's task is to find the index, i, such that for every sentence s in the target language $\mathcal{L}$, $TM_{UG}(i, s)$ halts in the accepting state. The learner must do so on the basis of a random sample (an input text) σ drawn from $\mathcal{L}$. Linguists should be particularly interested in compact descriptions relative to TM_{UG}. In the sections that follow, we will turn to the mathematics necessary to support this notion of compactness. In the following section, we turn to the general problem of data compression and show how it relates to entropy. This relation to entropy will allow us to formalize the notion of descriptive complexity, relate it to probability and use entropy to estimate complexity.

4.3.4 Data compression

Data compression involves assigning a short description to a source object. The description should be such that the object can be retrieved in a finite number of steps; in other words, the description cannot lose information about the object. On the other hand, the best description of an object will be one that exploits all the predictable structure available and, so, is significantly smaller than the object it is trying to describe.[15]

We can view data compression as a coding problem. That is, given that a random variable X can take its value in a set $\mathcal{X}$, we can write an encoding function C from $\mathcal{X} \rightarrow \mathcal{D}^*$, where $\mathcal{D}^*$ is the set of strings of finite length on an alphabet $\mathcal{D}$. For example, $\mathcal{X}$ could be the suits of a deck of cards, so $x \in$ {Clubs, Diamonds, Hearts, Spades}, $\mathcal{D}$ could be a binary alphabet and:

(148) $C(\text{Clubs}) = 00$ $C(\text{Hearts}) = 10$
         $C(\text{Diamonds}) = 01$ $C(\text{Spades}) = 11$

The suit of a card drawn at random could be encoded, then, as a sequence of binary numbers of length 2. Notice, however, that the chance of drawing a card of any one suit is the same as any other, one in four assuming a fair deck.

In general, code words of varying length are desirable if not all values of X are equiprobable. As a general principle of organization, we might want to reserve short code words for frequent items and allow infrequent items to be associated with longer code words. Intuitively, we would minimize our effort in coding a random variable if we reserved short code words for frequent outcomes which we would have to write down often and allowed less likely outcomes to be associated with longer code words.

In this light, the following quantity is of a good deal of interest:

(149)   The *expected length* $L(C)$ of a source code C for a random variable X and a probability distribution $p(x)$ is given by:

$$L(C) = \sum_{x \in \mathcal{X}} l(x)p(x)$$

where $l(x)$ is the length of the code word for x.

The quantity $L(C)$ defined in (149) gives the average length of a code word. Clearly, the most efficient code would be one where the expected length is lowest. Anticipating somewhat, we will be interested in taking the source code to be descriptions of the object x (a syntactic representation, for example). The best descriptions (the equivalent to codes in the above sense) will be those that have the lowest expected length.

There are a number of different types of codes. We will briefly review some of the different kinds here, as they will play a role in understanding later results. We turn first to *nonsingular* codes:

(150)   A code is *nonsingular* if every element of the range of the random variable X maps to a different string in $\mathcal{D}^*$:

$$x_i \neq x_j \Rightarrow C(x_i) \neq C(x_j).$$

The coding relation in (150) is a true function since each value that X takes on is uniquely related to a distinct code word. It seems like good common sense to have a nonsingular code since the fact that the coding relation is a function ensures decodability. Notice, however, that it might require adding punctuation between code words if we wish to concatenate code words reporting a sequence of outcomes of X, as in the case where X takes on letters of the alphabet as its value and we wish to transmit an encoded English text. If we are encoding sequences of values of X, we will need to define the *extension* of a code as follows:

(151)   An *extension*, C^*, of a code C is a mapping from finite length strings over $\mathcal{X}$ to finite length strings over $\mathcal{D}$, defined by:

$$C(x_1 x_2 \ldots x_n) = C(x_1)C(x_2) \ldots C(x_n)$$

where $C(x_1)C(x_2) \ldots C(x_n)$ is the concatenation of the code words for $x_1 x_2 \ldots x_n$.

Thus, the extension of a code is the concatenation of code words. Recall, for example, the code in (148) for encoding the suits of cards drawn randomly from a fair deck. Suppose we wish to encode the drawing of a club followed by a heart. Then $C(\text{Clubs Hearts}) = C(\text{Clubs})C(\text{Hearts}) = 0010$. We can now define a *uniquely decodable* code:

(152)   A code is *uniquely decodable* if its extension is nonsingular.

If a code is uniquely decodable, then any code string has only one possible source string associated with it; strings of code words are unambiguous.

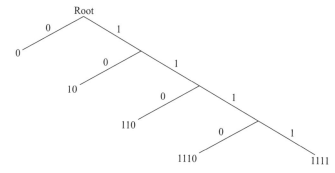

Figure 4.2 A code tree for a prefix code

Notice, however, that finding the source string associated with a code string may require looking at the entire code string. If this is so, then it may be quite slow to decode an entire encoded sequence. Consider the relationship between "pill" and "pillow" in English; the former is a prefix of the latter and, so, to distinguish them, we would require some amount of look ahead to see whether the prefix "pill" is followed by a space or an "o". A *prefix code* or *instantaneous code* allows for instant decoding without reference to future elements of the encoded string. Such a code can be defined as follows:

(153)   A code is a prefix or instantaneous code if no code word is a prefix of any other code word.

A prefix code can easily be decoded without reference to possible continuations of the code word precisely because the end of the code word can be immediately detected; it is a "self-punctuating" code.

Let us construct an example of a prefix code to illustrate the principle. To take an artificial example, suppose that we have discovered a flaw in the management of the local race-track; there is a split second between the end of the race and the close of betting, so that if we could place a bet in that brief moment of time, we could always beat the track. In this case, optimal coding is crucial since the time window within which we can place a bet is so brief that every millisecond counts. Imagine that there are five horses – Red, Orange, Black, Indigo, and Green. We can easily generate five code words to create a prefix code for the five horses, as shown in figure 4.2. Notice how the code tree is constructed. Only the leaf nodes are labeled; each leaf is labeled by a code word. Left branches are associated with a "0" while right branches are associated with a "1." Taking a left branch outputs a code word whose end is signaled by "0." Only one code word,

"1111," lacks this property. Its end is signaled by its length. Thus, the code is self-punctuating. Let us associate the horse with code words via the encoding function E : HORSES → CODE WORDS:

(154) $E(\text{Red}) = 0$
    $E(\text{Orange}) = 10$
    $E(\text{Black}) = 110$
    $E(\text{Indigo}) = 1110$
    $E(\text{Green}) = 1111$

Suppose that the sequence "11111100101110" is transmitted over the channel. This sequence can be unambiguously decomposed into the code words "1111" followed by "110" followed by "0" followed by "10" followed by "1110". Adopting the convention that order in the sequence corresponds to order across the finish line, then we can interpret the string as indicating that Green was first, followed by Black in second place, Red in third, Orange in fourth and Indigo in last place. A little experimentation should show that any sequence of the code words in (154) can be unambiguously segmented.

Notice that the code in (154) is not necessarily optimal. Recall, however, that we needed to report only the winner of the race and that we had only a very brief time to transmit the report and place the bet. In order to optimize our resources, we would want to assign the shortest code word to the most likely winner, and so on. Notice the association between shortness and probability and recall the discussion above concerning randomness and description length; the association between description length and probability apparent here. Suppose that we have the following probabilities of winning:

(155) $\Pr(X = \text{Red}) = \frac{1}{2}$
    $\Pr(X = \text{Orange}) = \frac{1}{4}$
    $\Pr(X = \text{Black}) = \frac{1}{8}$
    $\Pr(X = \text{Indigo}) = \frac{1}{16}$
    $\Pr(X = \text{Green}) = \frac{1}{16}$

Now the code given in (154) is optimal. The most likely winner, Red, is associated with the shortest code word since $E(\text{Red}) = 0$ which is of length 1. Analogously, the least likely winners, Indigo and Green, are both associated with code words of length 4. In other words, and this is the punch line, the optimality of the code is directly related to probabilities. The rest of this section will explore this point.

An optimal prefix code like the one in (154) can be constructed via an algorithm; it requires no special, transcendental computational properties to devise a prefix code for the values of a random variable. A good example of an algorithm for constructing prefix codes is the one discovered by Huffman. Here, the values of the random variable are ranked from most likely to least likely, as in (155). The two least likely values are processed and assigned a code word that differs only in the last bit. The process of combining the least likely values is repeated until values sum to 1. See Cover and Thomas (1991) for fully worked examples as well as proofs that the algorithm is optimal.

Before continuing, let us pause, try to collect our thoughts and consider why we are taking this detour into coding theory. We initially wanted a theory of the complexity of linguistic descriptions that we could relate to a formal theory of linguistic variation. Intuitively, the more complex a variant linguistic structure, the less likely it would be to occur in a text and the longer it would take a learner to master.[16] In order to develop this theory, we needed some computational architecture within which to compute linguistic representations. We have chosen the Turing machine architecture since it has ample computational power and a well-defined structure. We saw, in the preceding section, that Turing machines could be described using a restricted code. Thus, we can imagine a Turing machine designed to compute the representations of English sentences, for example. Intuitively, we would like a code that represented the minimum amount of information necessary; a Universal Turing machine could "unpack" this information and simulate the particular machine we are interested in. Universal Grammar could be treated as a special Turing machine which takes a specification of the contingent properties of an individual grammar, G, and constructs a language-particular machine that computes the representations of sentences in $L(G)$.

In this section, we started to consider the question of optimum codes. Clearly, we want our theory of grammar to be as succinct as possible in its specification of linguistically variable properties. What we have discovered is that optimum codes are related to probabilities in a nontrivial way: the shortest code words should be reserved for the likeliest outcomes. Since code words are related to descriptions, we would expect that the likeliest things should have the shortest descriptions. We are now in a position to consider the mathematics that backs up this claim. Let us first note the existence of the so-called *Kraft inequality* (see Cover and Thomas, 1991, for proof):

(156)   *Kraft Inequality*
For any prefix code over an alphabet of size D, the code word lengths $l_1, l_2 \ldots l_m$ must satisfy the inequality:

$$\sum_i D^{-l_i} \leq 1$$

Conversely, given a set of code word lengths that satisfy this inequality, there exists an instantaneous code with these word lengths.

Applying the Kraft inequality to our toy code in (154) we see that each code word length associated with a horse is crucially related to the probability that the horse will win according to the distribution in (155). Notice that D, the size of our code alphabet in (154), has two elements. Thus, we want to consider the sum of 2 raised to $-l_i$, the length of each code word in our code. In this case, we are interested in the following sum:

$$2^1 + 2^{-2} + 2^{-3} + 2^{-4} + 2^{-4}$$

since our code has one word of length 1, one word of length 2, one word of length 3 and two words of length 4. That is:

$$\frac{1}{2} + \frac{1}{4} + \frac{1}{8} + \frac{1}{16} + \frac{1}{16}$$

which sums to 1, exactly as one would expect of a probability measure as defined in (136) in section 4.3.1. Notice that these correspond exactly to the probability mass function given in (155). Thus, there is an interesting relationship between probabilities and code word lengths in an optimal prefix code. This relationship can be best understood by considering the *entropy* of the random variable ranging over the things we wish to encode; and this brings us back to entropy as we defined it in (138) above. Note that in our horse-race example in (155), the entropy is: $-(\frac{1}{2}\log\frac{1}{2} + \frac{1}{4}\log\frac{1}{4} + \frac{1}{8}\log\frac{1}{8} + \frac{1}{16}\log\frac{1}{16} + \frac{1}{16}\log\frac{1}{16}) = 1.875$ bits.

Naturally, there is a tight relationship between entropy and optimum codes. Intuitively, the best code is one which is just long enough to transmit a message and no longer. If a code is too short (below the number of bits required by entropy), then information is lost. If it is too long, then there are redundancies (and, hence, wasted effort) in the system. In fact, the following is a theorem (see Cover and Thomas, 1991, chapter 5, for a proof and discussion):[17]

(157) Let $l_1, l_2 \ldots l_m$ be the optimal code word lengths for a source distribution $\mathbf{p}$ and a D-ary alphabet and let L be the associated expected length of the optimal code ($L = \sum p_i l_i$). Then:

$$H_D(X) \leq L < H_D(X) + 1.$$

The theorem in (157) just says that entropy of the source provides a bound on the length of the optimum code words for encoding that source. Indeed, many data compression schemes rely on the relationship between entropy, probability and prefix codes to approach optimum compression. Returning to the code in (154) and the probability distribution in (155) we see that $L = \sum p_i l_i = ((\frac{1}{2} \times 1) + (\frac{1}{4} \times 2) + (\frac{1}{8} \times 3) + (\frac{1}{16} \times 4) + (\frac{1}{16} \times 4)) = 1.875$, which is the same as the entropy of the distribution; thus, the code given in (154) is optimal relative to the probability distribution in (155). The theorem in (157) implies that we can use empirical estimates of entropy of a random variable X to bound the length of optimum code to encode the values X takes. Since codes are related to our computational notion of description, this implies that we can use entropy to compute bounds on the length of optimal descriptions, as we shall see.

4.3.5   Putting it together

We have seen, so far, that there is an interesting mathematical relationship between probability mass functions and optimal schemes for encoding the possible values of a random variable. In fact, this relationship is exploited in compression algorithms, like Lempel-Ziv coding, familiar to dedicated computer users. Let us now reconsider the Turing machine. Despite the computational power of Turing machines, the vocabulary for building ("programming") them is quite restricted. It consists of a finite set of states, a finite vocabulary and a finite set of cursor moves. If we so choose, we can apply the methods discussed in section 4.3.4 to the symbols in $K \cup \Sigma \cup \{h, \text{``yes,''} \text{``no,''} \leftarrow, \rightarrow, -\}$ to encode Turing machines.

More specifically, we can create a code, $C : \mathcal{X} \rightarrow \mathcal{D}^*$ where the random variable $\mathcal{X}$ ranges over the symbols used in the δ (transition) function for Turing machines and $\mathcal{D}^*$ is the set of strings of finite length on a vocabulary $\mathcal{D}$. Indeed, let us assume that $\mathcal{D}$ is the set $\{0, 1\}$. The function C would take δ functions into strings of binary digits. In (158) I've given a prefix code for specifying δ functions over the vocabulary $\{0, 1\}$; note that q_i refers to states in K:

(158) $E(\sqcup) = 0$
$E(0) = 10$
$E(1) = 110$
$E(\triangleright) = 1110$
$E(\text{"yes"}) = 11110$
$E(\text{"no"}) = 111110$
$E(h) = 1111110$
$E(\rightarrow) = 11111110$
$E(\leftarrow) = 111111110$
$E(-) = 1111111110$
$E(s) = 11111111110$
$E(q_0) = 111111111110$
$E(q_1) = 1111111111110$
$E(q_n) = 1^n 111111111110$

Like the code in (154), the code in (158) is self-punctuating; thus, we can concatenate code words into longer strings without introducing ambiguity into the string. In fact, "0" acts as a form of punctuation, much like the space in plain English text. A receiver could easily translate a long bit string encoded according to (158) back into a program for a Universal Turing machine. Notice, however, that the code in (158) makes no reference to the relative likelihood of a symbol's occurrence in the space of Turing machine programs. Thus, it is unlikely that the code in (158) is optimal, but it will do in the absence of a precise distribution of symbols.

Let us return to the program for recognizing the palindrome language defined in (147). Recall that the program is for a two-string Turing machine. This means that all of the rules are of constant length, since each rule maps a triple (the state of the machine and the current symbols in each string) to a quintuple (the new state, the symbols written in each string and the cursor direction for each cursor). The receiver can exploit this fact and the fact that each symbol in the program is encoded unambiguously by the prefix code. Consider the first rule:

(159) $\delta(s, 0, \sqcup) = (s, 0, \rightarrow, 0, \rightarrow)$

Stripping away the δ, the parentheses, the commas and so forth, we need only encode the following sequence of symbols:

(160) $s0 \sqcup s0 \rightarrow 0 \rightarrow$

We can now step through the sequence in (160) and associate each symbol with its code word. This results in the sequence:

(161)   11111111110 10 0 11111111110 10 11111110 10 11111110

The sequence in (161) can be concatenated to yield a single binary number:

11111111110100111111111110101111110101011111110

This process can be repeated for each rule in (147) to encode it. Finally, all of the binary numbers in the program can be concatenated to yield a single binary number. Notice that this number could be taken as the index in the enumeration of Turing machines used by a Universal Turing machine.

The encoding procedures defined above dovetail nicely with the theory of computation described above. As we noted above, however, nothing guarantees that the code given in (158) is optimal. This property would hinge on the actual statistical distribution of the symbols in Turing machine programs. We could imagine that a random variable, X, was ranging over the symbols for encoding programs for a particular Universal Turing machine. We could then investigate the statistical distribution of these symbols in the programs and develop an optimal prefix code. The result could be used to transmit compressed versions of these programs or, indeed, act as the index for each encoded program.

We could imagine, for example, generating potential Turing machine programs by flipping a coin. One could theorize about the likelihood that a sequence of coin tosses results in a well-formed program. Notice, significantly, that the longer the sequence is, the less likely it is to result in a well-formed program; complex objects become increasingly unlikely. This fact has significance for issues of language learnability; the more complex a linguistic structure is, the harder it should be to learn, the less often the learner should encounter it and, thus, the longer it should take the learner to master it. The view we have been developing in this section combines the symbolic aspects of computation theory (Turing machines) with statistical properties (optimal prefix codes).

4.3.6   The complexity of descriptions

Suppose that x is a program written in the language D. We will let $U(x)$ stand for the process of running the Universal Turing machine U on x. For present purposes, we will conflate the description of an object with the object itself; thus, if x is a description of the object y in D then we will write $y = U(x)$, even though the output of $U(x)$ is a description of y and not necessarily y itself. Given this formalism, we give the following definition for *Kolmogorov complexity*:

(162)   The *Kolmogorov complexity* $K_\mathcal{U}(x)$ of a string x with respect to a universal computer $\mathcal{U}$ is defined as:

$$K_\mathcal{U}(x) = \min_{p\,:\,\mathcal{U}(p)\,=\,x} l(p)$$

where $l(p)$ denotes the length of the program p.

In other words, the Kolmogorov complexity of an object x is the length of the shortest program, p, for $\mathcal{U}$ that allows $\mathcal{U}$ to compute a description of x. It should be emphasized that x itself can be anything we can describe. For example, we might estimate the complexity of Marcel Duchamp's "Nude Descending a Staircase" by scanning the picture and performing our calculations on the resulting binary file. Similarly, we might say that the complexity of a linguistic representation is the length of the shortest program which outputs an acceptable encoding of that representation.

Let us pause for a moment to consider what the definition in (162) means for us. It says that the complexity of an object is the length of the shortest program for computing (a description of) that object. Thanks to our work in section 4.3.3 on the computational properties of Turing machines and section 4.3.4 on data compression, we have some idea of what this entails. In particular, we know from our discussion of data compression that we can optimize our computational description of an object by exploiting statistical regularities in its structure. In other words:

(163)   An object is random if its description cannot be compressed.

That is, there are no predictable regularities in the object's description. Thus, we have now formalized the intuitions discussed in section 4.3.2.

Exercise

4.10   Consider, once again, the description of a sequence of coin tosses discussed in section 4.3.2. Explain why such a description is random in terms of optimal codes and the definition in (162).

More generally, return to the ideas listed in (145) and explain how each one is accounted for in terms of optimal codes and Kolmogorov complexity.

Natural language structures will not, of course, be random. Given any particular sentence, much of its structure will be predictable from properties of Universal Grammar plus language-particular information. Thus, not only can we coherently talk about the Kolmogorov complexity of a linguistic structure x, but we can in general assume that its complexity $K(x)$ is lower than $l(x)$. In other words, suppose we take $l(x)$ to be the size of a conventional structural description of a sentence, a phrase marker for example. Since many aspects of the structural description are predictable, we can assume that $l(x)$ is an over-estimate of its true complexity so that $K(x) \leq l(x)$. Furthermore, we have argued that language-particular settings of parameters must be expressed (i.e., have an influence) on structural descriptions for particular sentences. We can now associate the complexity of a particular parameter value with the Kolmogorov complexity of the simplest structures that express that parameter value:

(164)   For all parameter values v_i in a system of parameters $\mathcal{P}$, there exists a syntactic structure τ_j that express v_i where the Kolmogorov complexity $K(\tau_j)$. Furthermore, for all τ_k that express v_i if $K(\tau_k)$ is greater than or equal to $K(\tau_j)$ then $K(\tau_j)$ is the complexity of v_i. We will denote this quantity as $K(v_i)$.

The Boundedness of Parameter Expression discussed in (134) can be restated as follows:

(165)   *Boundedness of Parameter Expression II*
For all parameter values v_i in a system of parameters $\mathcal{P}$, $K(v_i)$ is bounded from above by a fixed constant c.

It might seem as though the above definition of complexity is of only limited interest, since it is defined relative to a particular Universal Turing machine, $\mathcal{U}$. In fact, Kolmogorov complexity is machine-independent as shown by the following theorem (see Cover and Thomas, 1991, for a complete proof) which says that the complexity of an object x given two different Universal Turing machines $\mathcal{U}$ and $\mathcal{A}$ is bounded by a constant that depends only on the machine $\mathcal{A}$:

(166)   *Universality of Kolmogorov complexity*
If $\mathcal{U}$ is a universal computer, then for any other computer $\mathcal{A}$,

$$K_{\mathcal{U}}(x) \leq K_{\mathcal{A}}(x) + c_{\mathcal{A}}$$

for all strings $x \in \{0,1\}^*$, where the constant $c_{\mathcal{A}}$ does not depend on x.

It is surprisingly easy (and pleasing) to see why this is so. Briefly, suppose that $\mathcal{A}$ is a Turing machine and that $K_A(x)$ is the complexity of x relative to $\mathcal{A}$. Since $\mathcal{U}$ is a Universal Turing machine, it can simulate any other Turing machine. In particular, it can simulate $\mathcal{A}$. Let c_A be the Kolmogorov complexity of the program, y, that $\mathcal{U}$ uses to simulate $\mathcal{A}$. We can compute a description of x on machine $\mathcal{U}$ using the program we used to compute x on machine $\mathcal{A}$ plus y, the simulation program. Thus, the Kolmogorov complexity of x relative to $\mathcal{U}$ is bounded from above by the Kolmogorov complexity of x relative to machine $\mathcal{A}$ plus the Kolmogorov complexity of y. The absolute Kolmogorov complexity of x relative to $\mathcal{U}$ may well be less than this amount, but it can never exceed $K_A(x) + c_A$.

The theorem in (166) implies that our complexity calculations are independent of the architecture of the universal computer $\mathcal{U}$ we have chosen; any other choice would lead to a variation in the complexity bounded by a constant term and, thus, be well within the same order of magnitude as our estimate of complexity. Of course, the size of the constant might be quite large, particularly if we are bad programmers. Nevertheless, it is a fixed constant and we can always hire a better programmer to optimize our machine. Thus, given the result in (166), we can drop reference to the particular machine we use to run the programs on.

The Kolmogorov complexity of a particular linguistic structure is a quantity of some interest to linguists. If we could discover the Kolmogorov complexity of a structure, we would have some handle on its inherent complexity, since the Kolmogorov complexity of a structure is a provable invariant up to a constant across computing machines, as stated in (166). But how easy is it to discover this quantity? It might be that we could never make any useful estimates of this quantity. In the remainder of this section we will consider some general results that bound the complexity of descriptions. Let us first define *conditional Kolmogorov complexity* as in (167):

(167)   *Conditional Kolmogorov complexity*
         If $\mathcal{U}$ is a universal computer then the conditional Kolmogorov complexity of a string of known length x is:

$$K_{\mathcal{U}}(x|l(x)) = \min_{p\,:\,\mathcal{U}(p,l(x))\,=\,x} l(p)$$

The definition in (167) is the shortest description length if $\mathcal{U}$ has the length of x made available to it. For example, suppose we are interested in the complexity of a labeled bracketing for a particular sentence. We could encode the labeled bracketing, x, as a string with length $l(x)$. Given that we know the quantity $l(x)$, the conditional Kolmogorov complexity of x is the length of the shortest program out putting that structure.

From the definition in (167), it is a fairly routine matter to prove the following:

(168)   *Bound on conditional Kolmogorov complexity*

$$K(x|l(x)) \leq l(x) + c$$

In this case, the length of the string x is known beforehand. A trivial program for describing x would, therefore, be merely "Print the following $l(x)$ bits: $x_1 x_2 \ldots x_{l(x)}$." That is, we simply transmit the description along with a print instruction. The length of the above program is therefore $l(x)$ plus the print instruction, c. Hence, $K(x|l(x))$ is bounded from above by $l(x) + c$. This means that the conditional complexity of x is less than the length of the sequence x. Notice that the conditional complexity of x could be far less than $l(x)$; we have guaranteed that the complexity of an object will never exceed its own length.

The result in (168) may seem fairly useless. What happens if we don't know the length of x? In this case, the end of the description of x will have to be signaled or computed somehow. This will add to the complexity of the description, but by a bounded amount. Thus, the following is a theorem (see Cover and Thomas, 1991, for a formal proof):

(169)   *Upper bound on Kolmogorov complexity*

$$K(x) \leq K(x|l(x)) + 2\log l(x) + c$$

The addition term, $2\log l(x)$, comes from the punctuation scheme that signals the end of x.

We have seen so far that we can estimate the inherent descriptional complexity of an object by the expedient of using programs which compute a description of the object and, furthermore, that this metric is universal. Once a program that computes a description of the object has been discovered, we can use it as an upper bound on the actual Kolmogorov complexity of that object. Can we ever discover the actual Kolmogorov complexity of the object? It is perhaps surprising to realize that in general we cannot do so. Recall that we are measuring complexity relative to programs for a Universal Turing machine, $\mathcal{U}$. Suppose that we were to enumerate the possible programs in lexicographic order (starting from the shortest program and proceeding in alphabetical order). We could then run each program on $\mathcal{U}$. Suppose that:

$$\mathcal{U}(p_i) = y$$

That is, $\mathcal{U}$ halts on p_i, yielding a description of y; we can enter $l(p_i)$, the length of program p_i as an estimate of $K(y)$. But there may be programs shorter than p_i such that $\mathcal{U}$ has yet to halt on these programs. In particular, suppose that there is a program p_j such that $l(p_j) < l(p_i)$ and $\mathcal{U}(p_j)$ has not yet halted. It could be that $\mathcal{U}(p_j)$ will eventually halt with $\mathcal{U}(p_j) = y$. If so, then $l(p_j)$ is a better estimate of $K(y)$ than $l(p_i)$. If we could know that $\mathcal{U}(p_j) = y$ then we could find the actual Kolmogorov complexity of y. But this entails that we know that $\mathcal{U}(p_j)$ halts, which entails in turn that we have a solution to the halting problem. Since the halting problem is unsolvable, we cannot guarantee that we have arrived at the true Kolmogorov complexity of an object once we have a program which computes its description.[18] In other words:

(170)   An upper bound on the Kolmogorov complexity of an object can be found, but a lower bound cannot.

The result in (170) is not as bleak as it first may appear. We can still arrive at useful approximations of the descriptive complexity of an object, just as we can arrive at near optimal codes for compressing information. In fact, given that Kolmogorov complexity is concerned with optimum description length, it should come as no surprise that there is an intimate relationship between the theory of optimum codes (that is, data compression) and Kolmogorov complexity. Presumably, the shortest description of an object is already in its most compressed form. Otherwise, it wouldn't be the shortest description since there would have to be a better compression algorithm that we could use to shorten the description further. Let us assume that we encoded the programs for our Universal Turing machine, $\mathcal{U}$, using a prefix code. The following theorem can be seen as the complexity analog of the Kraft inequality in (156), which, it will be recalled, related encoding to probability measures:

(171)   For any computer $\mathcal{U}$:

$$\sum_{p\,:\,\mathcal{U}(p)\text{ halts}} 2^{-l(p)} \leq 1.$$

In fact, from (171) we see that the halting programs for our machine $\mathcal{U}$ must form a prefix code. In the theorem in (171) the halting programs for $\mathcal{U}$ have the same numeric property that words in a prefix code have. Indeed, if we recall that the likeliest outcomes of a random variable are encoded with the shortest code words in an optimal code, then we would expect that the shortest programs are the likeliest to halt on $\mathcal{U}$; as the programs lengthen, it becomes increasingly likely that the machine will not halt. If we take a sample of randomly generated programs of great length, for example, the overwhelming majority of them will fail to halt while only a few will correspond to intelligible programs. One might think of it as follows: the things that work well (halt) tend to be simple (short).[19]

Exercises

4.11   Relatively simple organisms, microbes, far outnumber more complex insects which vastly outnumber humans. Once again, simplicity seems correlated with probability. Give a Kolmogorov complexity account of why we should expect this.

4.12   Let us apply the above reasoning to linguistic constructions. We would expect constructions with more complex representations to be less frequent. Make a guess about the relative frequency of simple transitives, pronouns and nonpronominal NPs with and without relative clauses, yes/no questions, WH-questions, raising constructions and *tough* movement constructions based on your (informal) estimate of the relative complexity of their descriptions. Check your guess by calculating their frequencies in some real text.

4.13   Is syntactic complexity sufficient to estimate the relative frequencies of constructions? Will we, rather, have to include semantic and pragmatic information in our descriptions? Ponder and discuss.

Recall that we have established that there is a nonarbitrary relationship between optimal code word lengths and entropy in (157). From (171), the fact that the halting programs form a prefix code, we know that the halting programs are related in an interesting way to entropy. We would therefore expect that entropy of a random variable X ranging over an alphabet $\mathcal{X}$ should provide a useful bound on the Kolmogorov complexity of objects described by $\mathcal{X}$. This is indeed the case, as the following rather imposing-looking theorem states:

(172)   *The relationship between Kolmogorov complexity and entropy*
         Let the stochastic process $\{X_i\}$ be drawn in an independent identically distributed fashion according to the probability

mass function $f(x)$, $x \in \mathcal{X}$, where $\mathcal{X}$ is a finite alphabet. Let $f(x^n) = \prod_{i=1}^{n} f(x_i)$. Then there exists a constant c such that

$$H(X) \leq \frac{1}{n} \sum_{x^n} f(x^n) K(x^n | n) \leq H(X) + \frac{|\mathcal{X}| \log n}{n} + \frac{c}{n}$$

for all n. Thus

$$E \frac{1}{n} K(X^n | n) \to H(X).$$

That is, the average expected Kolmogorov complexity of length n descriptions should approach entropy as sample size grows. This means that we should be able to use texts to estimate the entropy of various linguistic variables and, therefore, place a bound on the complexity of their descriptions. In other words, linguists interested in the relationship between linguistic typology and learnability should be very interested in the results of corpus-based linguistics since studies of real corpora will provide hard limits on the amount of information that can be packed into a parameter.

We have so far noted a relationship between Kolmogorov complexity, prefix codes and entropy. The relationship is both surprising and deeply suggestive. Recall that Kolmogorov complexity is defined relative to symbolic objects, namely Turing machine programs; we can, in fact, think of these programs as programs for a physical computer if we like. Entropy is a statistical notion, a measure of the amount of uncertainty in a system. Nevertheless, as (172) shows, there is a systematic relationship between entropy and Kolmogorov complexity.

Let us return to a thought experiment briefly suggested above. Suppose we started feeding a computer randomly generated programs. Sticking to the binary programming language we have been using for Turing machines, we might generate these programs by tossing a coin and using "1" for *heads* and "0" for *tails*. In general, these programs will crash (halt with no output), but every once in a while one of them will halt with a sensible output. Thus, the following quantity is well-defined:

(173)   The *universal probability* of a string x is

$$P_{\mathcal{U}}(x) = \sum_{p \,:\, \mathcal{U}(p) = x} 2^{-l(p)} = Pr(\mathcal{U}(p) = x),$$

which is the probability that a program randomly drawn as a sequence of fair coin tosses $p_1, p_2, \ldots$ will print out the string x.

The definition in (173) is quite similar to the Kraft inequality in (156). Since the Kraft inequality guarantees that optimal prefix codes are related to probability measures and since Kolmogorov complexity is also related to probability measures by 18, it is to be expected that there would be a tight relationship between universal probability and Kolmogorov complexity. Indeed, the following is a theorem (see Cover and Thomas, 1991):

(174) $P_{\mathcal{U}}(x) \approx 2^{-K(x)}$

That is, we can approximate the universal probability of x by using its Kolmogorov complexity. Intuitively, this is because the high probability things are encoded by short strings, as we have seen. Thus, simple objects are much more likely than complex ones.

The relationship between Kolmogorov complexity and probability has a rather pleasing result for us. We defined the Kolmogorov complexity of a parameter value as the complexity of the smallest structure which expresses it (see (164)). We used this to formalize the constraint that all parameters must be expressed on a structure whose Kolmogorov complexity is bounded by a constant c in (165). The result in (174) means that the descriptive complexity of a parameter value – the size of the minimal structure that expresses it – is also a bound on its frequency in real texts.

We had initially required that in order for a parameter value to be discovered by a learner, the frequency with which it is expressed in the input text must exceed some threshold level. This was the content of the requirement in (132). If we let ϕ represent this "learnability threshold" then we can restate the requirement as follows:

(175)   For all parameter values v_i is a system of parameters $\mathcal{P}$, $2^{-K(v_i)} \geq \phi$.

We speculate that the constraint in (175) is related to the Boundedness of Parameter Expression (II) in (165), repeated here as (176) through the constant c which bounds the complexity of the structures which express parameter values.

(176)   *Boundedness of Parameter Expression II*
For all parameter values v_i in a system of parameters $\mathcal{P}$, $K(v_i)$ is bounded from above by a fixed constant c.

In particular:

(177) $\phi \approx 2^{-c}$

That is, the complexity bound on parameter values doubles as the minimal learnability threshold. If the Kolmogorov complexity of a parameter value is greater than c then its probability of occurring in a text will fall below the learnability threshold.

The constant c can, in principle, be estimated from actual texts. Grammatical constructions effectively partition sentences into types, which occur with particular frequencies in texts. The complexity of a particular parameter value can be estimated from the frequency of constructions that express that parameter value. The probabilities here should be additive, so that careful investigation of a wide variety of constructions over very large texts will be required. The predictions are as follows. Extremely simple parameter values – those that are associated with a low Kolmogorov complexity – should have a high universal probability, as we saw above in (174); that is, constructions expressing this parameter value should occur relatively frequently in texts. If frequency of exposure is related to mastery of the target value, we would expect parameters with low Kolmogorov complexity to be set relatively early by learners. This follows from the interaction between the Frequency of Parameter Expression (see (175)) and Boundedness of Parameter Expression II (see (176)). Complex parameter values – those associated with a high Kolmogorov complexity – should have a low universal probability according to (174). This means that constructions expressing this parameter value should occur with a relatively low frequency in texts, the learner will be exposed to this value relatively infrequently and, therefore, discovering this parameter value should occur relatively late in the acquisition process.

We have now formalized the relationship between simplicity of description, frequency in the input text and ease of learnability. The theory of Kolmogorov complexity, with its association with universal probability, is a powerful tool that relates the information content of parameter values to real world texts. When fully developed, the theory of the complexity of parameters will relate theoretical linguistics, corpus-based linguistics and developmental psycholinguistics.

NOTES

1 On pumping lemmas, see Hopcroft and Ullman (1979); see also Partee, ter Meulen and Wall (1990) which gives a brief introduction to formal languages and automata theory directed toward linguists.
2 See Gallistel (1990) for a review of such approaches in animal learning.
3 I have drawn these from two files on the Child Language Data Exchange, one early file (adam15) and one late file (adam40).

4 See the reference cited in Gleitman and Wanner (1982) for extensive discussion.

5 See Wexler and Culicover (1980), particularly their chapter 2, for an excellent discussion of the "motherese" hypothesis.

6 Chomsky (1981a) gives a good exposition of the fundamental ideas underlying the *P&P* approach. See also the references cited in this volume.

7 See Clark (1996) where the basic units are minimal trees which the learner combines in fixed ways in order to account for the input text. The idea was based on Tree Adjoining Grammars (TAGs); see Rambow (1994), Frank (1992), Joshi (1987) and the references cited in these works for a discussion of TAGs.

8 See Clark (1992) and Clark and Roberts (1993) for a model which assumes a population of hypotheses.

9 See Clark (1992) and Clark and Roberts (1993) for discussion of a learning model with these properties.

10 The limit, $\lim_{T \to \infty} \bar{\mu}_0(\mathcal{L}, T) = 1$, expresses convergence to the target sequence of parameter settings as time, T, goes to infinity, given a learning system $\mathcal{L}$ and a test for correctness $\bar{\mu}_0(\mathcal{L}, t)$ to be the number of parameters correctly set by $\mathcal{L}$ at time t.

11 See Hamming (1991) for some articulately defended views on the nature of probability.

12 The example raises the interesting problem of how to decide when a given string is random; in particular, effective tests for randomness (proportion of sequences like "00," "10," "01" and "11" in the string, and so forth) are not guaranteed to give the correct answer. Thus, the randomness of a string may not be decided (see Li and Vitanyi, 1993, for some discussion) which brings up the interesting relationship between Kolmogorov complexity and Gödel's incompleteness theorem.

13 Space prevents a more complete discussion of Turing machines and computation theory here. For a more detailed exposition, see Papadimitriou (1994). I will rely on Papadimitriou's formalism for the discussion here.

14 A simpler specification of Turing machines is given in Hopcroft and Ullman (1979). A simpler formalism would make the binary encoding in the programs easier, but I have used the richer formalism for ease of pedagogy.

15 In this section, we will rely on the presentation of data compression to be found in Cover and Thomas (1991). See, in particular, their chapter 5.

16 Invariant properties could, of course, be hard-wired and, so, be arbitrarily complex since the learner would not learn them from linguistic experience.

17 Note that $H_D(X)$ is the entropy of X calculated with a base D log.

18 A fundamental work in this area is Chaitin (1987), which relates Kolmogorov complexity to many interesting results in number theory and recursive function theory.

19 An amazing principle that has many applications. The workstation in my office crashes more frequently than my desktop computer at home. The former relies on its connection to a complex local area network while the latter does not. The home computer has proven itself more problematic than my ballpoint pen. The complexity relationship between the latter two needs no further elaboration.

5   The Structural Triggers Learner

William G. Sakas and Janet Dean Fodor

5.1   Introduction[1]

How much work does it take to acquire a human language? For most adults, the acquisition of a new language is a slow and effortful process. But what if one has the right learning equipment, as children evidently do? For first language learners most of the work is done in five or six years. Our research goal is to find out what goes on in those few years. To what extent does it involve the use of special-purpose computational systems that adults lack? What do the learning routines do that is so difficult for the human brain to simulate later in life?

We will argue here that very little need be done to acquire a language, over and above the normal processes of comprehension that are involved in all language use. At least, we will argue this for the acquisition of syntax, on the assumptions that the syntactic component of a natural language grammar is largely innate and that learning consists exclusively of the setting of parameters. Similar conclusions could apply to any other parameterized domain, such as phonology (see Dresher and Kaye, 1990; Dresher, 1999). Acquisition of the lexicon is likely to be a different and more labor-intensive project. And semantic principles possibly demand no learning at all.

Thus, we assume here the principles-and-parameters framework for language description (Chomsky, 1981a, 1988, and elsewhere) and consider the process by which syntactic parameters are set. This process is commonly described as triggering, and it is contrasted with more traditional modes of learning such as hypothesis formation and testing. The latter seemed to be the only way in which a grammar could be acquired, back when linguistic theory defined grammars as rule systems differing considerably from one language to another (Chomsky, 1965). Hypothesis formation clearly carries a very heavy workload, and appears in addition to be too unreliable a mode of learning to model the remarkably uniform achievements of human learners. By contrast, parameter setting is thought to be much less onerous and more uniform across individuals.

The work involved in parameter setting can be broken down into three phases:

I   trigger recognition;
II parameter value adoption;
III any necessary error correction or other relearning (possibly repeating I and II).

The amount of work that each subprocess requires can be measured in terms of the number of computational steps it takes, and/or the number of input sentences consumed before learning is complete. Note that there are both swings and roundabouts here: an obsessively cautious learner would be slow on I and II but would recoup time with respect to III, while a learner that takes chances may coast through I and II but have to put in a lot more work at stage III. Triggering, as originally conceived, was hailed as winning in every direction: it is thought to be fast, accurate, and virtually computation-free.

We will report here a sad conclusion that is a commonplace in computational learning theory but is not widely known in linguistics and psychology: that the classical notion of triggering cannot be effectively implemented for natural languages. This is because trigger recognition is much more difficult than has been recognized. In the following sections we examine stochastic models of a kind recently proposed by Gibson and Wexler (1994) to take the place of classical triggering, and show that they fall far short in terms of efficiency, faring badly with respect to both I and III. We then outline a very different approach to parameter setting, which amounts to just a slight twist on normal sentence parsing and which copes with the difficulty of I without paying heavily on III.

5.2   Triggering

Definitions of *a trigger* or *to trigger* are hard to find in the literature.[2] The general understanding appears to be roughly as follows. A trigger is a sentence (a word string) of the target language, perceived by the learner, which "automatically" flips a parameter switch to the correct value. That triggering is "automatic" or "mechanical" is regarded as important but is rarely explicated. We suppose what is intended is that some easily accessible property of the input word sequence is detected by the learning mechanism and causes a change in the value of a parameter without there being any intervening computation of the linguistic consequences or any evaluation of alternative moves. The property in question need not even have any contentful relation to the parameter it sets (cf. Atkinson, 1987). Imagine, for instance, an artificial language domain in which all and only verbs begin with /w/, and all and only sentences with null subjects are verb-initial. In that domain, a sensor that detects /w/ could reliably trigger the positive value of the null subject parameter.

Unfortunately, this supremely simple triggering mechanism for parameter setting is a workable possibility for artificial languages only. Natural languages are not built for it. The sentence properties correlated with syntactic parameter values in natural languages are often abstract structural properties, not immediately detectable in the word string.[3] Two factors in particular impede superficial triggering. We will call these (i) the depth-of-derivation problem, and (ii) the string-to-structure problem. We consider them in turn.

(i) The depth-of-derivation problem: The criterial property for establishing a parameter value may be obscured by later derivational operations. This does not arise for all parameters. For example, the fact that there is no overt subject in a sentence is normally apparent in the surface form.[4] (But see exercise 5.5 at the end of this chapter.) However, some parameters, such as the word-order parameters, control underlying properties of sentences. For instance, the head-position parameter for VP determines whether the verb precedes or follows the object in the underlying structure, and this cannot be read off the surface word sequence because movement transformations may have rearranged the constituents.[5] (Underlying order information is preserved in the positions of traces, but these are phonologically empty categories which are not perceptible; see below.) Thus, the information needed to set the parameter is present in the derivation but difficult or impossible for a learner to access.

(ii) The string-to-structure problem: Even surface structure is not overtly registered in the terminal string in all its detail. As a result, even some surface facts about a derivation may be undetectable to a learner. Traces and other empty categories are inaudible, and so are structural nodes unless they have characteristic lexical markers. For instance, in a superficially subject–verb–object (SVO) sentence the verb might be *in situ* within VP, as in English, or moved up to an inflectional head, as in French, or moved up to the C position in a verb-second language such as German (the subject also being moved in the latter case). (See Gibson and Wexler, 1994; Holmberg and Platzack, 1991; and Haegeman, 1994, or other textbook for details of these derivations.) From the SVO word string it is impossible for the learner to tell which of these structures is present. Other sentences in the language provide more specific cues to structure. For instance, it might be possible for a learner to locate the verb (as linguists do) by reference to fixed-locus constituents such as tense or negation or lexical complementizers (see Bertolo et al., 1997a). But the reasoning involved in these deductions is far from trivial.

These observations make it clear that trigger properties for setting natural language parameters are not always apparent in the linguistic stimuli that learners are exposed to. Hence, for natural languages there can be no simple routing of input sentences towards the right parameter switches by a bank of peripheral sensors or by any kind of simple computation-free sorting procedure. We may still speak of trigger sentences, and even very loosely of triggering; but it must be with the understanding that these are not as in the carefree classical model in which word strings trip parameter switches without any significant linguistic analysis having occurred. We may take a trigger $T_{v_i^m}$ for value v_i^m of parameter p_i to be a sentence which occurs in at least one language and is grammatical in any language only if the grammar for that language has p_i set to v_i^m. Better still, we may take $T_{v_i^m}$ to be the specific structural property within sentences that the value v_i^m is responsible for licensing. Either way, an encounter with $T_{v_i^m}$ in the target language would constitute reliable evidence for v_i^m in the target grammar (ignoring here the possibility of ungrammatical input). Whether the learning device can recognize this evidence, whether it adopts v_i^m, and if so by what mechanism, are matters deliberately left open by this process-neutral definition. They are what remain to be determined.

All that can be retained from the classical instant triggering model is the triviality of stage II above, i.e., grammar changes consequent on trigger recognition are computation-free. We can assume that once a trigger has been recognized, the relevant parameter value is established and it alters the set of sentences licensed by the learner's grammar without any monitoring of this change by the learning device. For stage II, then, the learning system need not be knowledgeable about the very intricate correlations that hold between languages and the grammars that license them.[6] By retaining the labor-free stage II from the switch-setting metaphor we thus benefit by its considerable simplification over more traditional hypothesis testing procedures, which require a detailed knowledge of the generative consequences of different grammars. However, no general conclusion about this can be secure until we have established how the learner can recognize triggers, for it remains an open question whether the trigger recognition operations of stage I will demand a comparable amount of metalinguistic sophistication.

To summarize the conclusions of this section: many natural language parameters control nonperceptible, often deep, structural properties of sentences. What makes a sentence a trigger for some parameter value is that it has the property in question. Trigger recognition is therefore far from trivial, and the metaphor of triggering as instant switch-flipping must be relinquished. The literature on learnability still commonly refers to triggering. This is a convenience which does no harm as long as it is clear that an input sentence could reliably flip a correct parameter switch only after it has undergone a significant amount of linguistic analysis.[7]

5.3   Using the parser to identify triggers

Gibson and Wexler (1994) had the idea of using the sentence-parsing mechanism to recognize trigger sentences. This makes excellent sense, since the sentence-processing device routinely computes relations between terminal strings and structural representations at all levels of derivation. During normal sentence comprehension, it takes as input a surface word string, and its job is to establish sufficient structure to permit semantic interpretation of the sentence. Plausibly, this involves establishing empty categories and underlying grammatical relations of just the kind needed for natural language parameter setting. Note that the output of the syntactic parse might be a representation of the whole derivation, a *structural description* in the sense of Chomsky (1995); or it might be some more compact representation of significant derivational properties, such as an S-structure as defined by Government and Binding (GB) theory, which contains movement chains. For present purposes the difference is not important. For concreteness, and greater parity between transformational and non-transformational models, we will assume here that the processor constructs a single-level parse tree with movement chains, as is common in many current parsing models.

It is not unreasonable to suppose that the human parsing mechanism is innate (see Fodor, 1998b). An infant's parsing routines may perhaps be limited in processing capacity at first, but we assume that the mechanism is ready to operate as soon as it is supplied with a grammar to work with. It would seem, then, that the ideal learning strategy would be for the learner, on encounter with a novel input string, to parse it so that any deep trigger properties it contains will become visible, and then use these properties to set the relevant parameters. However, this proposal for trigger recognition also faces some practical problems.

One is what we call *the parsing paradox*, first drawn to attention by Valian (1990). The sentence processing mechanism can parse (assign a complete structure to) only those sentences that are licensed by the grammar from which it is drawing its information about the language. Those sentences, however, do not demand that any learning take place. The sentences that should initiate learning are those which the learner's current grammar does *not* yet license. But these sentences the learner's parsing routines cannot parse. In short: the learner cannot parse the very sentences it should learn from.

A second problem, emphasized by Gibson and Wexler (1994), is the existence of parametric ambiguity. This would confound trigger recognition even if the parsing paradox were solved. A sentence is parametrically ambiguous if it is licensed by two or more distinct combinations of parameter values (specifically: values of *relevant* parameters).[8] For example, we have noted that an SVO string is structurally ambiguous; and it is also parametrically ambiguous. Each of the possible structures is licensed by a different set of parameter values. As Gibson and Wexler point out, SVO order can be licensed by the parameter value for verb-second (V2) structure, with any values for the parameters that control the underlying order of subject, verb and object (in German the underlying order is SOV), or else by the parameter values for underlying subject-before-verb and verb-before-object order without the +V2 value, as in English. By contrast, a VOS sentence is not parametrically ambiguous, at least with respect to these three parameters. It can be licensed only by the −V2 value, and the underlying verb-before-subject and verb-before-object values.

Let us consider a little further the fact that sentences that are parametrically ambiguous are commonly structurally ambiguous (perhaps necessarily so; see Fodor, 1998a), i.e., that the different grammars that license the same word string assign it different structural descriptions. As we have seen, the structure of an SVO string in German is very different from that of an SVO string in English (at least on standard analyses); in German, but not in English, the subject and verb are raised into the C projection. Because of this, the learner's parsing mechanism cannot determine what structure to assign to a parametrically ambiguous input string until it knows which grammar to apply to that string. However, for a novel sentence type the learner does not know which grammar is appropriate – that is precisely what it is trying to find out by parsing the sentence. Caught in this vicious circle, a bold learner might try to guess which structure (which grammar) is correct, while a cautious learner would rather avoid setting any parameters at all when there is danger that the input is ambiguous.

Current models of human language learning divide on just this point. Some ignore ambiguity and adopt any parameter settings that succeed, without concern for the fact that the success might turn out to be spurious and the settings incorrect. This is how Gibson and Wexler's model operates, as we explain in sections 5.4–5.7. By contrast, the model we advocate in sections 5.8–5.10 attempts always to be aware of ambiguity and to refrain from adopting parameter values unless it has unequivocal evidence for them.

In summary, the sentence parsing mechanism must exist independently of learning, and it is expert at assigning abstract structure to word strings. Putting it to work to identify the triggers for parameter setting is thus an excellent plan. But it can succeed only if two problems can be solved: the problem of how to parse sentences that fall beyond the licensing capacity of the learner's current grammar; and the problem of how to determine the right grammar when an input string can be licensed by two different (combinations of) parameter settings.

5.4   The Triggering Learning Algorithm

Gibson and Wexler's learning procedure is the *Triggering Learning Algorithm* (TLA). It neatly sidesteps the parsing paradox by turning to its own advantage the fact that it cannot parse the sentences from which it needs to learn. It uses this as a stimulus for experimenting with alternative grammars. On receiving an input string s it first tries to parse s with its current grammar G. If this succeeds, no learning is called for; though G may not be fully correct, the learner at least has no specific reason to believe that it is wrong. If the parsing attempt with G fails, the learner tries again with a modified grammar G' that it arrives at by resetting one parameter, chosen at random. (That only one parameter may be reset is the Single Value Constraint; see section 5.6.) If the parsing attempt with G' also fails, G' is no improvement over G, so the TLA retains G (this follows from the Greediness Constraint, which permits adoption of a grammar only if it licenses the current input; see section 5.5.1 for discussion). If G' does permit a successful parse of s, the TLA shifts from G to G'. Once again, the grammar that affords a parse is not necessarily correct for the target language, but it has at least the merit of being compatible with the current sentence. This is a necessary condition, though far from a sufficient one, for being the target grammar.

Gibson and Wexler make no specific assumptions about the nature of the parsing mechanism; they require only that it be capable of delivering a report of success or failure to the learning algorithm. It is not assumed that the parser presents the learning device with a structural description of the sentence in which it could recognize the deep structural properties that can reveal correct parameter values. But importantly, although deep structural properties are not explicitly consulted, they are what drive the outcome of the parsing test. Ambiguity aside, the reason why an attempted parse succeeds is that the sentence does have the properties associated with the parameter values that are being tested. Thus the TLA is able to employ the parser to detect, implicitly, any relevant trigger properties at all, regardless of whether or not they are superficially evident.

The TLA would be maximally effective if there were a perfect correlation between the correctness of a grammar for the target language and its success or failure in parsing input. In fact the relationship is only partial. If a grammar fails the parse test on some input it must be wrong, since there is at least one sentence of the target language that it cannot license. But if a grammar passes the parse test on some sentence, it is not necessarily correct for the language.[9] The input string might be parametrically ambiguous, and the TLA might by chance have picked for the parse-test a grammar which assigns the input a structure but not the structure it has in the target language. For instance, if the input were an SVO sentence from a $-$V2 target language, and a $+$V2 grammar were picked for testing, the parser would report success – even though the verb is analyzed as in C instead of in the VP, and the $+$V2 parameter value will overgenerate many nontarget sentences. The TLA is oblivious to such dangers. It behaves as if there were no such thing as parametric ambiguity. It selects a new parameter value to try out, and adopts it if it succeeds in converting parsing failure to parsing success. Because it picks only one candidate, it never knows whether that is the only one that would succeed, or whether it is merely one among many. And because it selects the candidate at random (respecting the Single Value Constraint), it is a matter of chance whether the one it picks constitutes the correct resolution of an ambiguity. If it chooses wrongly there is a penalty: it may unwittingly switch a parameter that was already set correctly, to an incorrect value.

The TLA's blissful ignorance about the danger of ambiguity is not necessarily a drawback, however, even in the face of the considerable parametric ambiguity that exists in natural languages. The TLA is designed as a nondeterministic system which routinely mis-sets parameters and then later sets them again (and perhaps again) until eventually all are correct. In the end, this might be more effective than fussing about which input sentences can be trusted and which cannot. However, a trial-and-error strategy works well only if the setting and resetting process is not too cumbersome or slow. In fact, as we will show below, this kind of learner may take a great many computational steps on average to change even one parameter value. Hence the cost of having to keep repeating the process is considerable. In short: the TLA's trigger recognition stage I is imprecise, its parameter adoption stage II is unaware of the imprecision and so inherits it, therefore there must be extensive error correction at stage III, but this is a laborious process.

Thus, the TLA solves one of the two problems we identified above, but in such a way that it is forced to give up on the other one. It solves the parsing paradox by testing out alternatives to the current grammar. But testing a grammar is work, and the learning system can only reasonably test one grammar at a time, and so it cannot in principle recognize parametric ambiguity. It could do so only if it were to run the parse test repeatedly on the same input sentence with different grammars until it either found a second successful grammar or exhausted *all* the possible grammars without having found one. This is presumably not a realistic possibility. But without an exhaustive test, a learner cannot recognize parametric ambiguity, so it cannot defend itself against it. So inevitably it makes mistakes. We see, then, that there is a clear connection between doing the work of trigger recognition by means of the parse test, and the fact that parameter setting is nondeterministic. This relationship is interesting and somewhat unexpected. In the classical instant-triggering model it was assumed that all property detectors were on the job at all times and could function in parallel, so the limitation of having to test grammars one by one did not arise.[10] But there was a lot of wishful thinking about trigger recognition in that model, as we have observed. It is only by taking the process seriously, as the TLA does, that we can see how arduous it actually is, and how much of it must be sacrificed to keep the workload within plausible limits.

In summary, the TLA is a significant advance on the classical model because its parse test can detect effects of parameter settings which are not accessible to any superficial property detector. But it purchases this sensitivity at a high price. Though it can achieve trigger recognition, it is then forced to close its eyes to trigger ambiguity. The TLA's parse test imposes only a necessary condition on correctness of a parameter value, not a sufficient condition. For the TLA to do more would tax its capacity beyond feasibility. But because it cannot do more, it makes errors on ambiguous triggers and so must engage in more work later on to correct those errors.

We turn now to the other significant aspect of the TLA's workload, which arises at stage I but which interacts with the ambiguity problem as we will show. It is very arduous for the TLA to find a parameter that is worth resetting. The consequence is that the TLA must expend a great deal of effort, and consume a great deal of input, to set even one parameter. To set 20 or 30 is harder still. And every error that is made at stage II due to ambiguity exacerbates this problem because it requires more parameter setting in order to correct the error. In the next section we establish some formal machinery to document these claims.

5.5 Performance of a TLA-like algorithm

Gibson and Wexler demonstrated that the TLA converges on the target grammar under some conditions, though not under all. We will suppose here, since it is not our main concern, that convergence is guaranteed. Even so, it is unclear that the TLA is a plausible model of the human language learning mechanism. This is because, as we now argue, it is very inefficient at extracting information from the input sentences it encounters. Correspondingly, it has to parse a great many input sentences, on average, before it finds the target grammar. Though its workload per input sentence is not excessive, the accumulated load across the enormous input sample is high.

Our strategy in this section will be to demonstrate the computational inefficiency of the TLA in two steps. For simplicity, we first calculate performance characteristics for an error-driven learning system which we will call TLA− ("TLA minus"). It obeys the Greediness Constraint and is like the TLA in all respects except that it does not obey the Single Value Constraint (SVC). We then estimate the effect on performance of converting this TLA− into the TLA proper, by imposing the SVC. This second stage of evaluation is necessarily less precise, since the effect of the SVC is heavily dependent on the character of the particular language domain, as noted by Berwick and Niyogi (1996). In Berwick and Niyogi's application of the TLA to the simple eight-language domain defined by Gibson and Wexler, the SVC increased the number of trials to convergence; but this doesn't rule out the possibility that there are circumstances under which it improves performance.[11] However, we do not believe that the SVC substantially affects the results presented here concerning the exponential complexity of trigger recognition in the TLA−.

Niyogi and Berwick (1996) formalized the behavior of the TLA as a Markov process. This is elegant and of some interest (though it can be difficult to manage for very large language domains); see section 5.11, and Niyogi and Berwick (1996) for details. For our goals, however, it is not ideal. We wish to establish a foundation for comparing the TLA with other models. We therefore develop a framework that articulates degrees of parametric ambiguity and parametric irrelevance, and that can distinguish among different sources of learning difficulty: grammar sampling problems, memory problems, parsing capacity problems, error rates, and so forth. However, our aims are too ambitious for us to achieve all this in this chapter. As will become clear, we must settle for formalizing simplified versions of the learning models we are interested in. We believe that even this offers some insight into the very different strategies that learning systems may adopt. But conclusions drawn here on the basis of the simplified models will not necessarily extend, of course, to the richer versions that have been proposed as models of human language learning.[12]

5.5.1   *TLA−* = *TLA without SVC*

We focus first on stage I, and later consider its impact on stages II and III. Although stage I serves the function of discovering the triggering information in input sentences, in the TLA− no particular role is played by the association of any sentence or sentence property with a particular parameter value. The TLA− in effect ignores the parameterization of the language domain, except insofar as it offers a finite and orderly array of possible grammars to hypothesize. The TLA− recognizes a sentence *s* as a trigger in the same way as the TLA does, by trying out grammars against it in hope of finding one that licenses it (see note 10). If it succeeds, it adopts that grammar. Thus it treats an input sentence, in effect, as a trigger for adopting all the new values which differentiate the successful grammar from the previous one that failed. The work expended per novel input (i.e., an input not licensed by the learner's current grammar) consists in trying to parse the sentence a second time with a new grammar, subsequent to the failed parse with the current grammar. If this second parse succeeds, some information is gained, and at relatively little cost. But every sentence from which the learner gains no information constitutes a waste of the effort that went into the second parse, as well as a waste of learning time.[13] If few input sentences were wasted, the TLA− would be quite an economical means of language acquisition. In fact it is very expensive.

We illustrate here with some particular numerical estimates, followed by general formulae in each case. We make the following background assumptions throughout these calculations. Their general trend is to impose homogeneity on the learning process, in order to simplify both the mathematics and the exposition. We do not assert that these points are true of natural languages; indeed, we very much doubt that some of them are. But they will allow us to take some initial steps towards what must ultimately be a more sophisticated formalization.

(i) The sample of the target language that a learner is exposed to entails the value of every parameter relevant to the target language (i.e., every parameter that needs to be set);

(ii) The learner's input sample does not necessarily exhaust the target language (e.g., it may be limited to sentences of two clauses or less), but the sample is uniformly distributed (i.e., no particular sentence type within it is systematically withheld or delayed);

(iii) Every language in the domain shares an equal number of sentence types with the target language;

(iv) If a target sentence is licensed by two grammars, then it is also licensed by every grammar which shares the parameter values they have in common;

(v) All sentences within the target language are ambiguous with respect to the same number of parameters. (We assume this to start with, but later we introduce some flexibility in this regard);

(vi) Grammars tested by the TLA− are selected with equal probability from the set of candidates (= all possible grammars other than the failed current grammar).

Suppose there are 30 binary syntactic parameters. (See chapter 3, page 89 on how many parameters it is reasonable to assume for natural language syntax.) Assuming that there are no constraints limiting which parameter values can cooccur, their combinations amount to 2^{30} (= 1,073,741,824) possible grammars. Suppose that only 25 out of the 30 parameters are relevant to the target language (irrelevant parameters control properties of phenomena not present in the target language, such as clitic order in a language without clitics). Then 5 parameters are irrelevant, and the consequence is that 2^5 (= 32) of the billion grammars count as equally correct for the target language. In general, for r relevant parameters out of a total of n parameters in the domain, the number of correct (target) grammars is 2^{n-r}. A useful way of considering irrelevance is that the total class of 2^n grammars is thereby clumped into 2^r equivalence classes, each containing 2^{n-r} grammars; the grammars within any one equivalence class have identical consequences for target language sentences. In the present case, there are 33,554,432 (= 2^{25}) equivalence classes each consisting of 32 ($= 2^5$) grammars; one of these equivalence classes constitutes the target.

Now let us consider parametric ambiguity. Suppose that all sentences of the target language are parametrically ambiguous. Specifically, let us suppose here that each is ambiguous with respect to eight parameters that are relevant to the target (not the same eight in every case). (Recall that between them the input sentences must provide unambiguous information about each relevant parameter; see assumption (i) above.) Then each input sentence is licensed by $2^8 * 2^5 = 2^{8+5} = 2^{13} = 8,192$ grammars; this follows from assumption (iv).[14] Of these, 2^5 ($= 32$) grammars are correct and $8,192 - 32 = 8,160$ are incorrect. In general, a target sentence that is ambiguous with respect to a parameters is assumed to be licensed by $2^a * 2^{n-r} = 2^{a+n-r}$ grammars, of which 2^{n-r} are correct and $2^{a+n-r} - 2^{n-r} = 2^{n-r} * (2^a - 1)$ are incorrect.[15]

Let us now cut to the point at which the TLA− adopts a grammar, and ask what the probability is that the grammar it adopts is one of the 2^{n-r} correct grammars. Suppose for the moment (though we will return to this below) that the learning algorithm has established already that its currently hypothesized grammar G does not parse the current input sentence s, and that the candidate new grammar G' does parse s. Given that 2^{n-r} grammars out of the 2^{a+n-r} grammars that could parse s are correct, the probability that G' is correct is $2^{n-r}/2^{a+n-r} = 1/2^a$. For our current estimates it is $1/2^8 = 1/256$, or a 0.39 percent chance of guessing correctly. It follows that on average the number of grammar changes that would be necessary to identify the target grammar is 256, or in general $1/(1/2^a) = 2^a$ (see section 5.11). Note that this value increases exponentially with the degree of ambiguity (i.e., with a, the number of parameters with respect to which an input is ambiguous).

Now let us unpack the two temporary assumptions we made above. We will take them in sequence. First, there is some probability that G will parse the input s so that no grammar change will be attempted. This must be factored into our calculations. Consider the probability that an arbitrary grammar G will be able to parse a given sentence s from the target language. Recall from above that an input sentence is licensed by 2^{a+n-r} grammars out of the total of 2^n grammars. Therefore, the probability that a grammar G can parse an input s is $2^{a+n-r}/2^n = 2^{a-r}$, or $2^a/2^r$. This is the probability that the current grammar G can parse the input and will not be given up. The probability that G fails to parse the input, so that the learner recognizes the need to switch to a new grammar, is thus $1 - (2^a/2^r)$. In the present case, this is 0.99999237.[16] In other words, with this degree of ambiguity the learner would be motivated to change grammars on almost every trial. Note that as ambiguity increases, the probability of a needed grammar change decreases, other things being equal; hence the number of inputs between attempted grammar changes increases. This is because at higher ambiguity levels, G will parse more sentences for which it is not in fact correct. Nevertheless, despite this increase, the number of inputs between attempted changes remains relatively low except at extremely high levels of ambiguity. For instance, the number of inputs per attempted change is increased only by a factor of approximately 2 (relative to total unambiguity of all inputs) if all sentences are ambiguous for all parameters except one. It is increased by a factor of 20 if 90 percent of sentences are fully ambiguous and 10 percent are ambiguous for all parameters except one (with an average ambiguity of 24.9 when $r = 25$, i.e., 99.6 percent ambiguity). Clearly, the range of this multiplier reflecting the effect of parametric ambiguity on the success rate of G is quite limited. As shown below, this factor does not have a major impact on how quickly on average a learner will identify the target grammar.

The other matter that needs to be brought into the equation is the probability that G', the grammar that is put through the parse test when G fails, does parse s. The calculation is similar to the general formula given above for the parsing success of G, except that only $2^n - 1$ grammars are under consideration because the current grammar G has disqualified itself by failing its parse test. For $n = 30$ (or for any other plausible size n) this number is very close to 2^n, so to simplify the calculations that follow we will substitute 2^n (or equivalently: we can simplify by assuming that G is included in the pool of grammars from which the learner selects after G has failed). Thus, the general formula shows that for any G' that the learner tries out when G fails, the probability that G' will parse the input s is 2^{a-r}. This is a very low probability except at high levels of ambiguity. Thus, very often when the learner needs to change to a new grammar, its candidate new grammar will fail the parse test. Because Greediness does not allow the TLA− to change to a grammar that fails the parse test, the rate of *actual* grammar change will be low. Grammar change occurs in the TLA− only when G fails and G' succeeds, and the probability of this is $(1 - 2^{a-r}) * 2^{a-r}$. Given our current estimates, it is approximately 0.000007629 or on average 1 actual grammar change every 131,073 input sentences.[17] Between these events, no learning occurs. As calculated above, 256 such changes would have to occur on average before convergence on the target grammar. This is not a great number,

Table 5.1. *Average number of inputs consumed by the TLA– before convergence (formula:* $2^r/(1 - 2^{a-r})$)

a	$r = 15$	$r = 20$	$r = 25$	$r = 30$
0	32,769	1,048,577	33,554,433	1,073,741,825
5	32,800	1,048,608	33,554,464	1,073,741,856
10	33,835	1,049,601	33,555,456	1,073,742,848
15	can't learn	1,082,401	33,587,232	1,073,774,593
20		can't learn	34,636,833	1,074,791,425
25			can't learn	1,108,378,657
30				can't learn

but the rarity with which Greediness is satisfied magnifies it considerably. The total number of inputs consumed before convergence is on average $256 * 131,073 = 33,554,688.$[18] In general, the average total number of inputs consumed before convergence is

$$2^a \frac{1}{(1 - 2^{a-r})(2^{a-r})} = \frac{1}{(1 - 2^{a-r})(2^{-r})} = \frac{2^r}{1 - 2^{a-r}}$$

Table 5.1 presents some figures for other values of a and r.

Note that the number of inputs required on average rises exponentially in r, the number of relevant parameters (= the number of parameters that need to be set for the target language), and is over a billion for 30 relevant parameters. As an informal rule of thumb, one can estimate the number of sentences to convergence as approximately 2^r (because the denominator in the formula above differs very little from 1 unless a is high relative to r). For 15 parameters the average cost in input is a little over 2,000 sentences per parameter; for 30 parameters it is over 35 million per parameter. Because efficiency is so much better at the lower end of the scale, it is important for this model that the number of parameters for natural language be low. Linguistic research has this as its goal and may ultimately show that it is so, but at present there would probably be broad agreement among linguists that 15 syntactic parameters underestimates the extent of natural language variation. Note that by the rule of thumb, each extra ten parameters multiplies the total number of inputs needed on average by about 1,000. So for 40 parameters, it would be in the order of a trillion, or about 25 billion per parameter.

The learning process is sketched in figure 5.1, as a probability tree with all three stages shown: the possible success or failure of the current grammar G to start with, then the success or failure in finding

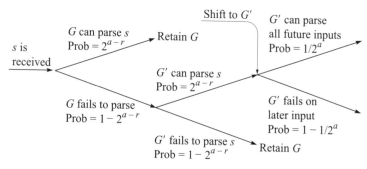

Figure 5.1 Probabilities of different outcomes of an encounter between the TLA− and an input sentence. Homogeneous ambiguity.

a new grammar G' that satisfies Greediness, and then the question of whether the grammar adopted is correct (in which case no more changes will ever be required) or incorrect (so that the process must be repeated on another input). Note that convergence on the current trial corresponds to the path on which G fails the parse test, G' passes the parse test, and G' is indeed correct. (We round the formulae for the probabilities of G' success or failure here, as noted above.)

With the structure of the situation thus outlined, we can elaborate it in various ways to make it capable of approximating real learning situations more closely. Suppose, for example, that sentences are not uniformly ambiguous. Perhaps 10 percent of the target language sample are parametrically unambiguous, while 90 percent are each ambiguous with respect to 8 parameters. We'll retain for now the assumption that only 25 of the 30 parameters are relevant to the language. This is sketched in figure 5.2 (see exercise 5.3 below for further examples). Note that this probability tree contains more branches, to represent the richer range of outcomes, but the calculations along each path are of the same kind as we worked through above. For the ambiguous sentences, the situation is exactly as in figure 5.1.

5.5.2   *Summary of TLA− performance*

The amount of work expended by the TLA− in attaining the target grammar is a function of the number of sentences it consumes before convergence. We have seen that, given the general assumptions made above, this increases exponentially with the number of parameters that need to be set (= r, the number of relevant parameters). To a lesser degree, it increases also with the degree of parametric ambiguity. It becomes implausibly high at levels of parameterization and ambiguity

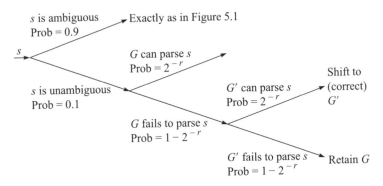

Figure 5.2 Probabilities of different outcomes of an encounter between the TLA− and an input sentence. 10 percent unambiguous sentences.

that seem to be not unreasonable (or perhaps overly modest) estimates for the human language domain. We will review the roles of these two factors, r and a, in turn. Note in general that in terms of the three-stage analysis of grammar acquisition in section 5.1, the TLA−'s grammar selection process at stage I and grammar adoption process at stage II have two distinct undesirable effects. They inhibit grammar change in many cases where change is necessary, and they permit change to a wrong grammar in response to ambiguous input. The latter necessitates further parameter setting to correct the errors, which inflates the workload at stage III. The costs of this stage III repair process are included in the estimates above of the amount of input consumed en route to the target grammar.

The exponential dependence of workload on the number of parameters to be set is due to the TLA−'s blind (i.e., merely error-driven) search through the field of all possible grammars for one that is compatible with the input. Where the classical instant-triggering model tested a sentence to see what its implications were for each parameter, the TLA− tests a grammar to see what its implications are for a given sentence. Without advance knowledge of what would be a good grammar to test, the latter is a slow business. If the learner had an oracle that would tell it which parameters most likely need to be reset to accommodate a given input, it could avoid the TLA−'s high rate of failure in the parse test, and the extreme waste of input sentences which that causes. How to improve on the TLA− in this respect is the topic of sections 5.8 and 5.9.

The dependence of the TLA−'s workload on the degree of parametric ambiguity is less extreme and more complex in nature. Greater ambiguity decreases the probability that the current grammar will fail, even if it is wrong and does need to be changed. This is not a fact about the TLA− alone, but is true of all error-driven learning systems: the spurious success of wrong hypotheses encourages complacency, and will slow down discovery of the correct hypothesis. We know of no data on this for human language learning, but at least at present there is no reason to doubt that it is true. As noted above, this consequence of the fact that learning is error-driven is predicted to be a relatively modest effect except at extremely high degrees of parametric ambiguity (approaching 100 percent); when ambiguity is moderate, it is just not very likely that a wrong grammar will survive many tests against target language sentences.

Once an error has been detected and G is known to be wrong, ambiguity has no further effect on the overall success rate of the TLA−. In our calculations above we examined stage I and stage II separately, and found that ambiguity has an effect on each; but that these effects cancel each other out. The rate of potential trigger recognition (i.e., of finding a new grammar G' that satisfies Greediness) in stage I increases exponentially with a, the degree of ambiguity. In other words, for higher ambiguity, grammar change will occur more often when grammar change is needed. However, there is no guarantee that the change that occurs will be the one that is needed. In fact, the probability of correct (target) grammar adoption from the candidates delivered to stage II decreases exponentially with the degree of ambiguity. These two effects are equal and opposite and so cancel out. (The respective formulae are: $2^a/2^r$ and $1/2^a$; see above.) The *only* net effect of parametric ambiguity within the TLA− is thus in the initial testing of the current grammar G.

This considerable indifference of the TLA− to ambiguity levels could be seen as encouraging, but what it amounts to is really that the TLA− succeeds equally rarely whether the language domain is ambiguous or not. This is because it does not actually make use of the fact that a given input is ambiguous or unambiguous; it simply ignores the matter. The TLA−, in effect, just picks randomly out of the 2^n total grammars, in the hope of hitting on one of the 2^{n-r} correct grammars for the target. This is a needle-in-a-haystack problem that gets exponentially worse as more parameters need to be set. It is clearly worth considering whether a solution might be found for the "sampling problem" of stage I (e.g., by means of some kind of pre-test to identify promising parameters worth checking; see discussion of a proposal by Valian, in Fodor, 1998a). Note, however, that the exponential cost of ambiguity would then emerge at stage II. All in all, then, the complexity characteristics of the TLA− do not commend it as a model of human language learning.

5.6   Adding in the SVC

Our remarks in this section are speculations only. The SVC is not our main focus of inquiry and so we can treat it only briefly. Moreover, it is particularly difficult to calculate any general effects of the SVC, since it interacts in an intricate way with Greediness and with the pattern of ambiguity distribution within a particular language domain. (If of interest, however, it would be possible to apply Berwick and Niyogi's Markov model to an algorithm with SVC in a language domain meeting the assumptions we have made here.) In the Structural Triggers model that we propose in section 5.8 the SVC does not apply (because it is not needed). We therefore leave it to other investigators to develop a more satisfactory theory of SVC effects than we are able to here. See Nyberg, 1992; Clark, 1992; Niyogi and Berwick, 1996, Sakas, 2000; see also exercise 5.2 at the end of this chapter.

Gibson and Wexler's TLA differs from the TLA− only in that the SVC forces the TLA to limit its choice of a new grammar to be tested; it must pick from among those that differ by only one parameter setting from the current (failed) grammar G. The SVC thus causes an uneven sampling of the class of possible grammars at stage I. It has the consequence that the learner will tend to perseverate, cycling through the same cluster of neighboring grammars to a greater extent than it would without the SVC. To the extent that this increases the rate at which the same grammar is tested repeatedly, or the chance of testing a grammar that differs from a failed one only by an irrelevant parameter, this could postpone convergence on the target. But such effects are probably minor compared with the more fundamental question of whether grammars that are similar tend to license languages that are similar, and the related but more pertinent question of whether successful grammars tend to be similar to other successful grammars.

To extrapolate to the TLA the performance measures computed above for the TLA−, we would need to answer two questions concerning the SVC. (1) Does the SVC alter the probability that a grammar selected for testing at stage I licenses the input sentence s? That is, are the n grammars that differ from G with respect to just one parameter (which we will call "1-adjacent" grammars; Nyberg, 1992) more likely to license s than any of the other grammars that differ from G? (2) Does the SVC alter the probability that G', a grammar selected at stage II, is the target grammar? That is, among the grammars that do parse s, is a grammar that is 1-adjacent to G more likely to be the correct grammar for s than a less similar grammar is? The answers to these questions are not simple, but we can indicate their general outlines. We emphasize again that this is a preliminary exploration only. And we will keep it as manageable as possible by taking advantage here of the point demonstrated in section 5.5.1, that the conceptual distinction between grammar sampling (stage I) and grammar adoption (stage II) has no substantial consequence in the TLA– and does not affect the overall likelihood of adoption of the target grammar. Thus we can conveniently combine the two questions and ask simply: (3) At a point in the learning process at which the learner's current grammar G has just failed the parse test, are grammars that are 1-adjacent to G more likely to be (or lead to) the target grammar than grammars less similar to G? If this is generally so, then adherence to the SVC facilitates convergence.

It is important to bear in mind that the notion of "n-adjacent" is defined over the parameter value combinations that constitute grammars, not over the sets of sentences that constitute languages. Whether and how the two are correlated is what is under consideration. Berwick and Niyogi (1996) refer to "smoothness" of the relation between grammars and the languages they license, when grammar similarity and language similarity are highly correlated.[19] We do not presuppose smoothness here, but regard it as an empirical issue to be evaluated. The considerations raised below suggest that in fact smoothness cannot be relied on by natural language learners.

To answer question (3) we must start with the properties of the failed current grammar G. What is certain is that G licenses at least one sentence of the target language but not all (a default or randomly chosen grammar at the very outset of learning may license none). In some cases the current grammar will have parsed several target sentences in a row. This is not a fact that a TLA learner has access to (since there is no memory for prior learning events), but it nevertheless has an indirect effect. The more target sentences a grammar licenses, the more likely it is in a greedy system to become the current grammar and to stay that way. Thus on average, over the long run, the learner's current grammar at any point is likely to license more target sentences than an arbitrary other grammar does. This did not figure in our calculations in section 5.5.1 because there we made the homogeneity assumption (iii) such that all grammars except the target grammar license exactly the same number of target sentences. The advantage of the current grammar may be very slight. It depends on the degree and distribution of ambiguity in the target language. For instance, if *all* grammars in the domain license most of the sentences in the target sample, then an arbitrary incorrect grammar could be the learner's current grammar for many trials; hence, being the current grammar would not be a strong predictor of ultimate success. It is clear, then, that being able to license many target sentences is not the same as being the target grammar, and nor does it entail having many parameter values in common with the target grammar.

For natural languages Chomsky has emphasized that small changes in parameter settings can have considerable effects on the languages generated, due to the rich interactions of principles, parameters and lexical properties in sentence derivations. For example, he writes (Chomsky, 1988: 63): "there is no simple relation between the value selected for a parameter and the consequence of this choice as it works its way through the intricate system of universal grammar. It may turn out that the change of a few parameters, or even of one, yields a language that seems to be quite different in character from the original." If this is so, the degree of overlap of the parameter settings in two grammars would *not* correlate highly with the degree of overlap of the languages they generate; the grammar/language relationship would not be a smooth one. But regardless of whether Chomsky's point establishes nonsmoothness in general, it is certainly the case that parametric ambiguity can introduce some significant bumps into the grammar/language correlation. In an ambiguous domain there may be several grammars dotted distantly around the grammar space all of which can license many sentences of the target language. Only one of them is G_t, the target grammar. It is very clear that a grammar that is successful for one target sentence, or even for many, need not in this case resemble G_t closely at all. For example, in Gibson and Wexler's small domain of three word order parameters, the sentence pattern SVO is licensed by grammars that differ from each other maximally: every one of their parameters is set differently. SVO order is licensed by the grammar SV, VO and −V2, and by the grammar VS, OV and +V2 (among others). In such a case, the SVC could do the learner more harm than good. For instance, if the starting state were VS, OV, −V2 and the target were SV, VO, −V2, then it would obviously *not* be most profitable for the learner to favor grammars 1-adjacent to G; in response to an SVO input, that would force a step in the wrong direction, to +V2.

In sum: adherence to the SVC gives the TLA a tendency to hover in one area of the total space of grammars, typically (because of Greediness) a promising area where some parsing success has occurred. If this area includes the target grammar, convergence is likely to be more rapid with the SVC than without it. But in a language space with parametric ambiguity, the SVC may unhelpfully focus the search on an area around a competing grammar, which functions as an attractor because it can parse many of the target sentences but which is nevertheless an incorrect (nontarget) grammar. In this case the SVC would retard convergence on the target: the learner needs to make a substantial shift to a very different grammar but is hindered from doing so by the SVC (and Greediness). In the most extreme case, a TLA learner that has gone astray can get permanently stuck, if it finds itself at a local maximum, i.e., a wrong grammar from which there is no possible route to the target grammar via a sequence of successful one-parameter changes as required by Greediness and the SVC. (See Gibson and Wexler (1994), for discussion, and Winston (1992) on local maxima in other types of learning systems.) Interestingly, this becomes more likely if the degree of parametric ambiguity is low, though in general a reduction in ambiguity would be expected to facilitate learning. In a fully unambiguous domain, the TLA is unable to change grammars at all, unless the target is exactly one parameter away from the starting grammar.

Translated into implications for human learning, a major consequence of the SVC would appear to be a considerable variability in acquisition outcomes. This would especially be so if individual learners can differ with respect to their starting state (e.g., if there are no innate defaults), and if the order of information received can vary substantially across children (i.e., if the frequency distribution of construction types in input to children is not very dependable). Some children could by good fortune arrive at the target grammar very rapidly, while other children would toil through many blind alleys before attaining the target, and some might never get there at all (unless the local maximum problem can be solved in some way that Gibson and Wexler suggest). Though we cannot quantify the discrepancy, this seems to us to be out of keeping with the remarkably uniform success of human language learners. Thus, even if the distribution of ambiguity in natural language should turn out to be such that the net effect of the SVC is a considerable improvement in average acquisition rates relative to the TLA−, it is arguable that the SVC does not improve the psychological fidelity of the learning algorithm.

In section 5.7 we will turn to issues concerning the isolation of individual parameters so that their contributions can be evaluated independently of the grammars in which they are embedded. In this connection it may appear that the SVC would be an unqualified blessing. For the TLA−, which lacks the SVC, a trigger sentence is a trigger for a collection of parameter values, even a whole grammar, as noted above. If a new grammar succeeds in parsing an input sentence, there is no way for the TLA— to tell which of its parameter settings was/were responsible for the success, and which were simply irrelevant (to this sentence, or to the whole language). So the TLA— must accept or reject the collection of parameter settings as a whole, without having any idea as to which of them are now correct. But in the TLA, the SVC makes it possible to attribute a parsing success to the one parameter whose value differs from the prior (failed) grammar. As we will see in section 5.7, however, the TLA is unable to take advantage of this ability to focus on specific parameters, because of a lack of certainty caused by ambiguity. The new parameter setting is the one that made the parse successful but still it might or might not be correct, because that parse might or might not be the correct parse. The TLA adopts the successful parameter setting, but it cannot do so with confidence; and as we will show, confidence has an important effect on efficiency. Thus in this respect, also, the SVC is not as helpful as might have been expected.

5.6.1   Evaluation of the TLA

Our assessment of the TLA in comparison with the TLA— has been that the TLA may well prove to be more efficient overall, but it seems likely to prove less plausible psychologically than the TLA— because of the greater variability of its routes to convergence in an unevenly ambiguous domain. In this respect the TLA may be more sensitive to parametric ambiguity than the TLA—. For the TLA— there is no sense of the learner making gradual progress toward the correct grammar; each hypothesis is randomly pulled from the total pool. By contrast, for the TLA, the SVC in combination with Greediness causes consistent shifting in the direction of locally more successful grammars. To the extent that smoothness reigns, this is beneficial. But the gradualness entailed by the SVC can be damaging if the learner is steadily converging on a wrong grammar because the domain is skewed due to ambiguity, and the SVC does not allow it an easy escape. In respects other than the SVC, the TLA is like the TLA— and thus it can be expected to exhibit the properties documented in sections 5.5.1 and 5.5.2. That is, on a high proportion of trials on which it knows it must switch to a new grammar it may fail to find a promising grammar to switch to. When it does switch, its blindness to parametric ambiguity can result in errors. Together, these problems appear to create an implausibly heavy workload for any reasonable number of natural language parameters. We would stress, however, that it would be valuable to check general remarks such as these by means of Markov modeling or simulations of particular cases (see exercise 5.2 below).

Note that for convenience in the following discussion we will not always distinguish now between the TLA and the TLA−, despite their partially different characteristics noted here. Our focus shifts now to the comparison between this class of nondeterministic grammar-testing systems and a class of systems which can detect parametric ambiguity and avoid errors.

5.7 The Parametric Principle

The fact that the workload of a learning device is exponential in the number of parameters betrays the fact that it is not really a parameter setting device. The TLA does assign values to parameters, but it does not incorporate the central insight of parameter theory. Parameterization has several advantages for learnability. The set of hypotheses for learners to consider is finite and orderly (while still allowing for a great variety of languages); there isn't an open-ended set of hypotheses that learners must devise from scratch. The testing of hypotheses does not require the learner to engage in a hunt for generalizations or a laborious comparison of minimal pairs of examples. Though we have seen that the learning machinery cannot be just "automatic" triggering, it is still true that once the relevant triggers have been identified in the input, the work is done. The TLA takes full advantage of both of these benefits of parametric theory. However, it does not abide by what we will call the *Parametric Principle: The value of each parameter is established independently of the values of all others.* This is what distinguishes a true parameter setting device from learning systems of other kinds, and it is the source of the enormous simplification of the learning task for which the principles-and-parameters model is renowned.

The essential point is familiar: if there are n binary parameters and the learning procedure is able to establish the value of each one independently of the others, then only n bits of information need to be extracted from the input sample for convergence on any one of 2^n grammars. In other words, given the Parametric Principle, the extent of the learning task depends only linearly on the number of parameters. It may take a little or a lot of work to set each one, but at least the workload per parameter is roughly constant. By contrast, any learning device that evaluates grammars rather than individual parameter values faces a task that expands linearly with the number of grammars, hence exponentially with the number of parameters. The workload per grammar would have to be vanishingly slight in order for the total labor not to spiral out of hand rapidly for any reasonable number of parameters. Gibson and Wexler tested the TLA on an artificially small domain of eight languages defined by three binary parameters, where the extreme difference in workload between setting parameters and selecting grammars did not become apparent. But if the estimate of 30 syntactic parameters for natural language is more realistic, then the disparity is between setting 30 parameters and checking more than a billion grammars.

A useful way to look at the difference between testing grammars and testing parameters is to see convergence as the elimination of all grammars other than the target, and to consider how effectively different procedures manage to eliminate grammars. A grammar-by-grammar test can eliminate them one at a time at best, so even if the learner kept track of the fate of every one, in the worst case it could take up to $2^n - 1$ eliminative steps to rule out all but the target. In fact, the TLA never eliminates any possible grammars at all, because it does not take the trouble to record negative outcomes of its parse tests. We assume that this is because the slight reduction in the search space that results from eliminating individual grammars does not compensate for the cost of record-keeping on such a vast scale.[20] Therefore all grammars remain in the pool from which the TLA selects a grammar to test, with the consequence that some incorrect grammars may be tried out many times. More importantly, the pool does not get any smaller as learning proceeds, so the stage I probability of finding a grammar that can parse the input does not improve (except for whatever contribution the SVC makes). This, as we saw, is a major source of the TLA's inefficiency.[21] Because it does not obey the Parametric Principle, the TLA gropes just as randomly later on in the learning process as it does at the beginning.

By contrast, true parameter setting permits a very rapid reduction of the pool of possible grammars. Each time a parameter is set, one parameter value is eliminated. And since half of all grammars have that parameter value, that eliminates from consideration half of the candidate grammars remaining.[22] In a domain of 30 parameters, setting one parameter rules out roughly 500 million grammars; setting the next one excludes another 250 million; setting 5 reduces the pool to roughly 3 percent of its original size. This is how the Parametric Principle makes such a great difference to the scale of the learning problem. Chomsky's insight was that if grammar acquisition is a selective rather than a creative process, its complexity need be no more than linear in the number of ways in which grammars can differ from each other.[23]

Nevertheless, very few existing learning models abide by the Parametric Principle. Statistical weighting systems such as those proposed by Valian (1994) and Kapur (1994) postpone setting a parameter for some time while evaluating the evidence, but do eventually settle on a value for each and set it permanently. The Structural Triggers Learner that we describe here in sections 5.8–5.10 also is designed to obey the Parametric Principle. It seems astonishing that a parameter-based learning model would *not* take advantage of the powerful reduction of the acquisition problem that the Parametric Principle makes possible. Why would this be so? There are no compensating advantages to be gained by searching through the vast space of grammars. At best, clever search strategies may make it less punishing. Such strategies are being sought in current research in frameworks such as genetic algorithms and neural networks. It remains to be seen, of course, but at present it seems unlikely that any improvement would rival that due to the Parametric Principle. The sole reason for violating the Parametric Principle, it appears, is that obeying it is too difficult. The literature on language learnability does not make this clear. The point is rarely addressed explicitly. As far as we know, only Clark (1994a) considers it, and he judges that the computational costs of respecting what we are calling the Parametric Principle "are too great to be acceptable." If true, this is a very consequential fact. Being forced to give up the idea of "instant" triggering does some damage to Chomsky's original elegant conception of parameter setting, but to give up the Parametric Principle would be to abandon its whole essence. If it cannot be avoided, then it must be accepted and we must reconcile it as best we can with the efficiency with which children learn language. But the stakes are high enough that it is worth some further thought before we give in. In the remainder of this chapter we will argue for an approach that permits true parameter setting in accord with the Parametric Principle.

In order to obey the Parametric Principle, a learner must be able to establish a parameter value with sufficient confidence to be prepared to rule out forever all grammars in which that parameter takes the opposite value.[24] To simplify here, we continue to set aside the possibility of errors due to faulty input or performance slips. We also make the standard assumption that the two values of a parameter are mutually exclusive in a grammar. Then there is no reason not to set a parameter permanently, and permanently discard its contrary value, as soon as clear evidence of its value is received. However, a stochastic learning device such as the TLA cannot do this because it does not *know* when it has received clear evidence for a parameter setting, i.e., evidence that some sentence of the target language cannot be licensed (parsed) without that value. The SVC helps it come close to this knowledge, but parametric ambiguity undermines it. The SVC isolates the contribution of an individual parameter value in the parse test, so the TLA (unlike the TLA−) knows exactly which value potentially earns support from the success of the parse. But the support is only potential, not reliable confirmation, because the sentence might have been ambiguous and the parse assigned to it might have been the wrong one. In that case the positive outcome of the parse test provides no evidence at all for that parameter value; for all the learning system can know, the sentence is equally compatible with the opposite value.

Is there any way out of this crippling uncertainty? The uncertainty would not arise if there were no parametric ambiguity in the domain and if the learner knew that were so; but that is not realistic for natural language. Alternatively, the uncertainty could be resolved if the parser could run an exhaustive check of all possible parses of a sentence. If the parameter value in question were present in every grammar that could parse the sentence, then it could be adopted with full confidence. However, as we noted in section 5.4, an exhaustive search through a billion grammars is hopelessly impractical if the parser can try out only one of them at a time; and attempting a billion parses simultaneously is presumably no more feasible than seriatim.[25] Finally, the uncertainty due to ambiguity could be avoided by the learner if it could establish which inputs were parametrically ambiguous and refrain from setting parameters in response to them. Learning would be based solely on unambiguous triggers. However, this too demands parsing with multiple grammars. Parametric ambiguity can be established by parsing with enough grammars to find two that parse the input; nonambiguity can be established only by parsing with all possible grammars and finding no more than one that parses the input. The consensus in sentence processing research is that even adults are capable of only limited parallel parsing if any (see Gibson, 1991), even when the alternative analyses all involve the same grammar. It does not seem plausible to suppose that a two-year-old can apply a billion grammars to each passing sentence.

In summary of section 5.7: we have considered *why* the efficiency of learning procedures such as the TLA is so low, and have found that it is not a trait that can easily be altered. It stems from the idea of putting the parser to work to identify triggers, which seemed like an essential breakthrough but now appears to cramp optimum performance. The inability of the human parser to cope with ambiguity on a large scale has a serious negative consequence for acquisition. It creates uncertainty, which entails indeterminacy of parameter evaluation, which precludes definitive setting of any parameters at all, which leaves the whole pool of grammars to be considered at every point. In other words, the search problem remains exponential because the Parametric Principle cannot be implemented.

To put it differently, we must find some way of imposing the Parametric Principle or else parameter setting is of little interest.

5.8   Structural triggers

Fodor (1998a) argues that parallel grammar testing would be feasible, however large the pool of grammars, if triggers and parameter values were the kinds of things that could be ingredients of grammars and ingredients of trees. If they were suitable ingredients of grammars, they could all be combined into one large grammar (termed a "supergrammar") which the parser could apply to the input in exactly the same way as any other grammar. No unusual parsing activity would be needed, yet all parameter values would be evaluated at once. If parameter values were suitable ingredients of trees, they could be detected in the parse trees output by the parser, so that the learning device would be able to see which of them had contributed to parsing an input sentence and would know which to adopt. What would fit the bill for both purposes is a subtree consisting of just a few nodes and/or feature specifications. A trigger and the parameter value it triggers could then be identical, so that only one innate specification would be needed, rather than linked specifications of parameter values and their triggers (as in cue-based learners; see Lightfoot, 1991). UG would provide a pool of these schematic treelets, one for each parameter value, and each natural language could choose to employ some subset of them. As trigger, a treelet would be detected in the structure of input sentences (i.e., "trigger sentences"). As parameter value, it would then be adopted into the learner's current grammar, and would be available for licensing new sentences.

Consider some examples. For the Complement-final value of the word order parameter for VP, the structural trigger/parameter value might be (178), i.e., a VP subtree with the verb preceding the object. For the Complement-initial value, the treelet would be the mirror image of (178).

(178)

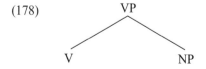

In order to cope with the depth-of-derivation problem (section 5.2), the treelet has to reflect underlying order in any language with that value. Assuming for convenience here that the parser's output is an S-structure tree with movement chains (see note in section 5.3), (178) will reflect underlying order as long as its terminals are not constrained in any way; when the underlying structure has been transformed, either NP or V or both could be traces. Thus (178) would contribute to parsing not only *I despise decaf* but also *Decaf, I despise* with the O moved out of VP, and not only *I have some change* but also *Have you any change?* with the V moved out. More appropriate than (178) as a parameter value is its ultimate source, i.e., whatever is responsible for the presence of (178) in derivations, according to the linguistic theory that is assumed to be correct. In a TAG framework it might be (178) itself; but in HPSG it might be a schematic version of (178) underspecified in terms of syntactic features; in a GB framework it might be a government direction feature of the verb; in the Minimalist Program (though the details are different, on the assumption that the deepest order is universal; see note 5) it might be a weak Agr$_O$ feature that does not attract the object forward for checking. For the purposes of learning, all that is required is that the trigger/parameter value be a piece of a tree; in other respects it is up to linguistic research to determine its properties. We assume that the structural triggers employed by the learner are exactly those elements, whatever they are, that UG specifies as the sources of possible cross-language variation. Some further examples are given for illustrative purposes in (179) and (180). Again, depending on the linguistic theory adopted, the mother-and-daughters configuration might be the real trigger, or it might be an intermediate representation, the true trigger being some ultimately responsible property such as a strong or weak feature value.

(179)   The +V2 trigger/parameter value

or just: C[+FIN] or C[+STRONG] or . . .

(180)   The null subject trigger/parameter value

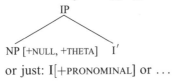

or just: I[+PRONOMINAL] or . . .

These structural triggers make it possible to attain the goal of efficient error-free learning. We now consider more carefully how this is so. We have observed that to set parameters accurately the learner must be able to conduct an exhaustive parse test of every grammar, against each input sentence. To run an exhaustive test the parser must try out all grammars simultaneously and yet be able to attribute success to individual parameters. This could seem to be patently unachievable, but in fact it is straightforward for the Structural Triggers Learner (STL). Suppose that the STL attempts (like the TLA) to parse each input with the current grammar G first. If that fails, it tries again with the supergrammar consisting of G with all UG-provided triggers/parameter values folded into it (or more precisely: all those not yet definitively disconfirmed by the input). Unlike the TLA model, the STL makes crucial use of the structural analyses assigned to strings by the parsing routines. To say that a parse with G fails is not to say that there is no structural output at all. The parser will build as much of the tree as G licenses before it is forced to a halt at the point at which it needs a new parameter value in order to proceed. It will then draw on the pool of treelets provided by UG to find one (or more) to patch the hole in the parse tree. Thus the learning device does not attempt to *spot* the trigger treelets in input sentences. Rather, it *contributes* the triggers to the input, when parsing cannot proceed without them. It knows that a treelet must be in the target grammar if it finds that that treelet and no other can enable an otherwise blocked parse.

But what if an input sentence is parametrically ambiguous? If it is, the supergrammar will define more than one parse tree for it. At some point in the parsing process, therefore, the parser will be faced with a choice between two (or more) analyses. So to detect parametric ambiguity, the parser needs to note when a choice point arises in parsing with the supergrammar, a point at which two (or more) analyses present themselves. If there is no such choice point, the input has just one supergrammar parse. It is parametrically unambiguous, and every parameter value present in the parse tree is correct; the learner should adopt all of them that are not already in G. The same applies to any parameter values involved in the analysis of the sentence prior to a choice point in the parse, since the sentence is unambiguous up to that point.[26] If and when a choice between alternative analyses does arise, there are two strategies the learner might adopt; we will call them the strong and weak strategies. If the parser is capable of pursuing all the possible analyses that present themselves, that can provide useful information. Specifically, if all the parses involve the *same* parameter values, then the sentence is structurally but not para-

Table 5.2. *Examples of STL responses to outcomes of supergrammar parse*

Target grammar	Input	Supergrammar parses	Action	
			Strong STL	Weak STL
a. −V2, SV, OV	Mary me saw	One, with −V2, SV, OV.	Adopt −V2, SV, OV	Adopt −V2, SV, OV
b. +V2, SV, OV	Mary has me seen	Two: both with +V2, OV. (But SV or VS)	Adopt +V2	Discard input
c. +V2, SV, OV	Mary saw me	Five: One with −V2, SV, VO; Four with +V2. (But SV or VS; OV or VO)	Discard input	Discard input

SV = Subject-initial; VS = Subject-final; OV = Complement-initial; VO = Complement-final; +V2 = Verb-second; −V2 = Not verb-second.

metrically ambiguous, and those parameter values can safely be adopted. Or the sentence may be parametrically ambiguous but one parameter value contributes to all of the possible parses; if so, that value is correct (it is essential to the licensing of that sentence) and can safely be adopted. Thus the strong strategy looks for the common denominator across all possible parses: treelets that are present in them all. In this way it extracts the maximum secure information out of the mix of reliable and unreliable parametric cues that natural language sentences typically present.

However, the assumption that the human parsing mechanism is capable of full parallel parsing, for sentences that could be multiply ambiguous, does not square with the empirical evidence on adult sentence processing. As noted above, it seems that even the adult parsing mechanism has little or no capacity for parallel parsing; and children, we presume, have no greater capacity in this respect than adults. So this strong learning strategy is not feasible. The weak strategy employs what is essentially a serial parser and is more realistic. When the parser notes a choice point in a sentence, it selects one analysis to pursue for purposes of comprehension and it ignores all other analyses. But it reports the presence of ambiguity to the learning mechanism, and the learner thereafter adopts no new parameter values on the basis of that sentence. Since it cannot know what parameter values might have been involved in the other parses, had it pursued them, it cannot be certain which values, if any, would be common to all analyses of the string, and so it cannot safely acquire any of them.

Note that in this weak version of the STL, alternative grammars are still tested in parallel, in order to detect and avoid ambiguity, even though the system *does not conduct a parallel parse* of the sentence. There is some parallelism but it is only momentary, as the parser registers the existence of more than one way of attaching the next input word into the tree structure it is building for the sentence. This kind of incipient parallelism is presupposed by any parsing system that selects between alternative analyses on the basis of preference strategies (such as Minimal Attachment). Most importantly, since the alternatives are not pursued in full, there is no consumption of exponential space or time resources even in the worst case; processing load for an ambiguous sentence is little or no greater than that for an unambiguous one. Of course, this parser delivers, in consequence, less information than a fully parallel one does, but we will show that in many circumstances it delivers sufficient for the needs of learning.

In table 5.2 some examples are given of the actions of the STL, strong and weak versions, in response to various outcomes of the supergrammar parse. Only the three parameters studied by Gibson and Wexler are considered in this illustration, so this is an artificially simple domain.

The weak STL does not find out as much about each sentence as the strong STL does, so there are sentences the strong STL can learn from that the weak STL can only discard. But what is important is that the weak STL is able to detect parametric ambiguity reliably, and can therefore avoid being misled by ambiguous inputs. So the weak STL is just as safe as the strong one.[27] What they have in common, and what gives them their ability to cope with parametric ambiguity, is that they approach an input sentence with all UG-permitted grammars at once, each one ready to parse the sentence if called on. This is feasible because these millions of grammars have been compacted into a single grammar, and the parser can call on the individual parameter values separately as and when they are needed to make the parse successful.

The parser the weak STL employs is very modest; it is hard to imagine that the human sentence parsing mechanism could do much less. Nevertheless, the weak STL (henceforth WSTL) can do two things that the TLA— can't do. It can *always* find a new grammar to parse an input for which the current grammar has failed. So it does not waste numerous inputs on a hunt for a successful grammar, as the TLA— does. In section 5.5.1 we wished for an oracle that would whisper to the parser which grammar is worth trying out in the parse test. The supergrammar parse of the STL acts like that oracle. The sentence parsing device is specialized in finding an analysis for a given sentence on the basis of structural resources available to it in the form of a grammar; this is the parser's normal job. Given the supergrammar, which makes all possible resources available, the parser exercises its usual skill, and establishes a parse for every sentence that has one (i.e., every sentence compatible with UG), except only for sentences which outstrip the parser's ability, such as multiple center-embeddings.[28] Second, because the STL knows which inputs are ambiguous it can *avoid guessing*, and so avoid errors, and so avoid having to keep resetting parameters until they are all correct at the same time, as the TLA— must do.

Most importantly, the WSTL obeys the Parametric Principle and reaps all the benefits thereof outlined above. Because the WSTL does not take chances it can set parameters with confidence, so it can be confident enough to discard incorrect values, and cut the size of the subsequent learning problem in half. Note that the WSTL is a true parameter setting device which obtains separate evidence (in the output parse tree) for each parameter involved in the derivation of a sentence.

It does not test grammars as wholes. The successive halving of the learning problem manifests itself in this system as a reduction in the number of alternative parses subsequent sentences will have. This will be high to start with, because all the UG parameter values are available to parse with and offer many alternative sentence structures, but the number will shrink as more and more parameters are set. Thus there is progressive disambiguation of the input as learning proceeds. For the strong STL this means fewer analyses to compute per sentence. Eventually, at the point of convergence on the adult (target) grammar, all sentences will be parametrically unambiguous; the only ambiguity that remains will be any structural ambiguity inherent in the target grammar itself. For the WSTL, the advantage of eliminating wrong parameter values is that the proportion of sentences that are fully unambiguous parametrically will increase as learning proceeds. A sentence that was unusable for acquisition due to ambiguity early on in the learning process could become usable some days or weeks or months later.[29]

We argued in section 5.7 that the Parametric Principle is the only way to defeat the potential exponential complexity of the learning task. Now that we have a true parameter setting device which respects the Parametric Principle, we can put this to the test. In the next section we check to see whether the WSTL does indeed reduce the learning problem to one whose workload is linear in the number of parameters, as Chomsky envisaged.

First, we make one more distinction among models of the STL variety. The WSTL that we have described is very weak. It throws away entirely any sentence that it suspects even might have an ambiguity in it. But the ambiguity might be only temporary. And in any case it does not impugn any part of the sentence preceding the ambiguity point. Even after the ambiguity point, the parser might be able to pick up the thread again and establish that there is only one parse of the final portion regardless of how an ambiguity in the middle of the sentence should have been resolved. What all this means is that there is more information in sentences that a parser (even a serial parser) could dig out if it were less rigidly programmed than we have described for the WSTL. It is this more flexible and opportunistic – though still conservative – system that we believe really models the human learner. We assume the parser finds unambiguous information about trigger treelets in the sentence's structure wherever and however it can, and when it does it informs the learning system. The learner adopts a treelet just in case the parser has solid information that it is necessary for parsing the language. However, this flexible system is more difficult to model mathematically and we will not attempt to do so here. The basic sorts of computations relevant to assessing the performance of the STL will be illustrated here with the weakest model as described above.

5.9   Performance of an STL-like learner

5.9.1   *Number of inputs to convergence for STL*

We are interested in calculating performance measures for the STL. For comparability to the TLA−, we employ the same framework of factors for representing ambiguity and relevance as we did in section 5.5.1, and we make some of the same simplifying background assumptions (section 5.1). We continue to assume (i), (ii) and (iv); (iii) and (vi) are unneeded; and (v) will be revised below. We consider here primarily the performance of a simple inflexible weak STL, as described above. We will comment briefly on the strong STL, which is of theoretical interest but which we do not regard as a plausible model for human learning. Of much more practical interest is the flexible weak variant of the STL which looks for unambiguous trigger properties even in a sentence which is partially ambiguous. This can be expected to learn faster than the simple weak model examined below, which does not even exploit available parametric information prior to an ambiguity in a sentence. Thus, like the relation between the TLA and the TLA− above, our formalization does not do full justice to the system actually proposed as a model of human learning. A more serious simplification in what follows is that we do not attempt to model dynamic aspects of the STL (all variants of). First, since the STL sets parameters with certainty, the input becomes progressively less parametrically ambiguous as learning proceeds. This is just the Parametric Principle at work. Without it, the STL is but a poor shadow of itself. The computations for the dynamically disambiguating system, though along the same lines as those below, would be more complex because of the need to capture the influence of each learning event on the size of the task that remains. A second point to note is that the complexity of a learner's input is likely to increase as learning proceeds (as the child develops). This will affect the rate of expression of parameters (see below), giving typically lower expression rates at the outset of learning where this would be most advantageous. This variable expression rate adds considerable complication to the calculations; it may prove more practical to study this aspect of the STL's performance by means of computer simulation techniques than by mathematical modeling. In the meantime, we establish performance estimates here only for the nondynamic variant, thus underestimating the dynamic STL's chance of encountering an unambiguous trigger, and hence the overall efficiency of STL learning. We will use the term STL− ("STL minus") in what follows to refer to the inflexible, weak version of the model without progressive disambiguation or variable expression in the input.

We now set out some basic calculations relevant to establishing how many sentences the STL− consumes on average before identifying the target grammar. A sentence that is ambiguous with respect to any parameter is discarded by the STL− for learning purposes. We need, therefore, to distinguish now between parametric ambiguity and parametric irrelevance. This was not important in section 5.5 because results for the TLA− are unaffected by it. But it makes a big difference to the STL−. This is because ambiguity with respect to a parameter increases the number of analyses a sentence has, thereby complicating the parser's task and disqualifying the sentence for learning, while irrelevance of a parameter to a sentence adds nothing to parsing complexity and does not impinge on what can be learned from the sentence about other parameter settings.

Consider, to start with, how learning will proceed if every parameter is relevant to every sentence (equivalently: every sentence expresses every parameter). In this case, all parameter values for the language will be established by a single sentence, the first unambiguous one encountered by the STL−. If every input sentence in the language is ambiguous with respect to at least a parameters, for $a > 0$, then learning is impossible. If, on the other hand, even one sentence in the input sample is parametrically *un*ambiguous, it will set all of the parameters and learning will be complete; no further inputs will be needed. The probability of encountering an unambiguous trigger in the input sample is thus the only factor of interest. For this we must define what we will call a degree of unambiguity, u, which is the proportion of sentences in the language that are fully unambiguous parametrically.

For comparability to the calculations for the TLA−, we will set u to the same value as in our second example at the end of section 5.5.1. We supposed there that 10 percent of inputs are parametrically unambiguous, i.e., that $u = 1/10$. Note that the degree of parametric ambiguity of the other 90 percent of sentences is not pertinent to the outcome for the STL− under the assumptions in place here (i.e., no learning takes place in response to ambiguous inputs; all parameters are expressed by every sentence). The only influence the ambiguity level could have, under present assumptions, is on the failure rate of the current grammar G, as noted in section 5.5.1 above; but this is masked here by the fact that grammar change is limited to a single shift to the correct grammar. Below, we show that the degree of ambiguity does enter in more interesting ways into the efficiency profile of the STL– under other more natural conditions.[30]

Given $u = 1/10$, and a representative sample of the language (as assumed throughout), the probability of encountering an unambiguous trigger is $1/10$, and the average number of sentences to convergence is therefore $1/u = 1/(1/10) = 10/1 = 10$ (regardless of how many parameters need to be set). For smaller u this rises proportionately; for example, if there are only 15 unambiguous triggers on average in every 10,000 input sentences, then $u = 15/10,000$, and so $10,000/15 = 667$ inputs are needed on average for convergence. Of course, this is not a psychologically realistic situation: as we have described it, nothing happens until suddenly the whole language is learned in one event. It is also not a linguistically realistic situation, since it is not usual for natural language sentences to express every parameter relevant to the language. For example, whatever parameter governs the acceptability or nonacceptability of multiple (overt) A'-movement (e.g., WH-fronting) in a clause will be irrelevant to any sentence without overt A'-movement, even if the target language as a whole exhibits overt A'-movement.[31] Up to now our calculations have not distinguished the number of parameters relevant to a sentence from the number of parameters relevant to the language. For example, in section 5.5.1 we assumed that $r = 25$ parameters were relevant to the target language, out of the $n = 30$ total parameters; and the value of a included not only parameters expressed ambiguously by a sentence, but also parameters not expressed by the sentence though relevant to the language as a whole (see note 8). Hence, an independent measure of parameters relevant to individual sentences was not needed. Now, however, we identify what we will call the expression rate for the target language, e, which is the number of parameters expressed by an input sentence. For simplicity, we will assume here (not realistically) that e is the same for all target sentences. The expression rate e contrasts with r, defined above, which is the number of parameters that are relevant to the whole target language.

To illustrate the effect of e, let us temporarily set $a = 0$ (i.e., no ambiguously expressed parameters), and let us set $e = 6$, with $n = 30$ and $r = 25$ as before. Now, a sentence expresses only 6 of the 25 parameters that need to be set, and it expresses them all unambiguously. The learner has to encounter enough batches of six parameter values, possibly (in fact, probably) overlapping with each other, to make up the full set of 25 parameter values that have to be

Table 5.3. *Average number of inputs consumed by STL— before convergence. All input sentences unambiguous.*

e	r = 15	20	25	30
1	50	72	95	120
5	9	13	18	23
10	4	6	8	11
15	1	3	5	6
20	–	1	3	4

established. So convergence is gradual, not a one-step process as above. Let $P(w|t, r, e)$ be the probability that an input sentence provides unambiguous evidence concerning w new (i.e., as yet unset) parameters, given that the learner has already set t parameters (correctly), for some r and e as defined above. In what follows, we will take r and e as given, and refer to this simply as $P(w|t)$. Note that $P(w|t)$ is in effect the probability that the STL— will add w new parameter values (treelets) to its current grammar on a given input, given that it had previously adopted t parameters. We present the formula for $P(w|t)$ in section 5.11; the details are not important here. Note that w will vary between 0 and e, and t will increase over time from 0 to r. $P(0|t)$ corresponds to success of the current grammar G on the current input, so this does not need to be separately calculated here (see section 5.11). The STL— is a memoryless system, like the TLA—, and so it can be modeled by means of a Markov chain (see section 5.5), which in turn can be cast as a probability transition matrix consisting of the values of $P(w|t)$ as learning progresses. In section 5.11 we outline the required matrix operations, which yield average numbers of inputs to convergence. Here, we present outcomes only.

Given a fully unambiguous target language with the values above, the necessary size of the input sample is 15. Table 5.3 gives expected sample sizes for other values of r, for different values of e, with no ambiguity. As expected, the fewer parameters expressed per sentence (the lower the value of e), the more input is needed to set them all. However, even for low expression rates the sample sizes are all quite small, and they are not exponential in r. If we consider the mean cost per parameter (in terms of number of inputs needed) we see that it increases very slightly for higher numbers of parameters; thus, it is almost (though not quite!) linear in the number of parameters needing to be set (see section 5.8). Note that even in the worst case here, four inputs are needed per parameter. (This contrasts with the exponential rise in table 5.1, where for unambiguous input the cost per parameter increases many thousandfold from 15 parameters to 30 parameters.) This performance reflects the fact that the STL−, with its "supergrammar" parsing ability, has no trouble identifying a grammar that licenses an input. Thus, unlike the TLA−, it does not have to discard potentially useful inputs just for inability to find a grammar that satisfies Greediness.

On the other hand, the STL− (unlike the TLA−) does discard sentences that fail its nonambiguity criterion. So now we must factor in the cost of ambiguity. Recall that for the TLA− we observed a potentially exponential cost of parametric ambiguity at stage II which was offset by improvement at stage I with respect to satisfaction of Greediness. For the STL− also we will see that there is a significant cost of ambiguity − not because ambiguity breeds errors in this case, but because the *avoidance* of ambiguity effectively limits a conservative learner like the STL− to just a portion of the input.

It is unimportant for the STL− *how* ambiguous an ambiguous sentence is. All that matters is how many unambiguous sentences there are in the learner's sample, and how much information each one provides. Let us retain $e = 6$, and let us suppose, as we did earlier, that 90 percent of sentences contain some ambiguity, by which we now mean that for each sentence in that 90 percent, at least one of the $e = 6$ parameters it expresses is expressed ambiguously. Then $u = 1/10$, and only the unambiguous 10 percent of the input sentences are usable for learning. So: on average, an unambiguous input occurs once every 10 inputs and brings information about 6 parameters. Calculating on these assumptions (see $P'(w|t)$ in section 5.11) we obtain an expected sample size of 150 (= ten times larger than with $u = 1$, all sentences unambiguous). If only 1 percent of sentences were unambiguous, the learner would need 1,500 inputs for convergence. Thus it's clear that as u declines, the number of sentences needed mounts in proportion. Let us consider this further. We know that if $u = 0$, learning is impossible for the STL−. Now we want to consider some other levels of unambiguity that could reasonably be expected for natural language, and compute the input sample sizes they call for.

In fact it is possible, given an average degree of parametric ambiguity and an expression rate, to calculate the probable distribution of unambiguous sentences in the target sample, rather than just stipulating a value for u as we have so far. What we establish is the chance that all the parameters expressed by some sentence happen to be expressed unambiguously, given the incidence of ambiguity in

Table 5.4. *Average number of inputs consumed by STL− before convergence. Ambiguous input.*

e	a (%)	$r = 15$	20	25	30
1	20	62	90	119	150
	40	83	120	159	200
	60	124	180	238	300
	80	249	360	477	599
5	20	27	40	55	69
	40	115	171	230	292
	60	871	1,296	1,747	2,218
	80	27,885	41,472	55,895	70,983
10	20	34	54	76	98
	40	604	964	1,342	1,738
	60	34,848	55,578	77,397	100,193
	80	35,683,968	56,912,149	79,254,943	102,597,823
15	20	28	91	135	181
	40	2,127	6,794	10,136	13,545
	60	931,323	2,975,115	4,438,464	5,931,148
	80	over 30 billion	. . .	. . .	almost 200 billion
20	20		87	256	366
	40		27,351	80,601	115,415
	60		90,949,470	268,017,383	383,783,455
	80		. . . in the trillions . . .		

general. Recall that this is what really matters to STL− performance. Once the pattern of unambiguity has been established for the language in this way, we can determine from it (via an adaptation of $P(w|t)$; see section 5.11) what the total sample size must be in order for all parameters to be correctly set. For brevity we will not present these calculations here. Table 5.4 relates expected sample size directly to the ambiguity and expression rates. Note that in table 5.4, a denotes the average number of ambiguously expressed parameters in a sentence as a percentage of the number of parameters expressed by that sentence (in section 5.5, a represented a constant number of ambiguous parameters in a sentence).

As before, the number of parameters to be set has relatively little effect. For this learner, the factors that dominate learning speed are the degree of ambiguity and the expression rate. When both ambiguity and expression rate are high, unambiguous inputs are very scarce. This is to be expected. Clearly, there is little chance of encountering a fully un-ambiguous sentence if every sentence expresses 24 parameters and the probability that each parameter is ambiguous is 99 percent (the probability would be $(1/100)^{24}$). As a result, for high e and a there are very few sentences that the learner can make use of, so the expected sample size is enormous, as can be seen in table 5.4. The effect of e is interesting. For ambiguous input it differs from the case of zero (or very low) ambiguity as in table 5.3. As e increases (holding the degree of ambiguity constant), it is rarer for the learner to encounter fully unambiguous triggers. Also, as e increases, the average payoff per unambiguous sentence improves: more parameter settings are acquired. The results here make clear, however, that the improved yield per sentence does not compensate for the longer wait between usable sentences.

The impact of ambiguity is also very sharp. Increasing ambiguity raises the sample size needed into several hundreds of thousands of sentences, and then into billions at the top end of the numerical scales considered here. This certainly does not look promising as an improvement on TLA-type models. Evidently, it can be even less efficient to wait for an un-ambiguous trigger than to cope with the errors that result from guessing on ambiguous ones. However, that is not true across the board. Fortunately, the generally severe effect of ambiguity is absent at lower expression rates. We see that humble sentences which reveal only a few parameter values are the most useful for a learner seeking reliable in-formation. This is important because expression rate is the one factor that might plausibly be low in real life learning. That a high degree of parametric ambiguity is characteristic of natural languages seems undeni-able. And, though linguistic research might prove otherwise, it seems vain to hope that the number of syntactic parameters will be reduced to less than a dozen. So there is not much prospect of a breakthrough in learning efficiency due to a reduction of either a or r. But it does seem within the realms of possibility that the expression rate for natural languages is as low as half a dozen parameters per sentence, particularly at the early stages of learning where the threat of parametric ambiguity is probably at its greatest.[32] It is encouraging, therefore, to find that in the Structural Triggers framework, a reduction in the expression rate has a beneficial effect on learning speed.

5.9.2   General assessment of the STL

Our calculations have illustrated some important facts about conserva-tive learning that relies on unambiguous structural triggers, at least for the rather undernourished version of the model that we have been able to formalize here. We see that the problem of finding a grammar that satisfies Greediness has dissolved. We see that performance is fairly constant up through large language domains with many parameters to be set. Of course, we have not demonstrated here that the needed sample size would not explode for domains with more than 30 parameters, but there is nothing in the mathematics to suggest that it will. (Concerned readers may check for themselves.) On the other hand, the problem of extracting trustworthy information from partially ambiguous input looms even larger than it did in section 5.5. We have found that to rely exclusively on unambiguous triggers is simply not feasible except at low expression rates. But at least it does appear to be feasible there. Though the worst case for the STL− is very bad indeed, there is also a more favorable region in which performance is efficient even for a sizeable number of parameters to be set. As long as there are sentences for which only a few parameters are relevant, the learner will have a good chance of encountering unambiguous triggers and converging rapidly on the target.

Whether this is so in real-life learning must be determined by empirical research. But as we have noted, the prospects seem tolerably good. It seems reasonable to suppose that learners, especially early learners, do not mostly encounter sentences that exhibit every syntactic phenomenon in the language, packed into three or four words or so. There are early child-directed sentences that contain negation, or overt WH-movement, or a subordinate clause, but probably few that involve them all, and those few the learner might ignore. We note for the record that the assumption that early input expresses fewer parameters per sentence than input to older children or adults constitutes a weakening of assumption (ii) above, which posits homogeneous input over time; that assumption has been convenient but is surely oversimplistic. In any case, even if the sentences directed to the child (or audible by the child) were independent of the child's stage of development, what the child is able to grasp and make use of almost certainly does increase with age.

These interesting possibilities are not captured by the computational results presented here, which have ignored completely the dynamic aspects of the STL. The latter will assist in pulling the learner down into the favorable zone in which the expression rate is low and the supply of unambiguous trigger sentences improves. Because the STL actually sets parameters, in accord with the Parametric Principle, every successful learning event decreases the number of parameters still to be set. To set up the mathematics for this we would need to change r to a variable whose value reflects the reduction, over time, in the number of parameters remaining to be set. Likewise, for a dynamic treatment we would need to replace *e* with a variable reflecting how many of the *parameters that remain to be set* are expressed by a sentence; only these parameters need to be expressed unambiguously in order for the input to qualify as unambiguous and usable as a trigger. It follows that, if the input were uniform, the probability of encountering an unambiguous trigger would rise as learning proceeds. The major concern for the STL is therefore to establish that there are sufficient unambiguous triggers to get parameter setting started, so that the Parametric Principle can then begin to shift the learner down into more comfortable regions of parametric expression where unambiguous triggers are more plentiful. Note that an ideal environment for the STL− would be one in which the number of novel (= previously unset) parameters expressed per sentence is roughly constant (and quite low) across the learning period. This means that the expression rate *e*, as it has been defined here (including parameters already set and not yet set), would ideally start low, but can increase without detriment to learning if it keeps pace with the proportion of parameters the learner has already mastered. An interesting speculation that might be empirically investigated is that one of the reasons why second language learning is apparently more arduous for adults than for children is that adults may be exposed early on to complex sentences that express too many novel parameter values.

The working out of this and many other aspects of STL performance must await further research. The STL offers two potential advantages for a learner, both due to its use of parameter value treelets to parse with. One is a virtually waste-free means of decoding sentences into the parameter values that license them, at stage I. The other is a test for parametric ambiguity. The value of the first seems unassailable. The value of the second is less evident, because recognizing ambiguity at stage I is only useful for purposes of discarding ambiguous stimuli before they engender errors at stage II, yet it appears that discarding them might be hardly more efficient than guessing at random. It is imaginable, then, that the optimal model would parse inputs as the STL does but respond to ambiguity as the TLA does (see Fodor, 1998c). On the other hand, the power of the treelet parsing procedure gives considerable scope for shaping up the STL system, in ways we have suggested and perhaps others too. Our best conjecture at present is that a more substantial analysis of it than we have been able to present here will show that it has considerable resilience to ambiguity. As we have noted, the main points yet to be undertaken are the formalization of the progressive disambiguation of triggers as parameters are set, an estimate of expression rates at the onset of learning, and an assessment of the parser's ability to extract as much reliable parametric information as possible from partially ambiguous inputs. Also, for the STL as for the TLA, it is important to keep an eye on the uniformity of learning success, by considering worst-case outcomes rather than just the average outcomes studied here.

5.10   Implications for linguistic research

How much work does it take to acquire a human language? Less than if grammars must be composed from scratch by hypothesis formation. But more, it seems, than was anticipated in early conceptions of parameter setting. The recent research that has developed explicit models of the parameter setting process has exposed some serious threats to the central idea, which was that acquiring one of 2^n grammars can be reduced to acquiring the values of n parameters. When the process of setting the n parameters is implemented, the workload shows a strong tendency toward an exponential *expansion* back to a cost proportional to the 2^n grammars. Efforts to beat this re-expansion can be seen as the impetus behind a number of interesting proposals for learning algorithms, such as the Genetic Algorithm of Clark (1992) and the cue-based models of Lightfoot (1991) and Dresher (1999). The Structural Triggers model aims to achieve this while respecting plausible capacity limits on the psychological mechanisms involved: no complex linguistic reasoning is required (in contrast to some versions of cue-based learning), no multiple parsing of each stimulus (in contrast to genetic algorithms), storage of outcomes is only by parameter not by grammar (also unlike genetic algorithms). Like many, but not all, other models it is also intended to be compatible with the absence of systematic negative evidence (direct or indirect), at most degree-1 input, and the severe restriction to learning from individual sentences without cross-sentence comparisons. Time will tell whether this can actually be pulled off. If so, language acquisition will be nearly effortless, as Chomsky proposed, though no longer a matter of just flipping switches.[33]

For linguistics there are tasks and conclusions, the most welcome conclusion being that – if our optimism is justified – a principles-and-parameters theory of UG does indeed fit nicely within a psychologically plausible performance model. The tasks for linguistics are of a kind that have been being given increasing attention in recent work: constant rethinking of the actual set of parameters and the way it organizes the space of language phenomena (see, for example, Frank and Kapur, 1996); and identification of unambiguous triggers for setting them. The STL puts especially heavy demands on the latter, since a trigger for parameter p_i must be unambiguous not only with respect to p_i but with respect to all other as-yet-unset parameters that are expressed by it. On the other hand, the STL does not demand that there be one simple, superficially identifiable cue property associated with each parameter value. The observable consequences of a parameter value may be extremely varied, as it interacts with other parameter values in derivations. As long as there is, somewhere in the derivation, a distinctive contribution from that parameter value, the STL will find it.

The one essential condition is that each parameter value be definable as (or inherently associated with) an ingredient of tree structures. Only this permits the efficient use of the parsing mechanism to decode sentences into their contributing parameter values. This is the most eccentric aspect of the STL among learning models, but it is very much in keeping with current linguistic theories, both transformational and monostratal.[34] In theories emphasizing phrase structure mechanisms, such as HPSG and TAG theory, there is little explicit talk of parameters, but it has always been natural to think of what differentiates one language from another as being a type of subtree, made available by UG, which is used in generating sentences in one language but not in another. How large a chunk of tree is involved, and whether it is underspecified or defined in full detail, differs between theories. The elementary trees of a TAG grammar are quite large and richly endowed (Joshi, 1987); the rule schemata that define treelets in HPSG specify just a small handful of syntactic feature values (Pollard and Sag, 1994).

GB theory was the original locus of parameters as switches, but has undergone an interesting transition from what we will call *freestanding* parameters to parameters as syntactic features, the limiting case of treelets. The earlier view is described by Clark and Roberts (1993). They write "A parameter can be thought of as a descriptive statement that may be either true or false of a given grammatical system" and give as example the statement "IP is a bounding node for Subjacency." This example also qualifies under a similar but more restricted characterization of parameters as points of variation in UG principles, or in the definitions that feed the principles. Another example is the proposal by Wexler and Manzini (1987) of five possible values for a variable in the definition of *governing category*, which feeds Binding Principles A and B. Another descriptive parametric statement is "Wh-movement occurs at Logical Form (and at S-structure)" in which the parentheses mark a parametric option (see Huang, 1981; Lasnik and Saito, 1984). This also counts as a prime example of a phase in which parameters offered choices as to the linguistic level at which certain constraints must be met, which led into the current concept of strong and weak syntactic features in the Minimalism framework (see below).

Constraints, definitions and levels of derivation are not building blocks of trees, so these early characterizations of parameters do not permit STL learning. Or at least, in order for them to do so there would need to be, in addition to an innate formulation of a parameter value, an innate specification of a treelet guaranteed to be present in sentence structures when and only when the parameter value in question is instantiated. But at about the same time, a conception of parameterization as directly concerned with the properties of elements in tree structures was emerging in the GB framework in work such as that by Rizzi (1982) and Hyams (1986, 1989) on the null subject parameter. It was proposed that a null subject is licensed by a pronominal feature of INFL. This clearly does lend itself to STL parameter setting. The positive value of the null subject parameter could be the treelet $I^0[+\text{pron}]$, and the negative value would be $I^0[-\text{pron}]$. Hyams (1989) shows (in an older notation) the treelets in (181); (181a) is for English and (181b) is for Italian. In (181b) the agreement features (AG) of INFL constitute the ungoverned empty category PRO.

(181)   a.   INFL   b.   INFL

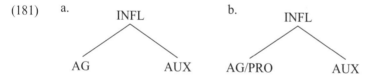

         AG   AUX   AG/PRO   AUX

These treelets for the null subject parameter make no mention of subjects, but that is appropriate since the claim is that the acceptability of null subjects is just one of a number of observable consequences of the treelet in (181b) as it interacts with UG principles in derivations.[35] This trend towards parameter values as structural elements (in the simplest case, a single feature specification) that are present in sentence derivations is embraced in the Minimalist Program of Chomsky (1995) where strong features of functional heads drive all overt movement operations.

Thus it seems that there is some significant convergence between the needs of efficient language learning and the conclusions of linguistic research. Linguistic theory need not be bent into unnatural forms to suit the learning device. We propose the following general characterization of parameters and triggers as most compatible with both linguistic theory and learnability concerns: a natural language parameter is the option of adopting a structural trigger into a grammar. A structural trigger is a partial tree that is made available by UG and is adopted into a learner's grammar if and only if it proves essential in parsing input sentences.

Exercises

Note that exercises designed for students with some mathematical expertise are marked (M); those which presuppose some knowledge of linguistics are marked (L). Some of the later questions are open-ended and could be the basis for research projects.

5.1   A nondeterministic learning device such as the TLA− may mis-set a parameter and have to reset it later.

(a) Using the background assumptions and numerical estimates of section 5.5.1, compute R = how many times the TLA− resets the same parameter on average before convergence. Note: you will need to estimate how many parameters on average the TLA− resets each time it changes grammars.

(b) Give the general formula for R for any number r of relevant parameters and any degree a of average parametric ambiguity.

(c) Graph the value of R relative to a and relative to r.

5.2   The probability tree in figure 5.1 gives the probability of attaining the target grammar in one step (one input sentence). Assume a learning domain of four languages (two binary parameters).

(a) Construct a Markov state diagram (as in section 5.11) depicting the transitions from one nontarget state to another (including itself), as well as from a nontarget state to the target.

(b) (M) Use the state diagram to construct a transition matrix, and calculate from it the fundamental matrix Q (as in section 5.11) and the average number of inputs needed for convergence by the TLA−.

For a readable presentation of Absorbing Markov Systems, see Waner and Costenoble (1996).

5.3   Assume as in section 5.5.1 that 25 parameters are relevant to the target language, and that all parameters are expressed (though perhaps ambiguously) by all sentences.

(a) Calculate the average number of sentences required for convergence by the TLA– for some more varied distributions of parametric ambiguity. For example: 10 percent of sentences unambiguous, 60 percent of sentences ambiguous with respect to 8 parameters each, 30 percent of sentences ambiguous with respect to 20 parameters each.

(b) Discuss informally (or calculate if you can, using Markov modeling; see exercise 5.2 and section 5.11), how these ambiguity distributions would affect the performance of the STL (weak or strong). For manageability, assume a low degree of parametric relevance and a low expression rate, e.g., $r = 5$, $e = 2$.

5.4   Suppose the prosodic contours of sentences provide learners with information about the surface bracketing (phrase structure) of every sentence (though not bracket labels). Assume also, as throughout this chapter, that the learner can recognize subject, verb and object, and other basic grammatical relations.

(a) (L) How much assistance would this be in setting the word-order parameters?

(b) (L) Are there other syntactic parameters it would be helpful for?

(c) How much more efficient would word-order learning be if learners had access to bracket labels also?

(d) To what extent would word-order learning be facilitated if learners could rely on implicational universals (such as "If the pronominal object follows the verb, so does the nominal object" or "Languages with dominant VSO order are prepositional, not postpositional") as proposed by Greenberg (1966), Hawkins (1983)?

For linguistic background on this question, read Nespor, Guasti and Christophe (1996); for mathematical background, read Levy and Joshi (1978).

5.5   For the null subject parameter the depth-of-derivation problem does not arise: the fact that there is no overt subject in a sentence is a fact about its surface structure (as well as its underlying structure). But the string-to-structure problem can be seen in examples such as (i) and (ii).

(i) Maria mangiava le olive e beveva il vino.
   "Maria ate the olives and drank the wine."

(ii) Maria ate the olives and drank the wine.

The Italian and English sentences mean essentially the same, but there is a structural ambiguity in the Italian (not in the English). The ambiguity in (i) is between a conjunction of verb phrases (technically, I-bars) with only one subject position in the sentence, as shown in (iii), and a conjunction of clauses with a null subject in the second one, as shown in (iv). In the latter case, assume the subjects of the two conjuncts are co-indexed.

(iii)

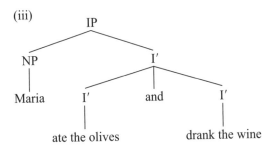

(iv)

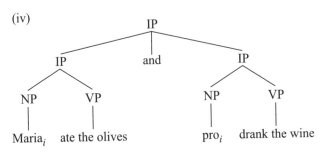

(a) (L) Try to establish which analysis is normally imposed on the word string (i) by native speakers of Italian. What linguistic tests (syntactic, semantic or prosodic) distinguish the two structures?

(b) (L) Would a learner be able to recognize which structure the word string (i) or (ii) has in the target language?

(c) Suppose structure (iii) is what the human parser prefers to compute when it has the choice. If learners imposed this structure on (i) or (ii), what consequences would this have for the learning of Italian? of English?

(d) Suppose instead that structure (iv) is preferred by the parser. What would the consequences be for the learning of Italian? of English?

(e) (L) Consider comparable questions for the word strings (v) and (vi), or any other examples you can construct of word strings that are ambiguous with respect to the null subject parameter (besides imperatives, and sentences in informal or diary register such as *Went home early. Forgot to buy chicken.*: see Haegeman, 1990).

(v) The policeman warned the woman that didn't have a valid driver's license.

(vi) Is John my friend (punctuation suppressed here)

For references on the null subject parameter, see note 4.

5.6   Consider a language L which has a variety of surface word orders, in a domain of languages such that each word order in L is the only permitted word order in some other language in the domain.

(a) Under what assumptions about the learning device would L and other languages in the domain be learnable?

(b) Are these assumptions plausible for human language learners?

(c) (L) Is there any reason to believe that the domain of natural languages has this character?

5.7   Natural language sentences are often structurally ambiguous even when generated by a fixed target grammar. For example, *He fed her dog biscuits* is ambiguous within English. For a constant degree of parametric ambiguity, estimate the effect of the degree of structural ambiguity within the target language on the performance of:

(a) the TLA or TLA−;

(b) a structural triggers learner with full parallel parsing capacity (a "strong STL");

(c) the weak STL (with a flagged serial parser).

(d) With *no* structural ambiguity, every target string is associated with exactly one target structure. It is presupposed for (a), (b) and (c), that structural ambiguity within the target is increased by increasing the number of associations between target strings and target structures, not by extending the set of target structures. Hence, parametric ambiguity is not thereby increased. Reconsider the answers to (a), (b) and (c) without this assumption.

5.8   (M) A strict hill-climbing learner adopts a hypothesis only if it offers improvement over the previous one (e.g., in terms of syntactic parameters: only if the resulting grammar has more parameter values in common with the target grammar than the previous grammar did). It has been shown (Berwick and Niyogi, 1996) that the TLA is not in fact a strict hill climber for arbitrary language domains.

(a) Are there domains in which the TLA does perform hill climbing? If so, what are their characteristics? For example: Can they contain parametric ambiguity? Is smoothness essential?

(b) Is the SVC essential? Is the TLA− a hill climber?

(c) Assume an error-driven learner which is a strict hill climber (regardless, for now, of how this is implemented), operating in an ambiguous domain. How does the number of input sentences between grammar-changes vary as a function of how close the learner is to success (i.e., how few parameters remain to be set)?

5.9   Start with the TLA. Add a recording device that keeps a running tally, for each parameter value, of how often a grammar containing it succeeds in parsing an input sentence.

(a) How accurate is this as a guide to whether a given parameter value is in the target grammar?

(b) How does its reliability vary with the degree of parametric ambiguity in the language domain?

(c) Would it be more useful or less useful to keep count, instead, of how often a parameter value being tested (in the sense of its being the one novel value in the grammar that the parser tries out after failure of the current grammar on some input sentence) is adopted?

(d) Given some such ranking of the frequency of success of each parameter value, how could the learner most profitably employ it in deciding which parameter to reset next? By a strategy of always switching to the highest-ranked parameter value not in the current grammar? By switching to a parameter value that is ranked much higher than the current value of that same parameter? By switching to higher ranked values with probabilities proportional to their relative advantage over others?

(e) Would any such strategy be useful for a parameter that is expressed only rarely in the target language? For example, the parameter that determines subject-auxiliary inversion in English imperatives when both subject and auxiliary are overt, which is quite rare; e.g., *Don't you touch that!*

Relevant reading: Clark (1992), Kapur (1994), Nyberg (1992).

5.10   (M) For the TLA−, with the numerical estimates of section
        5.5.1, compute the number of inputs necessary for the learner
        to identify the target with confidence greater than 50 percent,
        75 percent, 90 percent, and 99 percent. For the relevant mathe-
        matics, see Chung (1979).

5.11   Discuss whether average rates of convergence, or convergence
        at high degrees of confidence, is the more appropriate criterion
        for evaluating models of natural language learning.

5.11   Appendix

5.11.1   Time to first success

The "time to first success" of a series of independent success/failure
events is distributed geometrically where the expected value of the
number of trials (until the first success occurs) is simply the reciprocal
of the probability of success.

For example we could ask: on average, how many rolls does it take
to get a "6" on a six-sided die? The expected value, E, of the number
of die rolls required is:

$$E(\#\text{rolls}) = \sum_{i=1}^{\infty} iP(\neg 6)^{i-1}P(6)$$

Expanding this out we get:

$$E(\#\text{rolls}) = 1P(6) + 2P(\neg 6)P(6) + 3P(\neg 6)P(\neg 6)P(6) \ldots$$

where $P(6)$ is the probability of rolling a 6 and $P(\neg 6)$ is the probability of rolling something other than a 6. Note that $P(\neg 6)P(\neg 6)P(6)$ is
the probability that a 6 was rolled on the third roll (preceded by two
failed rolls). Solving this series (see Chung, 1979, for a good
description), we achieve the compact formula $1/P(6)$. Assuming a
"fair" die (all outcomes equally probable) and plugging in, we get:

$$E(\#\text{rolls}) = 1/(1/6) = 6$$

In general,

$$E(\text{time to success}) = 1/P(\text{success})$$

5.11.2   Calculations for the STL−: expected sample size to convergence

We present here one method for arriving at the expected size of the
input sample consumed by the STL−. This approach is related to dis-

cussions in the literature by Niyogi and Berwick (1996) and else-where.[36]

Assuming all input sentences are unambiguous, $P(w|t)$ can be thought of in terms of the following "urn problem":

There are 25 balls in an urn, of which t are black and $25 - t$ are white. We draw 6 balls. What's the probability that we'll have drawn exactly w white balls? It is equal to the number of ways we can draw w balls from the $25 - t$ white balls in the urn, times the number of ways we can draw $6 - w$ black balls from the t black ones in the urn, divided by the total number of ways we can draw 6 balls from 25. That is:

$$P(w|t) = \frac{\binom{25 - t}{w}\binom{t}{6 - w}}{\binom{25}{6}}$$

where

$$\binom{x}{y}$$

denotes the number of ways of choosing y items from a collection of x items. In general:

$$P(w|t) = \frac{\binom{r - t}{w}\binom{t}{e - w}}{\binom{r}{e}}$$

where e is the number chosen at each drawing and r is the number of balls in the urn.

Now we can ask the question that is really of interest. Start out with all r balls in the urn being white (corresponding to "unset" parameters). After drawing e balls, we paint them black ("set them") and return them to the urn. How many times do we need to draw before all the balls are black ("set")? We can use the states of a Markov system modeling the STL− (or the urn scheme above) to depict the number of parameters that have already been set. The system starts in state S_0 and on the first input (with no ambiguity) moves to state S_e. It may stay in state S_e or move on the next step to state $S_{e+1}, S_{e+2}, S_{e+3} \ldots S_{2e}$. This is illustrated in figure 5.3.

The probabilities of making the state transitions are calculated by plugging appropriate values into $P(w|t, e, r)$. The results can also be presented in matrix form, as in table 5.5.

Table 5.5. *A sample transition matrix for an STL− learner, where r = 5, e = 2 and no ambiguity.*

| | | TO: number of parameters set after an input $(t + w)$ | | | |
		2	3	4	5
FROM:	0	1.0	0	0	0
number of	2	0.1	0.6	0.3	0
parameters	3	0	0.3	0.6	0.1
currently	4	0	0	0.6	0.4
set	5	0	0	0	1.0

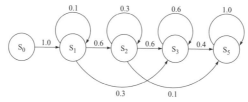

Figure 5.3 A Markov state diagram for an STL− learner, where $r = 5$, $e = 2$ and no ambiguity.

If we assume that the STL− in figure 5.3 has already set three parameters, then after receiving an input:

(i) it may not be able to set any additional parameters, or
(ii) it may be able to set one additional parameter, or
(iii) it sets two new parameters.

Thus, the probability of the STL− changing from having set three parameters to four is $P(1|3, 2, 5) = 0.6$.

Since the STL− is error-driven, once it has set all relevant parameters (i.e. once it achieves state S_r) it stays in state S_r. Markov chains that have absorbing or "sink" states such as this are referred to as absorbing systems.

A well-known result from Markov chain theory is that the fundamental submatrix of a transition matrix yields the waiting time of an absorbing system. The fundamental matrix Q is defined by means of an inverse function applied to the identity matrix, I (= 1 on the diagonal, 0 elsewhere), minus the (sub)matrix, N, that gives the transition probabilities of the nonsink state(s). That is:

$$Q = \text{inverse}(I - N)$$

Table 5.6. *The fundamental matrix Q for an STL–*
learner, where r = 5, e = 2 and there is no
ambiguity.

1	1.1111	0.9524	2.2619
	1.1111	0.9524	2.2619
		1.4286	2.1429
			2.5000

Deriving N from the matrix in table 5.5 above gives Q as in table 5.6. The sum of the first row of Q yields the average number of inputs required for the STL– starting in state S_0 (no parameters have been set), to enter the absorbing state S_5 (all parameters have been set). That sum here equals 5.3254.

In order to deal with ambiguity, we will change the definition of $P(w|t,e,r)$. We refer here to the new formula as $P'(w|t,e,e',r)$. Also, we use u' to refer to the probability that *all* e parameters expressed by a sentence are expressed unambiguously, given that on average e' parameters are expressed unambiguously per sentence. The probability that any one parameter is unambiguously expressed is e'/e. The probability that e parameters are unambiguously expressed is therefore $(e'/e)^e$. This is u'. We are now in a position to give the definition of $P'(w|t,e,e',r)$.

$$P'(w|t,e,e',r) = \begin{cases} (1-u') + P(w|t,e,r)u' & \text{if } w = 0 \\ P(w|t,e,r)u' & \text{otherwise} \end{cases}$$

For values of w other than 0, the probability of setting w new parameters is simply the probability that the sentence is usable for learning (i.e., all e parameters are unambiguously expressed $(= u')$) times the probability that w of those e parameters were previously unset $(= P(w|t,e,r))$. The probability of setting 0 parameters (i.e., $w = 0$) is the probability that not all e parameters are unambiguously expressed $(= 1 - u')$ plus the probability that even if the e parameters are unambiguously expressed $(= u')$ all of them had already been set $(= P(w = 0|t,e,r))$.

In calculating the transition matrix (as in figure 5.3) for the STL– operating in an ambiguous domain we substitute P' for P.

NOTES

1 We would like to thank Stefano Bertolo, Partha Niyogi and Cullen Schaffer for interesting discussion and technical advice on this work.

2 Chomsky (1981a) introduces the notation of parameters informally. Chomsky (1986) attributes to James Higginbotham the image of setting parametric switches. Atkinson (1987) offers conceptual clarification on the relation between triggering and other modes of learning. Clark (1994a: 478) observes: "Our folk-theoretic intuition, then, is that each parameter is associated with a trigger that *automatically* causes the learner to set a parameter to some value *immediately* upon exposure to it" (our emphases). Gibson and Wexler (1994) give a formal definition of *trigger* and of a learning procedure (see below) which they refer to as triggering but which does not reflect the familiar switch-setting metaphor.

3 Prosodic phrasing may be more directly perceptible, and could help learners establish phrase structure. See Mazuka (1996), Nespor, Guasti and Christophe (1996), and papers in Morgan and Demuth (1996).

4 The null subject parameter has attracted attention because it presents the opposite problem concerning reliability of evidence: some sentences that clearly lack overt subjects should not trigger the null subject setting. See Hyams (1986, 1994b), Valian (1990), and references given there. Also see exercise 5.5 at the end of this chapter.

5 In theories such as that of Kayne (1994) there is no variation in underlying word order, but the cross-language differences nevertheless show up at the surface level and must be determined by parameters controlling other aspects of derivations such as movement operations and/or what functional projections are present.

6 The relation between grammars and languages is apparently involved in application of the Subset Principle, which it is generally assumed that learners respect. If the language licensed by one grammar is a superset of the language licensed by another one, the former grammar should not be adopted; this is because of the impossibility of retreat from overgeneration without negative evidence. We will make the simplifying assumption here that learners can compute subset relationships solely by inspection of grammars, without needing to consult the languages they generate.

7 In cue-based models (Dresher and Kaye, 1990; Lightfoot, 1997), it is assumed that there is *another* property which is correlated with the true underlying trigger property, and *is* perceptible (cf. the artificial example of the /w/ cue for null subjects). We do not examine such models here. We doubt that simple superficial cues for syntactic parameters exist in all cases. We believe that cues are inherently related to the parameter values they trigger, and hence are abstract, and that the only feasible way to recognize them is by a mechanism such as the Structural Triggers Learner discussed in sections 5.8–5.10 below. We also set aside here the argument that natural language learning is not very accurate, as evidenced by the fact that languages change (see chapter 3 and references there). So we do not take inaccuracy as a goal of our model of how humans learn.

8 A parameter p_i is relevant to a sentence s (alternatively, the sentence expresses the parameter; see Clark (1992), and chapter 4: 13) if and only if there is a combination of values of the other parameters which licenses s if p_i takes one of its values but not if it takes the other. For example, by this definition the parameter controlling underlying word order in verb phrases

is relevant to an SVO sentence (since with $-$V2, SVO is licensed by underlying VO but not OV) but it is not relevant to an SV sentence (since for every VO grammar that licenses it there is an otherwise identical OV grammar that does). If a sentence is licensed by two grammars due to irrelevance of a parameter, the two grammars assign it the same derivation and both are equally correct (or incorrect) for that sentence. If a parameter is irrelevant to *all* sentences in the target language, then there are two equally correct grammars for the language. (If n parameters are irrelevant, there are 2^n correct grammars.) By contrast, if a sentence is licensed by two grammars due to parametric *ambiguity*, the two grammars will normally assign it different derivations, and one of the two grammars will be wrong for the target language. The TLA does not detect either parametric ambiguity or parametric irrelevance in input sentences, but the distinction nevertheless has an effect on its performance, as will emerge below. Note that we set aside, throughout this chapter, the existence of structural ambiguity of a sentence with respect to a single grammar.

9　There are two ways in which a grammar could afford a parse of an input sentence and nevertheless be wrong for the language. The input might be parametrically ambiguous; or the grammar being tested might contain false values of parameters that are not relevant to this input but are relevant to other sentences in the target language; see note 8. In either case, a learner that took parse test success as sufficient cause for adopting a parameter value could thereby mis-set a parameter that was previously set correctly; later it would have to relearn the correct value. Typically, when the TLA mis-sets parameters it does so because of ambiguity, not irrelevance, because the SVC provides it with a relevance filter (see Fodor, 1999). The TLA adopts a parameter value only if it is positively helpful in parsing at least one input string. However, ambiguity and irrelevance interact in ways that cannot be controlled even by the SVC and Greediness: a parameter that seems relevant may be so only on the wrong reading of an ambiguity.

10　There is a conceptual shift that we should point out in case it may cause confusion. The shift is from checking the parametric properties of *input sentences* (by running them through a bank of property detectors, in the original instant-triggering model), to testing *grammars* (by seeing whether they succeed or fail on the current input, as in the TLA). The two approaches are presumably intertranslatable, but their different emphases reflect different views of what is a feasible implementation.

11　The Greediness constraint, on the other hand, demonstrably inhibits convergence in the TLA$-$. See Sakas and Fodor (1997) for discussion.

12　There is a joke in the Mafia genre whose target is not the Mafia but applied mathematics. A Mafia boss kidnaps a mathematician, locks him into a dank cellar, says "I'll be back in six months and you must then give me a formula to predict whether my horse will win at the races. If you don't, I'll shoot you." He leaves. He returns in six months, asks the mathematician for the formula, the mathematician doesn't have it, the Mafia man pulls out his gun. But the mathematician says "No, don't shoot me. I don't have the formula yet but I have made significant progress. I have it worked out for the case of the perfectly spherical horse." We are still at the stage of modeling the perfectly spherical language learner.

13 It may appear to be the Greediness constraint that requires the second parse: a learner without Greediness does not attempt to evaluate the appropriateness of grammars before adopting them, so does not need to expend any effort on test-parsing candidate grammars. Berwick and Niyogi (1996) comment:

Further, not only does the greedy algorithm take more time, there is also a sense in which it requires more computation at any single step than a nongreedy one. Suppose the learner has received a sentence and is not able to analyze it in its current state. Greediness requires determining whether the new grammar can allow the learner to analyze the input or not" (p. 614).

However, it is reasonable to suppose that a learner, having picked a new grammar, would in any case then try to use it to parse the input, for the sake of understanding what was said. If so, then a nongreedy learner would also parse each novel sentence twice, once with the current grammar and once with a new one. The workload at each step is thus comparable (though the success rate may differ; see note 11). The way to save the labor of these double parses is to converge on the target grammar as soon as possible, so that over the course of learning, fewer sentences are encountered that are beyond the scope of the learner's current grammar. Input consumed and labor expended are thus related measures.

14 We are simplifying the discussion, throughout this section, by not distinguishing between the parametric ambiguity of a sentence and the irrelevance of a parameter to a sentence though it is relevant to the language as a whole. This sentence-level irrelevance (see note 8) is essentially folded into parametric ambiguity here. It is an interesting phenomenon, which we address in section 5.9, but it does not have a major impact on the outcomes of the TLA−.

15 In principle, a sentence that is indeterminate with respect to 8 parameters might be licensed by 256 grammars or by any lesser number between 256 and 2. In the minimum case, the two grammars would have opposite values for each of the indeterminate parameters. But assumption (iv) above entails the maximum, i.e., that every combination of values for those eight parameters is compatible with the sentence. This imposes a form of "smoothness" on the relation between languages and grammars (see discussion in section 5.6 below). It excludes, for example, the possibility that two very divergent grammars, and only they, could license the same sentence. To capture other assumptions formally, it would be necessary to distinguish two measures of ambiguity: a_g, the number of grammars that can license a given input; and a_p, the number of parameters whose values are not determined by a given input, where $a_g = 1$ if $a_p = 0$, and otherwise $2 \leq a_g \leq 2^{a_p}$. Assumption (iv) sets $a_g = 2^{a_p}$. For the TLA−, as analyzed above, a_g is the more useful measure; for the Structural Triggers model we consider below, a_p is more significant. A third measure of ambiguity that is sometimes appropriate is related

to assumption (iii). That is: a_l, the number of sentences or sentence types in common between different languages.

16 The probability that G is wrong and *ought* to be changed is $1 - (2^{n-r}/2^n) = 1 - (1/2^r)$, which is of course higher than the *recognized* need to change, which is $1 - 2^{a-r}$. The difference is $(2^a - 1)/2^r$, and is a measure of the extent to which the learner is lulled into a false sense of achievement due to ambiguity of the input.

17 For simplicity, we have assumed that the outcome of parsing s with G' is independent of the outcome of parsing it with G, which allows the corresponding probabilities to be multiplied together. In fact, the probability of a successful parse by G' is affected by the failure of the prior parse by G. For details, see Sakas (2000).

18 For a domain of three parameters, of which two per sentence are ambiguous on average, the average number of inputs to convergence by this calculation is 16. For Gibson and Wexler's three word-order parameters, Niyogi and Berwick (1996) showed that their implementation of the TLA needed approximately 100 sentences of child-directed adult speech from the CHILDES database (both English and German) for asymptotic (not average) convergence. However, these modest numbers should not distract attention from the high number of inputs needed for a more likely number of parameters for natural language. Success for small language domains is not a good prognosticator for whether performance will scale up appropriately.

19 Note that smoothness in this sense goes beyond the weaker phenomenon implied by assumption (iv) in section 5.5.1 above (see note 15), which concerns a single sentence. Smoothness has to do with the whole language licensed by a grammar and the extent to which it overlaps the languages licensed by neighboring grammars.

20 Nyberg (1992) proposes a model in which the learner's route through the grammar space is recorded, so that it doesn't (normally) retest a failed grammar. The learner tests all grammars one parameter distant from its most recent failed grammar, and performs an evaluation to select one of them to shift to. The learner's path through the grammar space could be reconstructed from a record of which parameter is reset at each step. Nyberg's model achieves very rapid learning rates (linear in the number of parameters), but it does so at the cost of an unrealistically heavy parsing load. For 30 parameters, each novel input is parsed by 30 grammars, and the outcomes recorded. This is repeated on successive inputs until a clear winner has been identified to shift to, or a dead heat is declared and a random choice made. Incidentally, we note that Nyberg precodes the input into the set of parameter values each sentence is compatible with. This is more than an expository convenience. It imports assumption (iv) of section 5.5.1 above. Suppose a sentence is licensed by two grammars, e.g. (for three parameters) by grammars 011 and 101. Then the sentence is coded as * * 1. This entails that the sentence is *also* licensed by grammars 001 and 111, i.e. by *all* combinations of parameter values compatible with this coding, of which there will be 2^i for $i =$ the number of asterisks (i.e., $i = a_p$ in the terms of note 15). This rules out the possibility that the target parameter

settings are quite unlike those of other grammars that succeed on some inputs, and it thereby facilitates this learner's systematic search through the grammar domain.

21 Fodor (1998a) notes that irrelevant parameters also inflate the size of the grammar pool; if they could be recognized as irrelevant and discarded, learning would be more efficient. However, Fodor wrongly implies that for the TLA the workload to convergence depends on the total number of parameters, whereas we have seen here in section 5.5.1 that it depends only on the number of parameters relevant to the target language (because irrelevance of some parameters affects the number of correct grammars in proportion to the total number of grammars). Thus, irrelevance of some parameters is helpful to the TLA, as it is for the STL model we present below.

22 For simplicity we make the common assumption here that exactly half of the remaining grammars are eliminated by each parameter that is set, but this would not be so if there were co-occurrence restrictions on parameter values or constraints on parameter accessibility such that a parameter does not freely admit of either value in combination with all other parameter values.

23 It is fair to raise the question of whether checking through millions of grammars could conceivably be faster or less effortful than setting one parameter. There can be no formal proof here, because it depends in principle on the cost of unit operations of noncomparable types. But it seems very unlikely that the answer could be positive (for any plausible number of parameters) – unless the parameter setting operation somehow smuggled in some individual grammar checking.

24 This does not rule out careful evaluation of the evidence before the irrevocable decision is made. It might even be combined with some sort of emergency retrieval of a previously discarded value if all else has failed, though we will not explore this possibility. Nondeterministic models like the TLA are of course able to freely return to past parameter values when necessary.

25 The learner cannot even usefully accumulate the results of parse tests over a succession of inputs. In principle it could count how often a given parameter value makes a contribution to licensing an input. But this interacts with how the *other* parameters are set in the grammars tested. So for decisive evidence in favor of that parameter value the learner would need to store the outcomes of half a billion parse tests, one for each possible combination of values of the other parameters. A learner with statistical capabilities might try to estimate reliability based on partial test data (see exercise 5.9 below), but even there the values of other parameters could skew the counts so it might take a very long time to distinguish between a parameter value that is correct and one that only seems to be so because of the company it keeps.

26 Future research should consider the possibility that the parser can pick up the analysis of a sentence again following an ambiguous substring. If it can perform accurately on the post-ambiguity fragment, despite not knowing what preceded it, it could provide additional reliable information for setting parameters.

27 Though both the strong and the weak STL are safe in that they do not commit errors, there are some circumstances in which an STL will fail to identify the correct grammar (see Bertolo et al., 1997a, b). For discussion, see Fodor (forthcoming).

28 See Fodor (1998c) on the consequences for acquisition of parser failure due to lack of needed lexical entries, garden paths and other processing problems.

29 Of course, the input itself (or that portion of it that the child is able to work with) may also be changing during that time. We conjecture that long sentences are typically less parametrically ambiguous than short sentences. So if it is assumed that the length and complexity of the sentences a learner is capable of processing increase with age then this will cause a decrease over time in the degree of input ambiguity. Stefano Bertolo has kindly checked this hypothesis in the domain of eight parameters for word order and movement which he and his colleagues have established at MIT (see Bertolo et al., 1997a). He reports the following distribution of the number of distinct languages that an input sentence type belongs to, for all the distinct sentence types in the domain under four words, and a sample of the sentence types of five words.

Sentence length in words	Number of distinct types in length	Number of distinct languages		
		min	max	mean
2	2	10	38	24
3	29	2	24	10.3
4	95	2	16	7.2
5	72 studied	1	9	3.9

Note that in this domain there are no fully unambiguous sentences shorter than five words long which the WSTL could use for setting parameters. In the smaller domain studied by Gibson and Wexler (1994) every language has at least one unambiguous trigger, ranging from three to five words.

30 The value u (degree of unambiguity) and the value a (degree of ambiguity) are to some extent independent, though they place outer bounds on each other. E.g., if $u > 0$, then $a < n$. Below, we give up the simplification of section 5.5.1 (assumption (v)) that all sentences are equally ambiguous, and consider a distribution of parametric ambiguity such that a represents the mean (average) number of ambiguous parameters per sentence.

31 This is only true, of course, if multiple A'-movement does not correlate reliably with some other phenomenon that can show up in nonmovement constructions. In general, a parameter that controls phenomenon p can be expressed by a sentence not exhibiting p if the sentence exhibits another phenomenon controlled by the same parameter.

32 The work of Bertolo et al. (1997a) suggests that there might be a linguistic limit on how far e can be reduced. This would be so if some substantial number of parameters are essential to every well-formed sentence. Bertolo et al. note that if these necessarily relevant parameters are ambiguously expressed, a conservative learner could be hung up indefinitely. This is a major reason for the high degree of ambiguity noted in note 29; see discussion in Bertolo et al. (1997a). We have been taking it for granted here (a) that all parameters have an equal chance of being irrelevant to an input sentence, and (b) that all expressed parameters have an equal chance of being expressed unambiguously. But if relevance and ambiguity are in fact unevenly distributed, then a few troublesome parameters might indeed be expressed ambiguously in many sentences, and depress the incidence of unambiguous triggers. A possible solution to this, if linguistic research supports it, is to revise the presumed parametrization of the language facts, so as to translate ambiguous parameters in some contexts into irrelevant parameters. See Fodor (1998c) for discussion.

33 See Fodor (1998c) for a proposal under which learners merely parse sentence (once each) for comprehension, as adults do but with the supergrammar, and the target grammar emerges as residue, with no additional procedures.

34 Only Optimality Theory seems incompatible with parameter values as treelets since it rejects parameter values altogether. Cross-language variation is captured in terms of different priority orderings of a UG-provided set of constraints on structure. Constraints are negative, quite unlike the positive ingredients of sentence derivations needed by the STL. See Tesar and Smolensky (1998) on acquisition in an OT framework.

35 If null subjects were characterized directly, in a different linguistic theory, that could be equally compatible with STL learning. For instance, the positive value of the null subject parameter might be a treelet consisting of the feature specification [+NULL] on an XP (NP or DP, depending on the theory) in characteristic subject position (again, at the choice of the theory), or perhaps an XP marked [CASE NOM], etc. Or, in a framework in which subjects are generated outside VP, the parametric treelets might offer a choice of VP or S as root categories or selected complements, etc. The learning theory does not dictate these details.

36 There is at least one other approach which can be used for establishing these results. It utilizes dynamic programming to compute the following recurrence relation: that the expected sample size required, on average, to set n parameters can be determined from the size required to set $n - i$, $0 < i < e$ parameters together with the possibility of setting i additional parameters given that $n - i$ have been set.

References

Allen, A. O. (1990). *Probability, Statistics and Queueing Theory with Computer Applications* (Academic Press, Boston).

Atkinson, M. (1987). Mechanisms for language acquisition: learning, parameter-setting and triggering, *First Language* **7**: 3–30.

——— (1992). *Children's Syntax: an Introduction to Principles and Parameters Theory* (Blackwell, Oxford).

——— (1996). Now hang on a minute: some reflections on emerging orthodoxies, in H. Clahsen (ed.) *Generative Perspectives in Language Acquisition* (John Benjamins, Amsterdam).

Baker, M. (1988). *Incorporation: A Theory of Grammatical-Function Changing* (Chicago University Press, Chicago).

Barber, C. L. (1976). *Early Modern English* (Andre Deutsch, London).

Benveniste, E. (1968). Mutations of linguistic categories, in W. Lehmann and Y. Malkiel (eds.), *Directions for Historical Linguistics: a Symposium* (University of Texas Press, Austin).

Bertolo, S. (1995a). Learnability properties of parametric models for natural language acquisition. Unpublished doctoral dissertation (Rutgers University).

——— (1995b). Maturation and learnability in parametric systems, *Language Acquisition* **4**(4): 277–318.

Bertolo, S., Broihier, K., Gibson, E. and Wexler, K. (1997a). Cue-based learners in parametric language systems: application of general results to a recently proposed learning algorithm based on unambiguous "superparsing," in M. G. Shafto and P. Langley (eds.), *Proceedings of the Nineteenth Annual Conference of the Cognitive Science Society* (Lawrence Erlbaum Associates, Mahwah, NJ).

——— (1997b). Characterizing learnability conditions for cue-based learners in parametric language systems (Technical Report D-97-02 Deutsches Forschungszentrum für Künstliche Intelligenz GmbH).

Berwick, R. and Niyogi, P. (1996). Learning from triggers, *Linguistic Inquiry* **27**: 605–22.

Bickerton, D. (1991). *Language and Species* (Chicago University Press, Chicago).

Blumer, A., Ehrenfeucht, A., Haussler, D. and Warmuth, M. K. (1987). Occam's razor, *Information Processing Letters* **24**: 377–80.

Bohannon, J. N. and Stanowicz, L. (1988). The issue of negative evidence: adult responses to children's language errors, *Developmental Psychology* **24**: 684–9.

Borer, H. (1984). *Parametric Syntax* (Foris, Dordrecht).

Borsley, R. D. and Roberts, I. (1996). *The Syntax of the Celtic Languages* (Cambridge University Press, Cambridge).

Bourciez, E. E. J. (1930). *Elements de linguistique romane* (Klincksieck, Paris).

Braine, M. D. S. (1971). On two types of models of the internalization of grammar, in D. I. Slobin (ed.), *The Ontogenesis of Grammar* (Academic Press, New York).

Brill, E. and Kapur, S. (1993). An information-theoretic solution to parameter setting (Unpublished manuscript, University of Pennsylvania).

Brown, R. (1977). Introduction, in C. E. Snow and C. A. Ferguson (eds.), *Talking to Children: Language Input and Acquisition* (Cambridge University Press, Cambridge).

Brown, R. and Hanlon, C. (1970). Derivational complexity and order of acquisition in child speech, in J. R. Hayes (ed.), *Cognition and the Development of Language* (Wiley, New York).

Chaitin, G. (1987). *Algorithmic Information Theory* (Cambridge University Press, Cambridge).

Cheng, L. (1991). On the typology of WH questions (Unpublished doctoral dissertation, MIT).

Chien, Y.-C. and Wexler, K. (1987). A comparison between Chinese-speaking and English-speaking children's acquisition of reflexives and pronouns (Unpublished manuscript, MIT).

(1990). Children's knowledge of locality conditions in binding as evidence for the modularity of syntax and pragmatics, *Language Acquisition* **1**: 225–95.

Chomsky, N. (1956). Three models for the description of language, *I. R. E. Transactions of Information Theory* **IT-2**:113–24.

(1965). *Aspects of the Theory of Syntax* (MIT Press, Cambridge, MA).

(1981a). *Lectures on Government and Binding* (Foris, Dordrecht).

(1981b). Principles and parameters in syntactic theory, in N. Hornstein and D. Lightfoot (eds.), *Explanation in Linguistics: the Logical Problem of Language Acquisition* (Longman, London).

(1986). *Knowledge of Language: its Nature, Origin and Use* (Praeger, New York).

(1987). On the nature, use and acquisition of language. Kyoto Lectures (Unpublished manuscript, MIT).

(1988). *Language and Problems of Knowledge: the Managua Lectures* (MIT Press, Cambridge, MA).

(1995). *The Minimalist Program* (MIT Press, Cambridge, MA).

(1996). Some observations on economy in Generative Grammar (Unpublished manuscript, Massachusetts Institute of Technology).

Chomsky, N. and Lasnik, H. (1995). The Theory of Principles and Parameters, in N. Chomsky, *The Minimalist Program* (MIT Press, Cambridge, MA).

Chung, K. L. (1979). *Elementary Probability Theory with Stochastic Processes* (Springer-Verlag, New York).

Cinque, G. (1989). Parameter setting in "instantaneous" and real-time acquisition, *Behavioral and Brain Sciences* **12**: 336.

(1997). Adverbs and the universal hierarchy of functional projections (Unpublished manuscript, University of Venice).

Clahsen, H. (ed.) (1996). *Generative Perspectives on Language Acquisition* (John Benjamins, Amsterdam).

Clark, R. (1990). Papers on learnability and natural selection (Technical Reports on Formal and Computational Linguistics 1; University of Geneva).

(1992).The selection of syntactic knowledge, *Language Acquisition* 2(2): 83–149.

(1994a). Finitude, boundedness and complexity: learnability and the study of first language acquisition, in B. Lust et al. (eds.), *Syntactic Theory and First Language Acquisition: Cross Linguistic Perspectives* (Lawrence Erlbaum, Mahwah, NJ).

(1994b). Kolmogorov complexity and the information content of parameters (IRCS Report 94-17; University of Pennsylvania).

Clark, R. (1996). Complexity and the induction of Tree Adjoining Grammars (IRCS Report 96-14; University of Pennsylvania).

Clark, R. and Roberts, I. (1993). A computational model of language learnability and language change, *Linguistic Inquiry* 24: 299–345.

(1997) Complexity is the engine of variation (unpublished manuscript, University of Pennsylvania and Wales).

Corbett, G. (1983). *Hierarchies, Targets and Controllers: Agreement Patterns in Slavic* (Croom Helm, London).

Cover, T. M. and Thomas, J. A. (1991). *Elements of Information Theory* (Wiley, New York).

Croft, W. (1994). *Language Typology* (Cambridge University Press, Cambridge).

Demetras, M. J., Post, K. N. and Snow, C. E. (1986). Feedback to first language learners: the role of repetitions and clarification questions, *Journal of Child Language* 13: 275–92.

Denison, D. (1985). The origins of periphrastic *do*: Ellegård and Visser reconsidered, in R. Eaton et al. (eds.), *Papers from the 4th International Conference on English Historical Linguistics* (John Benjamins, Amsterdam).

Déprez, V. and Pierce, A. (1993). Negation and functional projections in early grammar, *Linguistic Inquiry* 24: 25–67.

Dresher, E. (1999). Charting the learning path: cues to parameter setting, *Linguistic Inquiry*. 30(1): 27–67.

Dresher, E and Kaye, J. D. (1990). A computational learning model for metrical phonology, *Cognition* 34: 137–95.

Ellegård, A. (1953). *The auxiliary do, the establishment and regulation of its use in English* (Almquist and Wiksell, Stockholm).

Fintel, K. von (1995). The formal semantics of grammaticalization, *Proceedings of NELS* 25: 175–89.

Fodor, J. D. (1998a). Unambiguous triggers, *Linguistic Inquiry* 29(1): 1–36.

(1998b). Learning to parse?, *Journal of Psycholinguistic Research* 27(2): 285–319.

(1998c). Parsing to learn, *Journal of Psycholinguistic Research* 27(3): 339–74.

(1999). Learnability theory: triggers for parsing with, in E. C. Klein and G. Martohardjono (eds.), *The Development of Second Language Grammars: a Generative Approach*.

(forthcoming). Learnability theory: decoding trigger sentences. In R. C. Schwarz (ed.), *Linguistics, Cognitive Science, and Childhood Language Disorders* (Lawrence Erlbaum, Hillsdale, NJ).

Frank, R. (1992). Syntactic locality and Tree Adjoining Grammar: grammatical, acquisition and processing perspectives (IRCS Technical Report 92-47; University of Pennsylvania).

Frank, R. and Kapur, S. (1996). On the use of triggers in parameter setting, *Linguistic Inquiry* **27**(4): 623–60.

Gallistel, C. R. (1990). *The Organization of Learning* (MIT Press, Cambridge, MA).

Gibson, E. (1991). A computational theory of human linguistic processing: memory limitations and processing breakdown (doctoral dissertation, Carnegie Mellon University).

Gibson, E. and Wexler, K. (1994). Triggers, *Linguistic Inquiry* **25**(3): 407–54.

Giorgi, A. and Pianesi, F. (1998). *The Syntax of Tense* (Oxford University Press, Oxford).

Gleitman, L. and Wanner, E. (1982). The state of the state of the art, in E. Wanner and L. Gleitman (eds.), *Language Acquisition: the State of the Art* (Cambridge University Press, Cambridge).

Gold, M. E. (1967). Language identification in the limit, *Information and Control* **10**: 447–74.

Gray, D. (1985). *The Oxford Book of Late Medieval Verse and Prose* (Oxford University Press, Oxford).

Greenberg, J. (1966). Some universals of grammar with particular reference to the order of meaningful elements, in J. Greenberg (ed.), *Universals of Language* (2nd edition) (MIT Press, Cambridge, MA).

Grimshaw, J. and Pinker, S. (1989). Positive and negative evidence in language acquisition, *Behavioral and Brain Sciences* **12**: 341–2.

Grimshaw, J. and Rosen, S. (1990). Knowledge and obedience: the developmental status of the Binding Theory, *Linguistic Inquiry* **21**: 187–222.

Grodzinsky, J. and Reinhart, T. (1993). The innateness of binding and coreference, *Linguistic Inquiry* **24**: 69–101.

Haegeman, L. (1990). Understood subjects in English diaries, *Multilingua* **9**: 157–99.

(1994). *Introduction to Government and Binding Theory* (2nd edition) (Blackwell, Oxford).

Halle, M. and Marantz, A. (1993). Distributed Morphology and the pieces of inflection, in K. Hale and S. J. Keyser (eds.), *The View from Building 20: Essays in Honor of Sylvain Bromberger* (MIT Press, Cambridge, MA).

Hamming, R. W. (1991). *The Art of Probability for Engineers and Scientists* (Addison Wesley, Redwood City, CA).

Harris, T. and Wexler, K. (1996). The optional-infinitive stage in Child English: evidence from negation, in H. Clahsen (ed.), *Generative Perspectives in Language Acquisition* (John Benjamins, Amsterdam).

Hawkins, J. A. (1983). *Word Order Universals* (Academic Press, New York).

Heine, B., Claudi, U. and Hünnemeyer, F. (1991). *Grammaticalization: a Conceptual Framework* (Chicago University Press, Chicago).

Hirsh-Pasek, K., Treiman, R. and Schneiderman, M. (1984). Brown and Hanlon revisited: mothers' sensitivity to ungrammatical forms, *Journal of Child Language* **11**: 81–8.

Holmberg, A. and Platzack, C. (1991). On the role of inflection in Scandinavian syntax, in W. Abraham (ed.), *Issues in Germanic Syntax* (Mouton de Gruyter, Berlin).

Hopcroft, J. and Ullman, J. (1979). *Introduction to Automata Theory, Languages, and Computation* (Addison Wesley, Reading, MA).

Horning, J. J. (1969). A study of grammatical inference (doctoral dissertation, Stanford University).

Huang, C.-T. J. (1981). Move *WH* in a language without *WH* movement, *The Linguistic Review* **1**: 369–416.

Huang, C.-T. J. and Tang, C.-C. J. (1991). The local nature of the long-distance reflexive in Chinese, in J. Koster and E. Reuland (eds.), *Long-Distance Anaphora* (Cambridge University Press, Cambridge).

Hyams, N. (1986). *Language Acquisition and the Theory of Parameters* (Reidel, Dordrecht).

(1989). The null subject parameter in language acquisition, in O. Jaeggli and K. F. Safir (eds.), *The Null Subject Parameter* (Reidel, Dordrecht).

(1994a). VP, null arguments and Comp projections, in T. Hoekstra and B. D. Schwartz (eds.), *Language Acquisition: Studies in Generative Grammar* (John Benjamins, Amsterdam).

(1994b). Null subjects in child language and the implications of cross-linguistic variation, in B. Lust et al. (eds.), *Syntactic Theory and First Language Acquisition: Cross Linguistic Perspectives* (Lawrence Erlbaum, Mahwah, NJ).

(1996). The underspecification of functional categories in early grammar, in H. Clahsen (ed.), *Generative Perspectives in Language Acquisition* (John Benjamins, Amsterdam).

Jain, S., Osherson, D., Royer, J. S. and Sharma, A. (1999). *Systems That Learn – 2nd Edition: An Introduction to Learning Theory* (MIT Press, Cambridge, MA).

Jakubowicz, C. (1984). On markedness and binding principles, *Proceedings of the Northeastern Linguistics Society* **14**: 154–82.

Jespersen, O. (1954). *A Modern English Grammar on Historical Principles* (George Allen & Unwin, London).

Joshi, A. (1987). An introduction to Tree Adjoining Grammars, in A. Manaster-Ramer (ed.), *Mathematics of Language* (John Benjamins, Amsterdam).

Kapur, S. (1991). Computational learning of languages (Computer Science Technical Report 91-1234; Cornell University).

(1994). Some applications of formal learning theory results to natural language acquisition, in B. Lust et al. (eds.), *Syntactic Theory and First Language Acquisition: Cross Linguistic Perspectives* (Lawrence Erlbaum, Mahwah, NJ).

Kapur, S. and Clark, R. (1996). The automatic construction of a symbolic parser via statistical techniques, in J. Klavans and P. Resnik (eds.), *The Balancing Act: Combining Symbolic and Statistical Approaches to Language* (MIT Press, Cambridge, MA).

Kapur, S., Lust, B., Harbert, W. and Martohardjono, G. (1993). Universal Grammar and Learnability Theory: the case of binding domains and the "Subset Principle," in E. Reuland and W. Abraham (eds.), *Knowledge and Language: Vol. 1: From Orwell's Problem to Plato's Problem* (Kluwer, Dordrecht).

Katada, F. (1991). The LF representation of anaphors, *Linguistic Inquiry* **22**: 287–313.

Kauffman, S. (1995). *At Home in the Universe* (Viking, London).

Kayne, R. (1994). *The Antisymmetry of Syntax* (MIT Press, Cambridge, MA).

Kemenade, A. van (1987). *Syntactic Case and Morphological Case in the History of English* (Foris, Dordrecht).

Kiparsky, P. (1994). The Indo-European Origins of Germanic Syntax, in A. Battye and I. Roberts (eds.), *Clause Structure and Change* (Oxford University Press, Oxford).

Koopman, H. and Sportiche, D. (1991). The position of subjects, *Lingua* **85**: 211–58.

Koster, J. and Reuland, E. (eds.), (1991). *Long-Distance Anaphora* (Cambridge University Press, Cambridge).

Kroch, A. S. (1989). Reflexes of grammar in patterns of language change, *Journal of Language Variation and Change* **1**: 199–244.

Labov, W. (1972). *Language in the Inner City* (University of Pennsylvania Press, Philadelphia).

(1994). *Principles of Linguistic Change*, Vol. I: Internal Factors (Blackwell, Oxford).

Lasnik, H. and Saito, M. (1984). On the nature of proper government, *Linguistic Inquiry* **15**(2): 235–89.

Lehmann, C. (1985). Grammaticalization: synchronic variation and diachronic change, *Lingua e Stile* **20**(3): 303–18.

Lema, J. and Rivero, M.-L. (1991). Types of verbal movement in Old Spanish: modals, futures and perfects, *Probus* **3**(3): 237–78.

Levelt, W. M. (1975). *What Became of LAD?* (Peter de Ridder, Lisse).

Levy, L. S. and Joshi, A. K. (1978). Skeletal structural descriptions, *Information and Control* **39**(2): 192–211.

Li, M. and Vitanyi, P. (1993). *An Introduction to Kolmogorov Complexity and its Applications* (Springer-Verlag, New York).

Lightfoot, D. (1979). *Principles of Diachronic Syntax* (Cambridge University Press, Cambridge).

(1989). The child's trigger experience: degree-0 learnability, *Behavioral and Brain Sciences* **12**(2): 321–34.

(1991). *How to Set Parameters: Arguments from Language Change* (MIT Press, Cambridge, MA).

(1997). Catastrophic change and learning theory, *Lingua* **100**(2): 171–92.

Lockwood, W. (1964). *An Introduction to Modern Faroese* (Foeroyar Skulabøk-grunnur, Tørshavn).

Lyell, C. (1830–33). *Principles of Geology* (Murray, London).

Longobardi, G. (1994). Reference and proper names: a theory of N-movement in syntax and logical form, *Linguistic Inquiry* **24**: 299-345.

MacLaughlin, D. (1995). Language acquisition and the Subset Principle, *The Linguistic Review* **12**: 143–91.

McCarthy, J. and Prince, A. (1986). Prosodic morphology (unpublished manuscript, Brandeis University).

McCloskey, J. (1996). On the scope of verb movement in Irish, *Natural Language and Linguistic Theory* **14**: 47–104.

McNeill, D. (1966). Developmental psycholinguistics, in F. Smith and G. A. Miller (eds.), *The Genesis of Language: a Psycholinguistic Approach* (MIT Press, Cambridge, MA).

Manzini, R. (1995). From Merge and Move to Form Dependency, *UCL Working Papers in Linguistics* **8**: 323–46.

Manzini, R. and Wexler, K. (1987). Parameters, Binding Theory and Learnability, *Linguistic Inquiry* **18**: 413–44.

Marcus, G. (1993). Negative evidence in language acquisition, *Cognition* **46**(1): 53–85.

Matsuoka, K. (1997). Binding conditions in young children's grammar: interpretation of pronouns inside conjoined NPs, *Language Acquisition* **6**: 37–48.

May, R. (1985). *Logical Form: its Structure and Derivation* (MIT Press, Cambridge, MA).

Mazuka, R. (1996). Can a grammatical parameter be set before the first word? Prosodic contributions to early setting of a grammatical parameter, in J. L. Morgan and K. Demuth (eds.), *Signal to Syntax: Bootstrapping from Speech to Grammar in Early Acquisition* (Lawrence Erlbaum Associates, Hillsdale, NJ).

Morgan, J. L. (1989).Learnability considerations and the nature of trigger experiences in language acquisition, *Behavioral and Brain Sciences* **12**: 352–53.

Morgan, J. L. and Demuth, K. (eds.) (1996). *Signal to Syntax: Bootstrapping from Speech to Grammar in Early Acquisition* (Lawrence Erlbaum, Hillsdale, NJ).

Morgan, J. L. and Travis, L. (1989). Limits on negative information, *Journal of Child Language* **16**: 531–52.

Nespor, M., Guasti, M. T. and Christophe, A. (1996). Selecting word order: the rhythmic activation principle, in U. Kleinhenz (ed.), *Interfaces in Phonology* (Akademie Verlag, Berlin).

Newport, E., Gleitman, L. and Gleitman, H. (1977). Mother, I'd rather do it myself: some effects and non-effects of maternal speech style, in C. E. Snow and C. A. Ferguson (eds.), *Talking to Children: Language Input and Acquisition* (Cambridge University Press, Cambridge).

Newson, M. (1990). *Questions of Form and Learnability in Binding Theory* (doctoral dissertation, University of Essex).

Niyogi, P. and Berwick, R. C. (1995). The logical problem of language change (MIT A.I. Memo no. 1516).

(1996). A language learning model for finite parameter spaces, *Cognition* **61**: 161–93.

Nyberg, E. (1992). A non-deterministic success-driven model of parameter setting in language acquisition (doctoral dissertation, Carnegie Mellon University).

Papadimitriou, C. (1994). *Computational Complexity* (Addison-Wesley, Reading, MA).

Partee, B., ter Meulen, A. and Wall, R. (1990). *Mathematical Methods in Linguistics* (Kluwer Academic Publishers, Dordrecht).

Penner, S. (1987). Parental responses to grammatical and ungrammatical child utterances, *Child Development* **58**: 376–84.

Phillips, C. (1996). Order and structure (doctoral dissertation, MIT).

Pica, P. (1987). On the nature of the reflexivization cycle, *Proceedings of the Northeastern Linguistics Society* **17**: 483–99.

Pinker, S. (1989). *Learnability and Cognition: the Acquisition of Argument Structure* (MIT Press, Cambridge, MA).

Pintzuk, S. (1991). Phrase structures in competition: variation and change in Old English word order (doctoral dissertation, University of Pennsylvania).

Platzack, C. (1987). The Scandinavian languages and the null-subject parameter, *Natural Language and Linguistic Theory* **5**: 377–401.

(1994). The loss of verb second in French and English, in A. Battye and I. Roberts (eds.), *Clause Structure and Change* (Oxford University Press, Oxford).

(1996). The initial hypothesis of syntax: a minimalist perspective on language acquisition and attrition, in H. Clahsen (ed.), *Generative Perspectives in Language Acquisition* (John Benjamins, Amsterdam).

Poeppel, D. and Wexler, K. (1993). The Full Competence Hypothesis of clause structure in early German, *Language* **69**: 1–33.

Pollard, C. and Sag, I. A. (1994). *Head-driven Phrase Structure Grammar* (University of Chicago Press, Chicago).

Pollock, J. Y. (1989). Verb Movement, UG and the structure of IP, *Linguistic Inquiry* **20**: 365–424.

Radford, A. (1990). *Syntactic Theory and the Acquisition of English Syntax: the Nature of Early Child Grammar in English* (Blackwell, Oxford).

Rambow, O. (1994). *Formal and Computational Aspects of Natural Language Syntax* (IRCS Technical Report 94-08; University of Pennsylvania).

Reinhart, T. and Reuland, E. (1991). Anaphors and logophors: an argument structure perspective, in J. Koster and E. Reuland (eds.), *Long Distance Anaphora* (Cambridge University Press, Cambridge).

(1993). Reflexivity, *Linguistic Inquiry* **24**: 657–720.

Resnik, P. (1993). *Selection and Information: a Class-Based Approach to Lexical Relationships* (IRCS Technical Report 93-42; University of Pennsylvania).

Rizzi, L. (1982). *Issues in Italian Syntax* (Foris, Dordrecht).

(1989). On the format for parameters, *Behavioural and Brain Sciences* **12**: 355–6.

(1994). Some notes on linguistic theory and language development: the case of root infinitives (unpublished manuscript, University of Geneva).

(1997). The fine structure of the left periphery, in L. Haegeman (ed.), *Elements of Grammar* (Kluwer, Dordrecht).

Roberts, I. (1985). Agreement parameters and the development of English modal auxiliaries, *Natural Language and Linguistic Theory* **3**: 21–58.

(1992). *Verbs and Diachronic Syntax* (Kluwer, Dordrecht).

(1998). Verb-movement and markedness, in M. Degraff and A. Pierce (eds.), *Language Acquisition, Creoles and Language Change* (MIT Press, Cambridge, MA).

Roberts, I., and Roussou, A. (1997). Interface interpretation (unpublished manuscript, Universities of Wales and Stuttgart).

Rogers, H. (1967). *Theory of Recursive Functions and Effective Computability* (MIT Press, Cambridge, MA).

Ruhlen, M. (1987). *A Guide to the World's Languages, Vol. I: Classification* (Edward Arnold, London).

Saffran, J., Aslin, R. and Newport, E. (1996). Statistical learning by 8-month-old infants, *Science* **274**: 1926–28.

Safir, K. (1987). Comments on Wexler and Manzini, in T. Roeper and E. Williams (eds.), *Parameter Setting* (Reidel, Dordrecht).

(1996). Semantic atoms of anaphors, *Natural Language and Linguistic Theory* **14**: 545–89.

Sakas, W. G. (2000). Ambiguity and the Computational Feasibility of Syntax Acquisition (doctoral dissertation, The City University of New York).

Sakas, W. G. and Fodor, J. D. (1997). Triggering, hill-climbing and the conservative learner: can a stochastic trigger-based learner afford Greediness as a constraint? (unpublished manuscript, Graduate Center of the City University of New York; paper presented at First Annual Conference on Computational Psycholinguistics (CPL97), Berkeley, CA).

Shlonsky, U. (1997). *Clause Structure and Word Order in Hebrew and Arabic. An Essay In Comparative Semitic Syntax* (Oxford University Press, Oxford).

Sigurjónsdóttir, S. and Hyams, N. (1992). Reflexivization and logophoricity: evidence from the acquisition of Icelandic, *Language Acquisition* **2**: 359–413.

Snow, C. E. and Ferguson, C. A. (eds.) (1977). *Talking to Children: Language Input and Acquisition* (Cambridge University Press, Cambridge).

Sportiche, D. (1981). Bounding nodes in French, *The Linguistic Review* **1**: 219–46.

Tekavcic, P. (1980). *Grammatica Storica dell'Italiano* (Il Mulino, Bologna).

Tesar, B. and Smolensky, P. (1998). Learnability in Optimality Theory, *Linguistic Inquiry* **29**: 229–68.

Thráinsson, H. (1991). Long distance reflexives and the typology of NPs, in J. Koster and E. Reuland (eds.), *Long-Distance Anaphora* (Cambridge University Press, Cambridge).

Traugott, E. and Heine, B. (1991). *Approaches to Grammaticalization* (Typological Studies in Language 19; John Benjamins, Amsterdam).

Travis, L. (1984). Parameters and Effects of Word Order Variation (doctoral dissertation, MIT).

Valian, V. (1990). Logical and psychological constraints on the acquisition of syntax, in L. Frazier and J. de Villiers (eds.), *Language Processing and Language Acquisition* (Kluwer, Dordrecht).

(1994). Children's postulation of null subjects: parameter setting and language acquisition, in B. Lust et al. (eds.), *Syntactic Theory and First Language Acquisition: Cross Linguistic Perspectives*, Vol. II: *Binding, Dependencies, and Learnability* (Lawrence Erlbaum, Mahwah, NJ).

Valiant, L. G. (1984). A theory of the learnable, *Communications of the ACM* **27**: 1134–42.

Vikner, S. (1995). V-to-I movement and inflection for person in all tenses, *Working Papers in Scandinavian Syntax* **55**: 1–27.

Vincent, N. (1991). Latin and the Romance Languages, in K. Börjars and N. Vincent (eds.), *Complement Structures in the Languages of Europe* (EURO-TYP Working Papers III,1).

Visser, F. T. (1960–63). *An Historical Syntax of the English Language* (Brill, Leiden).

Waner, S. and Costenoble, S. R. (1996). *Finite Mathematics Applied to the Real World* (Harper Collins, New York).

Watkins, C. (1963). Preliminaries to the historical and comparative analysis of the syntax of the Old Irish verb, *Celtica* **6**: 11–49.

(1964). Preliminaries to the Reconstruction of the Indo-European Sentence Structure, in H. G. Lunt (ed.), *Proceedings of the Ninth International Congress of Linguistics* (Mouton, The Hague).

Wexler, K. (1993). The Subset Principle is an intensional principle, in E. Reuland and W. Abraham (eds.), *Knowledge and Language*, Vol. I: From Orwell's Problem to Plato's Problem (Kluwer, Dordrecht).

(1994). Finiteness and head movement in early child grammars, in D. Lightfoot and N. Hornstein (eds.), *Verb Movement* (Cambridge University Press, Cambridge).

Wexler, K. and Culicover, P. (1980). *Formal Principles of Language Acquisition* (MIT Press, Cambridge, MA).

Wexler, K. and Manzini, R. (1987). Parameters and learnability in Binding Theory, in T. Roeper and E. Williams (eds.), *Parameter Setting* (Reidel, Dordrecht).

Winston, P. (1992). *Artificial Intelligence* (3rd edition) (Addison Wesley, Reading, MA).

Zwart, J. W. (1994). Dutch Syntax (doctoral dissertation, University of Groningen).

Index